D0410170

Simpson & I

Simpson & I

BETWEEN TWO WORLDS

OGGY BOYTCHEV

QUARTET

First published in 2014 by Quartet Books Limited
A member of the Namara Group
27 Goodge Street, London W1T 2LD

A catalogue record for this book
is available from the British Library
ISBN 978 0 7043 7352 5
Typeset by Josh Bryson
Printed and bound in Great Britain by
T J International Ltd, Padstow, Cornwall

CONTENTS

For Julian

PROLOGUE

BULGARIA, JANUARY 1986

From my bedroom window I could see over the rooftops of downtown Sofia. The terracotta roof tiles, discoloured with age, glistened under the sleet which fell from the low, oppressive clouds. The black steel dome of the synagogue loomed close but through the blurry window I could only just make out the hexagram perched on a spike at its highest point. Beyond it was the five-pointed star over the Communist Party Central Committee, the symbol of the party's domination over the city. The ruby-coloured star was lit from the inside and had an uncanny glow around it, like a halo. The rest of the picture was drab – peeling façades of dilapidated Vienna Secession buildings, metal sheet French-style mansard roofs badly in need of repair, the remnants of a house hit by a bomb dropped by Allied aircraft forty-five years ago when Bulgaria was on the wrong side in the Second World War. I knew every detail of this picture framed by my third floor window. As a bookish child I stared at it while doing my homework and later as a young adult contemplating my future. And that early January evening I stared at it one last time because I knew that if all went well I would never see it again.

The white Volga taxi was waiting downstairs. I kissed my parents goodbye and carried my old-fashioned leather suitcase down the concrete staircase of this 1960s building where I'd lived since I was 10. At the first landing, I stopped and turned. They stood next to each other smiling with pride that I was embarking on a business trip abroad, the ultimate accolade to be awarded to anyone under the communist regime. I felt nothing. No guilt. No remorse. I had two hundred dollars in my pocket and a passport stamped at the Interior Ministry, 'Tous les Pays du Monde' – my exit visa. My salvation.

In a weird historical aberration, Bulgaria had declared itself a Francophone country after it gained independence from the Ottoman Empire in the 19th century, so even under communism all the diplomatic correspondence was still in French. 'All the countries of the world.' I smiled at the thought. I took one last look at my parents. In my heart I knew that this might be the last time I'd ever see them. I turned and rushed down the stairs towards the waiting taxi.

The gas guzzling Volga – spacious but basic inside – the pride of Soviet engineering, drove through grey cobblestoned streets. As a teenager I was embarrassed to tell my friends at school where I lived. Most of them had flats in newly built developments with tarmac roads outside. They were symbolic of the new order and the people living in them were the 'new people'. We were known as the 'former people', which meant that we belonged to the previous system. 'Former people' like us lived in the old city, the Jewish quarter, or the Armenian neighbourhood, depending on who they wanted to insult. I used to walk the cobbled streets in the summer and look at the dates engraved on the top of the buildings. Most of them were almost a hundred years old, originally merchant houses, opulently decorated in their time.

The Volga turned left into the main street opposite the Communist Party Central Committee, the Largo, and the tyres hit the yellow cobblestones, an idiosyncratic feature of Sofia. We drove between the two monolithic limestone Stalinist buildings, Grand Hotel Balkan and The Central Department Store, ZUM, the equivalent of GUM on Red Square in Moscow. The yellow ceramic blocks were notoriously slippery when wet but, ignoring the hazard, the taxi driver accelerated hard through the evening street towards the airport. As we passed the pale neo-Renaissance building of the National Assembly on the left, the visibility became poor as the sleet turned to snow. Suddenly I was jolted from my reflections by a screeching noise and the sound of crashing glass and metal. The Volga had skidded into the car in front. The blood drained from my face. *I'm going to miss my flight. Missing the flight could mean cancelling the trip*... I didn't want to think about it. The two drivers got out. They looked at the damage, and at each other, impassively. The damp, cold weather was not conducive to heated arguments.

I opened the door of the taxi and said sternly to the taxi driver, 'Can you please get my suitcase out of the boot? I don't want to miss my flight. I'll get another cab.' Faced with the prospect of losing his fare, he tried to persuade the other driver not to wait for the police. He wrote down on a piece of paper the taxi's registration and his telephone number but the other man insisted that they wait. I grew impatient as they argued, got out and started tugging at the boot lock to get my suitcase. The three of us must have looked like characters in a pantomime, but for me this was serious, a matter of life or death.

The dented Volga eventually pulled up in front of the departures hall of Sofia airport, about twenty minutes later than planned. The building was dark and dingy. There were no shops except for one souvenir stall. This was the third time I'd flown. There was a police cordon before you even reached the check-in counter of BGA Balkan (Bulgarian State Airlines). Two arrogant policemen stared at me and laughed. 'You look like you've seen a ghost. Why are you so nervous? What are you hiding?' one of them said.

I sighed. 'My taxi has just been involved in an accident. I was lucky I wasn't seriously injured,' I exaggerated, hoping to divert their interest in my purpose.

'Where are you travelling today?' the other one said.

'Cairo,' I replied.

'How much hard currency have you got on you?'

'Two hundred dollars.'

'That's not much for a trip to Cairo,' the other sneered.

'Well, the firm I'm visiting will meet all my costs.'

The policeman looked me up and down. 'Please show me the document for legal possession of your currency. And I want to see the money, too.'

My indignation slowly brought colour to my face. I vowed never to be subjected to such humiliation again but I had to endure such interrogation twice more before I got on the flight – once at customs and the second time at border control. By the time I reached the plane, I was exhausted. I slept all the way to Cairo, despite the bumpy ride in the ageing Russian-built Tupolev aircraft.

I had dreamt many times of seeing the free world but Port Said was not as exotic as I expected, except for the palm trees. It was the first time I'd seen real palm trees growing in the sand, and not the anaemic ones in wooden caskets outside hotels in Bulgarian seaside resorts.

As a child, my only escape from reality was books. I dreamt that one day I would be able to walk under the Eiffel Tower, climb to the top of the Empire State Building, visit Westminster Abbey, sail through the Suez Canal, or round the Cape of Good Hope. I had a hunger for freedom, which fuelled an indefinable anger from an early age. How disappointed I felt now, sitting in a dreary room in a cheap hotel in Port Said.

The shipping agent who acted on behalf of the Bulgarian vessel unloading grain flour at the port had arranged for an air-conditioned car to take me from Cairo airport to the hotel in the early hours of the morning. I was a junior executive with a Bulgarian shipping company and there to arrange the speedy release of the vessel. It had been involved in a collision with a tugboat and Egyptian bureaucracy threatened a lengthy delay and loss of earnings. But of course I had other, more pressing things on my mind.

My trip was supposed to last 10 days. I knew what I had to do and I did it quickly. All the relevant insurance documents were signed and lodged with the insurance company.

‘The job has been done,’ I said, walking into the shipping agent’s office on the fifth morning.

He wasn’t pleased that I was there and that everything had been done so efficiently. He wouldn’t be able to claim such a large fee.

‘There is no need for me to stay here any longer. Can you buy me a cheap air ticket to London for tomorrow? I’ve got another job in Tilbury.’

‘Shall I put it on the ship’s account?’ he said.

‘No,’ I replied and took out my wallet. ‘Let me know how much it costs and I’ll pay you cash in US dollars.’

After calling the travel agent he told me that it would cost $130 one way. I counted the money. He didn’t ask if I had a UK visa. For the first time, I was reassured that my scheme was actually going to work. However, I did worry that the agent might mention to the office in Sofia that I’d bought a ticket to London. Once I’d got the ticket in my hand, what could the Bulgarian authorities do? Send armed secret agents from the embassy in Cairo to find me in Port Said, drug me and bundle me onto the first plane back to Sofia?

I considered changing hotels. But that would only arouse suspicion with the shipping agent, and anyway I had no money to spare for a new hotel room. I packed my suitcase, left it at reception and spent the time hidden under the shade of a teahouse opposite to see if anybody came looking for me. By lunchtime nothing had happened and I walked to the agent’s office to collect my ticket. He seemed very friendly and that made me even more paranoid. Did he suspect anything? In the end, I would change hotels anyway: he told me that a car would pick me up at 6 pm to take me to the Novotel at Cairo airport. I was to spend the night there because my flight to London was very early the next morning.

I spent the rest of the day in the same teahouse watching the hotel. My head was buzzing. I could not know my future, and my mind fell back to my past. A godforsaken place in northern Bulgaria called Red Riverbank was my first memory when I was four. I woke up early one summer’s morning. It was Sunday and the house smelled of fried eggy bread. In the kitchen my father was crouched by our old vacuum tube radio set, furnished in oak veneer. The crackling voice, which came out of it, was Bulgarian but there was something strange about it. I sensed there was a great deal of secrecy about what my father was doing. My mother tried to usher me out but my dad stopped her and told me, ‘This is the BBC World Service. We can listen to the news together but you must not tell anybody. Otherwise, I’ll go to jail.’ We huddled close to the radio and listened in silence.

By the age of 10 I already led a double life. We listened secretly to the BBC and Radio Free Europe and we discussed world events. My father treated me as an equal. He told me about why we lived in Red Riverbank. He had been interned there since 1948, long before I was born, accused of espionage. At the time, I wasn't sure if there was any truth in this accusation or whether, like so many others, he'd been arrested on trumped-up charges. At the beginning he was forced to break stones in the local quarry. He then worked as a labourer on the roads, repairing and paving the streets of that forlorn place, Red Riverbank. He often said that there was nothing shameful about doing heavy physical labour. 'It keeps the circulation going,' he joked.

In the few years after my first encounter with the secret short wave radio transmissions, I learned from my father about past events in Hungary where the people tried to overthrow the communist regime, only to be suppressed even more viciously with the help of the Soviet Union. This contradicted what I was taught at school, but I kept quiet about what I knew to be the truth. While my friends were learning to ride bicycles, my father was telling me about a Bulgarian double agent who worked for the CIA. This agent had told the Americans about the forthcoming split between Khrushchev and Mao but they didn't believe him. The Sino-Soviet split had a profound effect on the future shape of the world and the Americans. The CIA director, Allen Dulles, learned to trust him, but not for long. He was uncovered by the Russian KGB, kidnapped from a hotel in Moscow, and shot dead in a Bulgarian prison following a short trial. Our man who had worked at the United Nations in New York believed that to preserve the balance in the Cold War no side should be given the impression that it had an advantage. Otherwise our world would not survive.

In the teahouse, in the warmth of the Egyptian afternoon, I continued to watch the hotel entrance. I thought that carrying these separate realities, keeping quiet about one while pretending to follow the other, was, perhaps, a lot of baggage for a 10-year-old child to carry. But I never felt the burden. What bothered me at the time was that I didn't understand the need for 'balance'. Why not let the free world win? I couldn't understand why the American citizens, Julius and Ethel Rosenberg, passed on the secrets of the atomic bomb to the Soviet Union. But my dad said they were driven by the same desire to achieve equilibrium in the world because no government could be trusted. They were later executed for treason in the electric chair in the notorious Sing-Sing prison in New York State in 1953.

My taxi to Cairo airport arrived at 6 pm on the dot. There was no sign that anybody knew anything about what I was planning to do. As I picked up my suitcase, I asked the receptionist if there had been any calls for me. He said there had been none. My heart was in my throat throughout the journey to Cairo. The driver spoke rudimentary English and tried to tell me something as we approached the airport but I was too uptight to understand. My pulse began to race when instead of heading towards the Novotel he took a back road among airport warehouses. I tried to remonstrate with him but he ignored me. We stopped in front of a small office building and he motioned at me to get out. My legs were heavy and the vein in my neck throbbed to bursting point.

I tried to look calm as I walked into the building. A young man in his late twenties, dressed in a grey oversized suit and open-neck shirt was sitting behind a desk. He asked for my passport in perfect English. I gave it to him. He looked at every page and said, 'Why are you travelling to London?'

This is it, I thought. It's what I feared most. *They have caught up with me. I'll be forced onto a Bulgarian plane back to Sofia. Interrogation, torture, jail…*

I decided to adopt an aggressive stance and said, 'I've got a valid passport to travel anywhere in the world. There is a job my company wants me to do in London.'

He fixed his gaze on my eyes and said, 'There is a national police strike in Egypt. The army has taken control of the airport. There may be delays.' And he handed my passport back to me. I could hardly believe it. He gave me his business card. I noticed that he belonged to the same shipping agency which looked after the Bulgarian vessel in Port Said.

I spent the evening in the Novotel restaurant and then in the lobby discreetly watching the lifts for any suspicious characters who might have been sent to find me. Eventually, I dragged myself to the room but could not rest, waiting for the proverbial 'knock on the door'. Early in the morning, about four hours before my flight, I made my way through the airport. The shops were closed. It was eerily quiet. Just before the check-in desks there was an army soldier checking passports. He was a young recruit with an intelligent face, brushed by the wind, and rough chapped hands. He took my passport and started to leaf through every single page. What was it with these airport security people? Everybody wanted to see every page of my passport. He handed it back to me without saying anything. The check-in clerk, an elderly man, looked frazzled. I had a story ready in my head but he only asked, 'Are you transiting through Heathrow?' 'Yes,' I said, and I was through. The next hurdle was passport control but I felt more relaxed. An army sergeant took my passport and my boarding pass and stamped them both without hesitation.

When the aircraft started to descend over London, what struck me was how green the ground was. The pretty rows of terraced houses nestled in the green trees around them gave an air of tranquility. I had watched an old black and white documentary about London on Bulgarian television some years previously. What had impressed me then was the idea that most people lived in houses, not in apartments, and that every house had a milk bottle delivered to the doorstep every morning.

Once out of the Egypt Air aircraft, a tremendous weight lifted from my shoulders. The worst was behind me.

I was dressed in my best double-breasted, dark blue pinstriped suit and a navy tie. Before I reached passport control, I stopped at a British Airways information desk, showed my Bulgarian passport to a lady with grey hair and said, 'I am a Bulgarian citizen and I would like to claim political asylum in Britain.' It sounded preposterous, like a line from a movie. She went all red in the face, took my passport and politely asked me to wait. A few minutes later she returned with two men in airport uniforms. One of them, the immigration officer, looked carefully at every page in my passport and asked me where I had come from. He was surprised that I had managed to get on a flight to London without a valid British visa. I said I had told everybody that I was transiting through London. 'But where is your onward ticket?' he said. I said that I didn't have one. He put my passport in his pocket and said to the other man, 'Let's go and get his baggage.'

We took a convoluted back door route to the baggage hall. The immigration officer had to lock and unlock many doors along the way. My suitcase was the only one still circulating on the baggage belt. The other man, who turned out to be a customs officer, asked me to open the case and examined its contents carefully. He turned to his colleague, pointed at the suitcase and, perhaps without realising that I spoke English, said the following words, which would stay with me for the rest of my life: 'He's got everything he needs for the English weather, except an umbrella.'

For the next five days, I was detained at Heathrow and interrogated twice daily. My interrogators alternated. A dark-haired woman, who I assumed to be an immigration officer, was mainly interested in the way I got on the Air Egypt flight without a British visa and whether I had planned to claim political asylum before I left Bulgaria.

My second interrogator was a smartly dressed woman in her thirties, with straight blonde hair and piercing blue eyes. Her questions were different. From them I inferred a deep knowledge of Eastern Europe. The questions were cleverly designed to check out my story: from little details about my journey to names and places she had teased out of me in previous conversations. She kept asking about my father: when was he interned, when was he allowed to return to Sofia, how he made a living, where he was born, what languages he spoke, who knew about the spying accusations, how he had managed to avoid execution as an enemy of the state. She basically asked the same questions over and over again but under different guises. There was an iron logic to them, although they were asked in a deliberately chaotic way. I suspected she was from MI5.

I told her everything I knew.

The blonde-haired woman was the one who told me that I would be released from detention. She handed me a piece of paper with the address of a hostel in Victoria, originally set up for Polish war veterans, and said they were expecting me. I had to pay a deposit from my own money and the hostel would advise me on how to start claiming help from the state. I sheepishly asked, 'But I've got no ID documents on me. You've kept everything. What if the police stop me?' She smiled and said something which took me completely by surprise, 'Police in this country don't normally stop people in the street and ask for documents.'

I was so excited about embarking on my first London Underground journey to Victoria. It was the evening of 14th January when I emerged from Victoria Station. The weather was unusually warm. I just stood in the street in my pin-striped suit and admired the evening traffic. The cars, clean and shiny, waited their turn at the traffic lights in an orderly manner. Their yellow number plates were spectacularly different from any I'd seen before. Then a red double-decker bus passed in front of me. My heart leapt: I was finally in London! Somebody stopped and kindly asked if I needed directions.

I didn't call my parents straight away. I didn't know what I was going to say. I knew that they would have been questioned by the police after I failed to return. A quick phone call to Port Said by the authorities would have established that I had boarded a plane to London. And I knew that their phone calls would be monitored.

A few days later, I summoned the courage to call them. Choosing a phone box took me a whole afternoon. Victoria train station, an obvious choice, was out of the question. It was too noisy. A couple of red phone boxes, one in Buckingham Palace Road, the other one in Eccleston Square, both within easy walking distance of the hostel, were too solitary. Then I realised that choosing a phone box was only a delaying tactic to avoid calling them.

I waited until the evening to make sure that they were at home. There was a row of modern phone boxes at Victoria Coach Station nearby where you could put your head under a clear plastic hemi-sphere to make the call. I chose the furthest one, in the corner. At that time of the evening the station hall was quiet. My mother answered. Her voice was steady, crisp and clear like that of a radio announcer. There was a strange indifference in her tone almost as if she was talking to someone else and not to me. My mum liked to think that she was a good actress but she was easy to read. I knew she was putting this on for the benefit of those who monitored the call. 'Where are you?' she said casually. 'London,' I answered trying to put some enthusiasm into the tone of my voice.

She said they knew that I had travelled to London but they were not sure if I was still there. The police had told them to report immediately my whereabouts. My father was listening on the other receiver in the sitting room. When he finally spoke his voice sounded a bit hollow but he was true to form: 'I thought you were roughing it in some refugee camp. That's why you hadn't called.'

'I was in detention for five days at the airport but they let me go,' I said.

'What are you doing for money?'

'Don't worry,' I said, 'I've got somewhere to live and I've got enough to eat. I've registered for government help. This will be enough until I find a job.'

'A bit humiliating to live on state handouts for someone in your position, isn't it?'

It was my contrarian dad speaking. This sounded like a rebuke for defecting from Bulgaria. I though he'd be pleased. Was he trying to hide his genuine concern about my well-being? He never liked overt expressions of emotion. Did he genuinely think I'd made the wrong decision? Or was he angry that I hadn't told him in advance?

'What is my position?'

'Highly educated…'

'I'm sorry,' I said, 'I'm running out of change. The line will go down in a second.'

'Take care and look after yourself,' my mother intervened. 'You know we love you.'

I hung up even before my two pounds were fully used.

I stayed in the hostel for the next few months and started sending handwritten letters to newspapers and magazines offering my services as a journalist or political analyst. I wrote to maritime companies and shipping agents trying to capitalise on my paltry business experience in Bulgaria. At best, I got flat rejections; at worst – no replies at all. The *Economist* wrote back affectionately to advise me that they would love to hear from me in a few years after I'd gained some British experience.

In my eighth week at the hostel, a letter arrived which would change my life forever. The hostel manager delivered it personally to me and, winking conspiratorially, said, 'You've got a letter from the BBC.' The letter was very short, typed on a small A5 sheet of headed paper, with the BBC coat of arms at the top. The BBC motto 'Nation shall speak peace unto Nation' was just about discernable under the shield. I must have stared at it for hours, examining with great precision every little detail as if trying to convince myself that it was real. It was from the Head of the Bulgarian Section of the World Service inviting me for an interview.

The iconic edifice of Bush House in Aldwych, where the World Service had been based since the bleak wartime winter of 1941, was awe-inspiring. I stood on the pavement in front of the grand portico and read the inscription over the entrance: 'To the friendship of English speaking peoples.' I didn't understand it. Years later, I would discover that the two Greek-style statues over the entrance of Bush House symbolised Anglo-American friendship.

I reported to the main reception desk and was asked to wait. I looked at the high ceilings and marble walls around me. From where I was sitting I could see beyond the security guard into the great atrium flanked by two grand marble staircases unfolding in opposite directions. The smell, the echo from the passing footsteps and the dark ambience around me made me feel as if I was in a place of worship, a shrine of something indefinable.

This spiritual exultation was shattered by a middle-aged man in a tweed jacket, crumpled blue trousers and very thick glasses. He stood in front of me, stretched his arm for a handshake and said something. I had difficulty understanding his accent because he spoke very quickly and no English teacher in Bulgaria had prepared me for the glottal stops. His name was John W, the Head of the Bulgarian Section. He signed me in at the reception desk and I followed him down a marble corridor into an internal courtyard and then into another part of the building.

The Bulgarian Section of the World Service was situated on the fifth floor of the South East Wing of Bush House. It comprised four interconnected rooms – one of which was the section Head's office. I was ushered inside and he shut the door, to the obvious annoyance of a couple of Bulgarian émigrés huddled over the only computer in the Section positioned in the secretary's room in front of his office. John W tried his heavily accented Bulgarian on me but I had even greater difficulty understanding him. Then he reverted to Russian. He was a fluent Russian speaker and I had no problem with his accent there. Behind John's unassuming façade I was to discover a powerful intellect and no nonsense attitude. I liked him straight away. He would become my mentor at the BBC and would eventually encourage me to leave the Section and work in the main World Service newsroom. That would be my first big break into mainstream British journalism.

A former RAF intelligence officer, he instilled in me a rigid work discipline and determination to succeed. Before long, he introduced me to his family at his house in Hendon and our shared love of opera would frequently take us to the English National Opera and the Royal Opera House in Covent Garden. But at that first meeting in the spring of 1986 he was terse and cold. 'Before anything,' he said, 'we must test your language skills in a written exam. You must also undergo a voice test. If you pass, we can discuss what employment opportunities there might be for you here.' I said I was ready to sit the test immediately.

Two weeks later, John W telephoned me personally at the hostel to tell me that I had passed the tests. There was, however, he explained, another hurdle: a rigorous security check by the BBC and MI5, which would take about three months. I was sanguine about it and just very grateful that the BBC had even considered me for a broadcasting position.

I wasn't prepared to do nothing for three months and I took a job in an art shop in Highgate. It turned out to be another lucky break. The shop sold top quality artists' materials and had an illustrious clientele of well-known painters, interior designers and restorers. Lucian Freud bought his canvases there but he hardly spoke to anyone. I met Leon Kossoff, the great British expressionist painter, and an exiled Russian avant-garde artist, Oleg Kudryashov, who had left the Soviet Union some twelve years previously. Oleg was allowed to leave during a brief spell of détente under Leonid Brezhnev but was not permitted to take any of his works with him. Years later, at his home in south London, his wife would tell me that he had destroyed about six thousand of his works before he left rather than leave them to the Soviets.

The work in the art shop improved my English and gave me that elusive thing, 'the British experience'. I was not ashamed to ask basic questions about British life. The most frightening experience was taking credit card payments on the phone. It was nerve-racking trying to understand people's accents. My brain went into overdrive about simple things like the names of places, post-codes and Royal Mail rates.

By the middle of the summer of 1986, just after the royal wedding of Prince Andrew to Sarah Ferguson, the BBC security checks were completed. John W offered me a casual contract, which meant that I was to come and do a shift in the section whenever they needed me. I opted to receive my payment in cash at the end of each week because I still didn't have a bank account.

On my first day at the Bulgarian Section, everybody looked at me suspiciously. I chose an empty desk in an empty room and started preparing my material for broadcasting. I was given two dispatches from BBC foreign correspondents, which I had to translate into Bulgarian and read out live on air during a half-hour news programme. My name would not be mentioned. It would be like doing two anonymous voice-overs. I thought that only my parents might be able to recognise my voice. But it was a time when almost everybody in Bulgaria listened to the BBC.

Just as I started typing my translations, an elderly man opened the door and introduced himself. He looked at me, and said: 'Not sure if you know, but you've chosen a very inauspicious desk.' I stared at him inquisitively. 'This was Georgi Markov's desk. No one has used it since his murder.'

Markov was a Bulgarian writer and dissident who defected to the West in the early 1970s. His inexplicable murder on Waterloo Bridge in London in 1978 introduced a new dimension at the height of the Cold War. A micro-engineered pellet containing the deadly poison ricin was fired from an umbrella into his leg while he was waiting for a bus. The murder coined a new phrase in the English language: 'The Bulgarian Umbrella.'

A few weeks after my first anonymous voice-over, John W took me aside in the corridor and said, 'Our presenter has just called in sick. How do you feel about presenting the programme this afternoon?' I was shocked but spotted an opportunity. There were two other people on duty that day who had been with the Section for many years but John W had chosen to approach me. I had already heard mutterings of discontent about my being fast-tracked. Some people had gone further and insinuated that there was something fishy about my good English. One even said that he knew about my school in Sofia: 'This is where top communists send their children. It's not for everybody. How did you manage to get in?' I didn't even try to explain that my father encouraged me to apply against all odds. It was the most prestigious high school in Sofia. At the age of fourteen anybody above a certain academic score could apply but that wasn't all. We had to sit two rigorous exams: maths and Bulgarian. My dad said, 'Most places are reserved for the sons and daughters of the nomenklatura [people appointed by the party] but there is a tiny percentage open for ordinary people. You've got to be head and shoulders above the rest if you want to get in.' I scored the top mark in maths and got a place.

There was no training, nor dry run for my live presenting debut. I was promised a rehearsal 10 minutes before the transmission. Almost all studios at Bush House were situated underground, perhaps a legacy of the wartime years. I put on a calm face when I took the lift to the basement but my heart was about to burst out of my chest. John W who was directing the transmission was sitting in the control room next to the studio manager, an elderly woman, slightly hippy-ish with long grey hair and no make-up. Just before I went into the audio room for the rehearsal John W peered into my face through his thick-lens glasses and said, 'Do you want to broadcast under your own name or do you want to choose an alias? Most people here prefer not to divulge their real names so that their families behind the iron curtain will not be persecuted.' I shrugged my shoulders thinking, if they delude themselves that the KGB doesn't know who they are, they live in cloud cuckoo land. But I didn't want to disappoint John W and said, 'I'll be Boyan Atanasov.' The name just jumped out of my brain because I knew that my dad would recognise it instantly. It was a homophonic pun on his own name.

The transmission went without a single hitch. John W was very generous in his praise. I knew I had sounded a bit uptight and nervous but I had instinctively timed my links with precision and managed to wind up the programme exactly on time.

I called my parents the following day from the same telephone box at Victoria from which I had called them that first time. I always called them from that same box. I had become superstitious about it. I thought it brought me luck. That's why I circled around for a bit until it became available. They had already been questioned again by the police. My mother didn't make any comment on the phone. My dad only said, 'Boyan Atanasov, huh!'

His old-fashioned veneered radio set had long been replaced by a modern Hitachi transistor radio with a more powerful short wave range and reception had been clear for years. He no longer had to put his ear to the speaker's membrane in an effort to decipher the crackling voice of the broadcasts. Despite his typically terse response, from now on I knew he wouldn't miss a single transmission.

TRIPOLI, LIBYA, MARCH 2011

My room at the opulently decorated Rixos Hotel is on the ground floor to the left of the main entrance. Although it's my first time here, I feel at home with the Soviet-style management of this establishment. You see the same men in ill-fitting overcoats milling around in the lobby or drinking endless cups of tea in the café. Their coats are too big in order to conceal the weapons they think no one knows they carry. Occasionally, you can spot severe-looking women in the inevitable dark trouser suits. They are not hotel staff and describe themselves as volunteer translators. One of them, appropriately named Huda ('guidance' in Arabic), approached me the other day and offered to help us with any stories we were doing. When I asked if she could assist in going out to do some filming in the city, she replied that she had to check with the security people. 'For your own safety,' she added.

When my dad first came to London in 1991, after communism had collapsed in Europe, he said something casually, true to style: 'Any Bulgarian exile could've joined the World Service in the Cold War, but do you have what it takes to make it outside, in the real world?' It still rings in my ears.

Tripoli under bombardment by NATO planes is my last assignment for the BBC after twenty-five years with the corporation. On that fateful day at Bush House when I was an anonymous voice reading a translation of a news dispatch for the Bulgarian Section of the World Service, I couldn't even dream that work as a journalist at the BBC would eventually take me from Belgrade and Kosovo to Baghdad, Kabul and Tehran, from Moscow and Beijing to Washington and Buenos Aires and, finally, here, to Tripoli today. A quarter of a century ago, it was inconceivable to think that one day I would meet the king of Saudi Arabia or the presidents of Russia and the USA. I wish my father had lived longer to see me travelling from the caves of Tora Bora in Afghanistan to the Toromocho Mountain in Peru or produce a political obituary for Tony Blair on the Ten O'Clock News when he stepped down as prime minister.

The Rixos Hotel is part of a Turkish chain and despite the bombing there are still some Turkish staff working at reception and in the café. They are all young men in tight black trousers, greased hair and astonishingly similar pointy black shoes. I am amazed that the restaurant still serves fresh food and there's no shortage of soft drinks. There are no other guests at the hotel except us, the foreign media. We are not free to come and go as we wish. In fact, we are under house arrest.

I am waiting for John Simpson in the hotel lobby. His room is on the first floor, and I am watching the grand staircase, which leads into the lobby. We've arranged to meet at 10.30. There he comes, clutching his leather-bound notebook. His movements are slightly out of sync as he is trying to force a hurried youthful stride. His tall figure is imposing and commands respect. His very English, old-fashioned, almost colonial looks, with white hair carefully combed back, immaculate cream shirt and chino trousers, make people turn their heads.

The memory of a young man chasing Simpson through Heathrow airport a few years previously shouting, 'Sir David, Sir David, I so much admire your film about the gorillas,' brings a smile to my face. The incident was prolonged because Simpson ignored him and walked determinedly towards our departure gate without uttering a word. I walked next to him trying to subdue my chuckles. I know it annoys him when people mistake him for another broadcaster, the natural history presenter, Sir David Attenborough, not least because Attenborough is almost 20 years older than him. But on that day, as now, he looked exactly like him.

The young man at Heathrow airport was not to know that we were not on our way to film gorillas, but to war-torn Baghdad where at the time a thousand people died each month in a vicious civil war. Simply being in Baghdad in those tumultuous days was seen as reckless bravery.

Over the last few years Simpson and I have developed a close working relationship – a 'partnership' as he puts it, to the annoyance of my colleagues and the bosses at the BBC. There was a period in our work, dubbed by jealous colleagues as 'The Simpson World Tour', when we spent more time together on the road than with our families and partners at home in London. A very senior BBC boss once told me that I was seen as personally loyal to Simpson and not to the BBC.

There's tension on this trip, too. The cameraman on the team thinks that he can do all the production and editorial work and I shouldn't be here at all. Some of the long-serving cameramen have in recent years been designated as video producers and production, at least nominally, is seen as part of their duties. They are good skilled operators, some of them very brave, but most of them, with very few exceptions, are cameramen first and foremost, not journalists.

'Hello, Oggy.' Simpson drops his heavy frame on the big leather sofa. 'Shall we have some tea?' After years of travelling together, I am now used to drinking gallons of tea on every trip. Simpson loves his tea. And I have learned a lot about tea, from his favourite strong Darjeeling to the dark Chinese Pu-erh and delicately powerful Ti Kuan Yin. Unfortunately, the Rixos only serves Lipton's tea bags.

'I have hardly slept,' he continues. 'Spent all night talking to some guys from the Information Ministry who threatened to expel me.'

I shake my head and say that I was woken up at about 2 am by a phone call. The man, whose voice and accent I vaguely recognised, asked me to come to the lobby immediately. I asked why and he said that I might be expelled in the morning. Feeling grumpy, I said I was not leaving my room in the middle of the night and that he would do me a favour if he expelled me from this dump, and put the phone down. No one called after that. And there's no sign of us being expelled this morning.

Simpson looks at me with tired eyes. I say we have been the victims of minor intimidation. He says there was a real danger of him being expelled but he'd persuaded them not to. I don't pursue it any further. We both agree that in Gaddafi's Libya nothing is what it seems. Sometimes, people who nominally hold menial jobs wield a lot of power. The question is, how do you find out?

In the afternoon, we are told we are being taken by bus to Green Square to do some filming. It always takes ages for the journalists to assemble by the bus. And there's no urgency on the part of our minders, either.

I am irritable and ignore the cameraman's instructions to help him with the gear. Normally, as a producer, I've got the distinguished job of carrying the tripod. I mumble that I have to go back to my room. As soon as I'm back in the room, I inspect the skin rash on the back of my right leg. It's getting bigger and almost looks like shingles but it doesn't itch. I know it's not shingles because I had this rash in the same place just a few weeks ago when I was skiing in Italy, and a few months earlier after a trip to Peshawar. You can't have shingles at the same spot on your skin only a few weeks apart. I try to calm myself down. But what is it then? I make a promise to see a doctor when I get back to London. For the moment, there's not a lot I can do about it.

When I'm back at the bus, Simpson is talking to somebody I haven't seen before. He is a middle-aged, casually dressed Libyan man with a moustache and very sad, dark eyes. They are standing on the grass in front of the hotel. As I approach, Simpson introduces me immediately as his producer. The man shakes my hand warmly and says: 'Fuad.' The conversation proceeds in a very cryptic way, so I decide to leave them to it and board the bus, deliberately choosing a seat on the other side so that they can't see me. A few minutes later, just moments before the bus is about to depart, Simpson sits next to me and whispers, 'I'll tell you all about it later.'

The trip to Green Square takes only a few minutes and I relish every second of it. We've only been in Tripoli for a few days but, due to our virtual house arrest, it seems like ages. It seems like ages since we left London, too. It was on Monday, 21st March, two days after the NATO aerial bombardment on Libya had started. Tripoli airport was closed. The Libyan embassy in London was also shut down, so we had to seek visas from the Libyan consulate in Sfax, Tunisia. After a night at Charles de Gaulle airport in Paris, we arrived in Tunis, early on Tuesday morning. A car and driver waited for us and we immediately set off on a four-hour drive to Sfax. When we arrived the consulate was closed. With the invaluable assistance of a highly over-worked and undoubtedly underpaid young man on the BBC foreign desk in London who made all the calls to the powers that be in Tripoli, visas were stamped in our passports before the end of the working day. Another five-hour drive east took us to the town of Zarzis on the Mediterranean coast. A night in a down-market all-inclusive hotel and we were again on the road the following morning to the Libyan border. When we arrived at the border crossing of Ras Ajdir, I felt like a zombie. I didn't care how long the formalities would take. Simply being on Libyan territory was an enormous relief. After two intensive days in transit our mission was accomplished – Simpson and I, and a cameraman, were again in a place which was closed to the outside world. The rest would take care of itself.

Coverage so far has consisted of live injects into BBC continuous news channels – News24 and BBC World, with the occasional radio two-way. Not being allowed to go out was an impediment to original newsgathering so until this trip to Green Square we'd been unable to offer a self-contained film.

The streets of downtown Tripoli are deserted except for occasional people going about their business. Most of the shops are closed. Although it's nice to get out and about, every trip in a government bus carries the risk of being bombed by NATO planes. Most of the bombardment happens during the night, but there's no guarantee that we are safe in the streets in daylight, especially when we are being driven in government buses.

Green Square is bedecked with an enormous poster of Gaddafi in sunshades. The banner is draped from the roof to the first floor along the front of a multi-storey building. It flutters with the breeze coming from the sea front. Does he really think he looks cool in his colonel's uniform and these ridiculous dark glasses? I can't believe that no one can tell him how preposterous he looks. His sons have been educated in the West. They should know what's cool. Can't they say, 'Dad, you look funny in these sunglasses. Let the people see your eyes'?

With these thoughts, I carry the tri-pod across the square, trying to find a suitable place to record Simpson's piece-to-camera. Cars and pick-up trucks occasionally race across the square full of screaming youths waving the green banner and holding portraits of the colonel. For our benefit, some of the youths kiss Gaddafi's image to demonstrate their love as they pass by the camera. The sound of the car horns is unbearable. There's a huge sound deck playing loud patriotic music in one corner of the square. Although there are very few people milling around, the noise is designed to give the impression that there are thousands of people here. I approach the cameraman and suggest that he raise the camera and pan across the square to capture how empty it is. He looks grumpily at me: 'I know what I'm doing.'

After we've recorded enough government propaganda and screaming people declaring their loyalty to Gaddafi, I ask our minder if we can go to the old quarter to buy some souvenirs. That's become my favourite pastime during these foreign trips. Simpson loves it, too. He has a remarkable collection of memorabilia connected with dictators, past and present. One of his most talked about conquests is Ceausescu's fountain pen which he says he nicked from the presidential palace in Bucharest when it was ransacked in the revolution of 1989. I once asked a welder in Kirkuk, northern Iraq, when it fell to Kurdish forces in April 2003, to cut out Saddam Hussein's face from a monument in the centre of the city so that Simpson could take it back as a souvenir. The Kurds were all too happy to oblige. They saw it as their duty to desecrate Saddam's monuments in revenge for the brutality he'd inflicted on their people. Years later, Simpson told me it was lost en route and never made it to his collection in London.

We are determined to buy souvenirs glorifying Gaddafi's power. Both of us are convinced that this is our last chance. We've often talked about how their value isn't important. What counts is the memory of when and how we bought them.

A short distance away from Green Square there is a warren of little streets with small craft shops, blacksmiths and other workshops, all government sponsored. Our minder is a lot calmer. Here, we are not likely to be exposed to approaches by random people, who might say something nasty about the regime. The people who work here have been trained to handle foreigners. He keeps close to Simpson because he's the main target to watch. I peel off accompanied by our security advisor. We walk into a small empty shop selling metalwork. The man is hammering a piece of iron.

'Do you have anything with Gaddafi's image on it?' I say in English.

He shakes his head. 'All gone.'

The man is dirty. His nails are soiled. But his eyes are alive and piercing. I stare at him. He then puts his hand behind a cupboard and pulls out a metal plate with an engraved picture of a young Gaddafi in tribal gear and dark shades. There are still bits of blue, green and black enamel on it but most of it has been rubbed off. A small hook is welded on the back so that you can hang it on the wall. I wonder how many people over the years have bought these plates and hung them voluntarily.

'How much?' I ask. 'Ten dollars,' he says looking straight into my eyes.

The inevitable haggling process begins. I can tell he hasn't had this pleasure for a long while. He enjoys it. Eventually, I give him a five-dollar note and he wraps the plate in a bit of brown paper.

'What will happen with Gaddafi?' I say casually, deliberately not looking at him.

He throws a glance over my shoulder to see the street through the open door behind me and says, 'He's finished.'

I ask him what will happen with the shop, with him, with his family. He just shakes his head. 'Inshallah!'

At that moment the minder storms into the shop. He looks worried. What have we been talking about? We should stick together as a group. This will get him in trouble. I show him the plate and he calms down.

Out in the street, I ask him about his education. He loves the question. He studied political economy in Moscow in the early 1980s. I ask him in Russian if he enjoyed his time in Moscow. He is shocked and instead of answering the question he says, 'You're not English, are you? You look Turkish. What are you?'

I explain that I was born in Bulgaria but that my father was from northern Greece, and that in the Balkans we are all mixed as we've been part of the Ottoman Empire for a long time. He is more relaxed now. We start a conversation in Russian. He is a very thin man with high cheekbones, more Berber-looking than Arab. His clothes are too big for him and, although civilian, the colours are military green and beige. He looks like a Soviet secret agent from the 1970s.

Now it's my turn to investigate his ethnic origins. 'You look Berber to me. Do you come from the desert?'

His broad smile reveals strong white teeth. He puts his arm around my shoulder to the consternation of the others. By that time the whole group is assembled together. Simpson has bought a glass panel with Gaddafi's face carved on it, quite expensive by the look of it. It is mounted on a wooden stand, something that a high-ranking official would've put on his desk. It's very similar to engravings of Lenin and Stalin I have seen in Russia. The Soviet influence in Gaddafi's Libya is staggering. I have often noticed this influence in other countries, like Sudan, Iraq, Egypt, even Turkey – countries which historically have not been in the USSR's direct sphere of influence. But they had successfully copied the Soviet style propaganda, the Soviet way of organising and running the security apparatus, even the way their secret police look.

As teenagers in Bulgaria, hungry for information and personal freedoms, and fed up with economic austerity, my friends and I looked at these quasi-socialist dictatorships as an economic model to admire. 'Socialism with dollars,' we used to call the countries, which fell between the two worlds – the Soviet Bloc and the Western alliance, countries like Tito's Yugoslavia, Saddam's Iraq, Gaddafi's Libya, Mengistu's Ethiopia and even Siad Barre's Somalia. In the 1970s, Bulgarian medical workers and engineers went with starry eyes to sell their labour for US dollars in those countries. They came back with stories of shops bursting with Western goods and freedom of travel. That affluence seemed to be within the reach of ordinary people. But no one talked about freedom of expression. No one talked about political prisoners. No one talked about how desperately poor most of those countries were.

How desperately misinformed we were!

But we weren't so naïve as not to understand that the world had been divided into spheres of influence and that Soviet support for one country or another had nothing to do with high political ideals. Marxism was used as a tool in the global race for domination of the world. The Soviets even changed the Marxist doctrine to allow nasty regimes to use it as an excuse for heavy-handed oppression. They called it 'adapting the socialist theory to the needs of each individual country' – with hindsight, this was a carte blanche for tin-pot dictators to preserve a seemingly market economy and dress up their outright repression as a struggle for the liberation of the working classes.

What's unfolding in the Middle East today is a direct consequence of the Cold War. Tunisia, Libya, Egypt and Syria were the last bastions of the old order, entrenched during the post-war Soviet era, when old colonial empires were collapsing and young charismatic leaders with socialist leanings emerged. However, after the collapse of communism in Europe there was no external pressure to reform and their economies failed. Those once charismatic leaders had turned their countries unashamedly into family-run businesses while milking the support from both Russia and the West. But now the young generation, which does not remember the Cold War and the anti-colonial struggles, demands the same freedoms and economic benefits as their Western peers. And they are not prepared to take 'No' for an answer. Delayed perhaps by the Western military interventions in Afghanistan and Iraq, the political and economic mismanagement of the old ruling families is catching up with them. The only unknown in the new equation is the latent Islamic fervour in certain sections of the population, suppressed for so long by dictatorial regimes. This has now become the new battleground for the hearts and minds of restless nations.

The next stop is a clothes shop selling traditional Libyan garments. I want to buy a burnus, a traditional cape with a hood, worn widely by men in the Maghreb countries. Gaddafi is often pictured in traditional Libyan dress – either a burnus, a bisht, or a barrakan. His wacky fashion style has evolved over the years and has ranged from a simple military uniform, early on, to elaborate Arab or African costumes, depending on whether he wanted to emphasise his Arab or African credentials. Even *Vanity Fair* felt obliged to do a special article about his dress sense.

I try a brown burnus but it's too big for me. They haven't got a smaller one and I buy it anyway. Simpson buys a black one. There is not much haggling here because the minder is in charge of the negotiations. We just have to pay the asking price. The shop assistants are three burly well-fed Arab men who look more like army sergeants than shopkeepers. I then play my last card: 'I'm sorry I didn't bring enough cash with me.' That causes bewilderment on everyone's face. The minder, however, is quick to suggest that he'll pay and I'll give him the money at the hotel. Clever. That's settled then.

Back at the Rixos, the minder follows me to my room. At the door, I turn around and say that he should meet me at John Simpson's room in 15 minutes. I would like witnesses that I've paid him back the money. I check my emails on the laptop set up on the hotel's slow WiFi. There are long rants from London about how I should focus on getting a permit for a BBC satellite dish instead of following any stories. At the morning's conference call, a little jumped up man who had already done a stint in Tripoli before me, gave me a lecture about who the main players were at the Information Ministry. I told him that all that had changed and there was a new man in charge, Musa Ibrahim.

Remember that name. In the last days of the regime, Musa Ibrahim was on television screens around the world all the time. He would give press conferences, sometimes several times a day. And because we couldn't leave the hotel, these gatherings would become the only events we filmed. I am still not sure what motivated him to stick by the Gaddafi family until the very last moments. He was an unpleasant character but undoubtedly skilful at his job. His main advantage was that he understood the Western media and spoke excellent English. At the time of writing this chapter, Musa Ibrahim is still at large, after all the main players of the Gaddafi regime had either been captured, killed or changed sides.

I was told during the conference call that Musa Ibrahim was nobody and I should work on another guy, Mr El Dursi, Head of the Government Media Section. Although I had spoken to El Dursi the day before, an affable older man with very good manners and perfect English, and he had told me he was leaving his job in order to go to Benghazi and find his family, I didn't mention anything about that at the conference call. El Dursi was out, either by choice or because he was pushed. But life was too short for lengthy explanations on the phone. I didn't have the patience. Let them stew in their own self-important ignorance if they think that they know better, sitting in their offices thousands of miles away.

This has been a permanent feature of my relationship with the so-called 'middle-management' at the BBC. They are normally a bunch of people who spend most of their time in various meetings or conference calls, regurgitating the scraps of information that people like Simpson and I feed them at our choosing. They know they should be worried about their vacuous jobs and they cling to them by stopping at nothing to justify their existence. Controlling the flow of information internally is one way of clinging to your job. And they hide their insecurity behind a wall of aggressive behaviour. The bane of the BBC is its fat layer of management, which generally consists of mediocre people who have generally failed in their reporting or editorial careers or, as a former Chairman of the BBC trust put it, 'those whose creative juices have run out'. Most of them are viciously opposed to talent – scared that talented people might outshine them.

A long time ago, there was this particular person who was so outraged that a foreign-born journalist like me should be promoted on the domestic side of the BBC, i.e. the part which produces material for consumption by UK audiences, that I was told through an intermediary that I should move back to the World Service where I 'belonged'. She thought that I was too 'foreign' to understand the 'domestic' agenda. I was determined to prove her wrong. Over the years, I have often wondered how on earth it's possible for the BBC, a bastion of managerial mediocrity, to produce such outstanding programmes. Perhaps there are enough in-built checks and balances in the system to allow the talented to produce fantastic programmes despite the management, not because of them.

A couple of months ago, after I had already put in motion the process of leaving the BBC, I was summoned to a sandwich lunch with the new boss of the World Affairs Unit, the outfit within BBC News where Simpson and I nominally belonged. 'Sandwich lunch' meant that I bought my own sandwiches and tea, and he bought his, and we ate them on a bench outside Television Centre. He had just been parachuted into the unit because, I suspected, his previous department wanted to get rid of him. He wanted me to start reporting to him every week about my plans with Simpson, something I had never done with any of his predecessors.

'No way! Absolutely not!' I said. 'We work in a very competitive industry. Even within the same organisation we constantly compete against each other. This is the nature of journalism. I don't want to discuss with you our plans in advance only to be told that another correspondent is already thinking or even planning to do the same story. Simpson holds a special place in BBC News and he should be allowed a greater degree of autonomy.'

The poor bloke was visibly shocked. I pushed even further: 'You may think you are our manager but you are not authorised to approve any of our trips because you don't have a budget, and neither can you give me a pay rise. So, why am I going to account to you?'

He looked embarrassed. 'But I can help you sell your stories to programme editors…' he started.

I interrupted him: 'I can speak to programme editors directly. It's much more productive cutting out the middle man. And Simpson can speak to very senior people right at the top of the BBC who are beyond your reach. You should take some lessons from your predecessor,' I continued, 'he managed to look busy even though he wasn't doing anything. And he left us alone.'

I wrap the metal plate with Gaddafi's faded image in a T-shirt and put it in the suitcase. When I travel on work assignments I never unpack. Everything stays in the suitcase and it has its permanent place so that I can find things even in the dark. My lucky black rucksack is always by my bedside so that I can grab it in an emergency and get out. It has my passports, money and some emergency supplies – a bottle of water, high-energy snacks and medication. And I always sleep with light clothing on regardless of the season. The indignity of being found naked in the rubble if the hotel is hit by a bomb or arrested in my underpants in the middle of the night is a far too worrying prospect to ignore.

It's happened to me only once in my career – in Baghdad at the end of 2003. One early morning I was lying in bed in my room on one of the top floors of the Sheraton Hotel, in the centre of Baghdad between the Tigris and Firdos Square. Needless to say there was no air conditioning, so I was almost naked when the building was shaken by an almighty explosion. What happened next was almost beyond description – the swishing noise of a collapsing structure just outside my door. For a minute I thought the building had been detonated. With indifference bordering on serenity I lay in bed waiting to be buried under the rubble. But nothing else happened. A mortar fired from a donkey cart across the square had struck the lift shaft on the roof, severing the cables and the lift cabin dropped twenty floors down into the basement.

The brown burnus is too bulky to fit in the suitcase, so I stuff it in the bag in which I carry my flak jacket. I hardly show my exotic purchases to anyone in London. Frankly, not many people are that interested. I have a cupboard full of trophy souvenirs like a box of gold cufflinks and a tie clip, which Saddam gave to his air force officers, a set of plates with his image in military uniform and, my favourite, a couple of police toy cars which were stuck with blue tack on a city map of Tikrit, which I found in the police station's control room in his home town.

Before I leave, I check again the inflamed patch on the back of my leg. There's no change. I feel the onset of a headache and take a couple of painkillers.

With pent up anger in my chest, I make my way to Simpson's room. The minder is waiting outside. Simpson is not there. I take a card key and open the door of the adjacent room, which belongs to our cameraman. It is our edit suite and from its balcony we do our live injects into programmes in London. The cameraman is not there either. I can't be bothered to wait for witnesses and put my hand in my pocket and take a few US dollar notes. The minder's eyes follow my every movement. I owe him $140, not cheap for some poor quality ethnic clothes, probably made in China. He looks around the room like a frightened animal, takes the money, looks around again and says, 'Thank you,' and promptly leaves. It's not a hanging offence to take money from foreigners in Gaddafi's Libya. What he doesn't want to do is to share it with his bosses.

On my way out of Libya a few days later, I learned that some of the broadcasters, who already had satellite dishes in the hotel, had paid significant bribes to get them in. Apparently, it had been a big scam right from the beginning: if you wanted to increase the number of people on your team or you wanted to import more equipment, one of the head translators was designated to negotiate and take the money, which was then presumably shared between senior people in the government media office.

Simpson is sitting in the café. I sit opposite and burn with impatience to find out about the man he was talking with by the bus earlier. But I wait. We order tea.

'We might be on to something here,' Simpson says. 'The man I was talking to by the bus is very close to Gaddafi. He was his personal translator during my last visit here a few years ago. I don't even know his name but he recognised me and started talking to me. I only heard his name when he introduced himself to you. Fuad. He gave me his number.'

My heart leaps with excitement. We could have a high-profile interview. Is Gaddafi still in Tripoli? I have heard that Saif al-Islam, Gaddafi's second son, an LSE doctorate holder, is here and is allegedly in command. Saif doesn't hold any official position in the government but somehow everybody in the regime obeys his orders. He looks like a thug with his shaved head. He has recently ditched his suit and now can be seen in casual clothes – jumpers or T-shirts – similar to any trendy Arab man you may see on the Edgware Road in London. The last time I saw him in a television interview, his eyes looked manic like a man on drugs. And his rants are just as good as his dad's. To get an interview with him would make our trip to Tripoli worthwhile.

'Fuad will come to the hotel tomorrow morning for a chat at about 11 o'clock,' Simpson says casually and we move on to another topic.

He knows that I am leaving the BBC at the end of this assignment but nothing has prepared us for the frantic few days ahead, which will strain not only my relationship with my current bosses but will have a bearing on my future relationship with Simpson himself.

We edit a short anodyne piece for the Ten O'Clock News, based on our trip to Green Square. There is no bang-bang in it, therefore it is judged to be less newsworthy than a similarly anodyne piece from Benghazi, where the frontline is at the moment. It's hard to provide news if you can't get out and about, and you can't keep repeating that we are virtually under house arrest. With cut-throat competition in the media marketplace, viewers have become very fickle. And editors have become very insecure. They want certainty.

The following morning, having had my breakfast very early, I am sitting in the lobby waiting for Fuad to turn up. Our cameraman walks past on his way to the breakfast room and wants to chat about plans for the day. I only indicate that Simpson and I are meeting an important contact who might be able to bring us the 'big interview'. Knowingly, he winks at me and wishes me good luck. Simpson turns up after 10 am and we wait over a cup of pale tea. I am so glad that I have something to look forward to. It's been a week since we arrived and we've hardly had any excitement. No adrenalin rush in the pursuit of a story. I don't even register the constant bombardment by NATO planes at night.

Gaddafi's compound, Bab al-Azizia, The Splendid Gate, is about half a mile away. It's been pounded relentlessly every night and my bed shakes every time a bomb lands on it. The original barracks were built by Libya's previous ruler, King Idris, the first and only king of Libya, who was deposed in the 1969 *coup d'état* led by the then unknown young officer, Muammar Gaddafi. Gaddafi was only 27. The compound has been reinforced and rebuilt over the years, and rumour has it that its vast underground tunnels have been designed to link the bunkers with various government buildings so that Gaddafi can appear and disappear without having to drive through the city. There's even a rumour that a tunnel links his bunker to our hotel. Some people working at the Rixos talk about a door opposite the conference room where all press briefings are being held, which leads to a tiled tunnel at the end of which there is a door with no handle.

An hour later, Fuad enters the lobby through the front door. Simpson and I shake his hand and offer him some tea. I lean back and listen to their conversation. It revolves around their meeting some years ago and how things have changed now. No politics. Has he been to London recently? Yes, but not since the bombardment started. Most of his trips abroad recently have been to neighbouring Tunisia.

After a while, I lean forward and ask, 'How did you arrive at the hotel?'

He looks me in the eye and says, 'I drove in my car.'

Well, it only confirms what we've been hearing. Everybody in the Gaddafi circle has abandoned the armoured limousines, including the Brotherly Leader himself, and drives around town in inconspicuous private cars. It reminds me of the last days of Saddam Hussein before the fall of Baghdad. It was said that Saddam drove in an old Nissan, wearing tribal clothes.

Looking at Fuad's intelligent face and sad eyes, I am wondering if he knows that the game is up. He can, of course, switch sides. The NATO governments will welcome someone like him. Later, I found a picture of Fuad, posted on the internet, in an elegant suit and dark shades, standing between Tony Blair and Colonel Gaddafi in happier days when the British prime minister visited Libya to bring Gaddafi into the fold. But today he is dressed in a beige zip-up jacket and checked shirt underneath – quite bland and unassuming. He looks like somebody's uncle.

Fuad is close to Gaddafi, a senior diplomat. Like most of the inner circle he probably doesn't hold any official position. Simpson asks him if the Leader is in Tripoli. He says yes, he is. How recently has he seen him? Yesterday, he says. Is it possible to talk to him on camera? That will be very difficult, impossible at this stage, but the Leader is in high spirits and full of optimism. Might it be possible to talk to Mr Saif, his son, who runs the defence of Tripoli? Silence. My ears prick up.

'That may be possible,' he says, 'but I have to check with him.'

Does he see him regularly?

'Yes, every day.'

Wow!

Simpson gets up and says that he has to do some radio interviews but Mr Fuad can talk to me about arranging to see Saif. After Simpson has gone, I look around at the dozens of Western journalists in the lobby seemingly oblivious to the fact that one of Gaddafi's closest confidants is here. No one has recognised him. The only one who gave me an inquisitive look as he passed by our sofa was the *Guardian* Middle East Editor. Did he recognise him?

Fuad asks me how long I have been working with 'Mr John'. We briefly talk about my work with Simpson in Iraq, Afghanistan and Zimbabwe, but I can tell that he is not interested. Then suddenly he bursts into a quiet monologue. 'Why are they doing this to him? Why? He gave them everything they wanted. He gave them the oil, he abolished the weapons of mass destruction. He gave them everything! He made peace with Tony Blair. He doesn't understand why they are doing this to him.'

I look into his eyes and inexplicably I feel sorry for him. I can understand that his whole world has crumbled under him but instead of running away he is still here. It's the same unidentifiable and ambiguous feeling that I had when

I first saw the footage of the execution of the Ceausescus on Christmas Day, 1989. Just before the bullets of the firing squad riddled his body, there was total bewilderment in Ceausescu's eyes. It wasn't so much fear as incomprehension that this was happening to him. Ceausescu was a vicious, brutal dictator but in that brief moment before his execution he looked like an ordinary old man, a grandfather, who had just realised he was about to die.

I want to tell Fuad that his boss is totally bonkers. Everything, from his wacky dress sense to the unpalatable, often rude, rhetoric he has employed during his 42 years in power, goes against every Western instinct of civilised behaviour.

Over the years, he called his opponents cockroaches and threatened to squash them mercilessly. His famous speech a few weeks ago in the wake of the Benghazi uprising, threatening to exterminate all those who dared to rebel against him, proved his undoing. It gave the West a reason to intervene. But much more importantly, he made one very simple mistake, which other dictators repeat time and time again: he stayed in power for far too long and lost touch with reality. He thought he was infallible.

When he came to power in a bloodless coup in 1969 he was a handsome and charismatic young officer intent on changing the world. A passionate disciple of the Egyptian president, Gamal Abdel Nasser, he set about changing the legacy of foreign domination. He threatened to shut down Libya's oil production unless foreign companies renegotiated their contracts with his government. The bluff paid off and Libya became the first developing state to secure a majority share from its oil revenue. This was followed by other Arab states, which sparked the petro-boom in the region. Gaddafi suddenly found himself sitting on an enormous amount of cash and that went to his head. He could be anything he wanted. Despite his limited education – reading the Koran and military training – he decided to be a political philosopher solving the contradictions between capitalism and communism. His famous Green Book is an unreadable and incoherent piece of diatribe but if you were persistent enough to go through it you would find that he dismisses electoral representation as 'dictatorship of the biggest party' and proposes instead a system in which every aspect of life is run by unelected 'people's committees' much like Lenin's Bolshevik 'soviets', which were in fact an instrument of terror.

At the top of the pyramid in Libya, of course, was the people's committee of the Gaddafi family. Torture, jail, disappearances and executions were meted out ruthlessly on those who dared to challenge his rule. A global network of Libyan spies began killing off any outspoken Libyan exiles. Awash with petro-dollars and not content with absolute power at home, he took his campaign abroad, funding terrorist and resistance groups around the world. The Soviets tolerated him because he was a thorn in the side of the Western powers.

Although he was allowed to thrive as an aberration of the Cold War, no one really knew where his allegiances were. On ordering US airstrikes against Tripoli and Benghazi in April 1986, President Reagan famously described him as the Mad Dog of the Middle East. The strikes were designed to kill Gaddafi in retaliation for the bombing of a Berlin nightclub used by US soldiers, which was blamed on Libyan agents. Two soldiers and one civilian died in the attack. Gaddafi survived and as is often the case with such a heavy-handed approach by the Americans, it actually backfired. Gaddafi emerged with an enhanced reputation among those who saw the United States as a global gendarme. The garish monument Gaddafi built in the central square of Bab al-Azizia to celebrate his survival is a golden Libyan fist crunching an American fighter jet. It is puny in size and looks quite ridiculous.

Gaddafi ruined the Libyan economy and frittered away his country's oil wealth. His pet project, The Great Man-Made River, was started in the early 1980s and, as ever, divided opinion. Gaddafi was described either as a mad man or ecological visionary. The project's idea was to bring underground water from under the Sahara desert in the south, trapped there since the last Ice Age, to the arid northern parts of the country through a system of wells, reservoirs, pumping stations and underground pipes. The buzzwords then were 'fossil water' and 'aquifers', referring to the type of fresh water and the geological formations in which it was preserved. Despite being derided as the project of an eccentric megalomaniac, the river still supplies 70 per cent of fresh water to Libya's coastal cities. However, no precise calculations were made about the quantity of fossil water. The pipes were designed to last only 50 years and, like many other projects in Gaddafi's Libya, this one is still unfinished.

I want to tell Fuad that I think that most Libyan people don't love his boss. They have realised that they have been left out of the oil boom. Even a project like providing every Libyan family with a home, which led to a recent construction boom and an influx of cheap Chinese labour, has run out of money. During our road trip from the Tunisian border to Tripoli, we spotted lots of unfinished housing estates, consisting of Soviet type apartment blocks. Our government minders blamed the uprising for the suspension but it's clear the project was half-baked and mismanaged.

If Gaddafi knew anything about how Western power worked he should have known that he would never be forgiven for the bombing of Pan Am flight 103 over Lockerbie in 1988, the worst single act of terrorism on British soil, in which 270 people died. Nor for the murder of PC Yvonne Fletcher outside the Libyan embassy in London in 1984. That he would never be forgiven for supplying the IRA with weapons, training and explosives. That he would never be forgiven for trying to assassinate the Saudi Crown Prince, who is now at the forefront of the coalition of Arab nations against his regime.

I want to tell Fuad that his Leader allowed himself to be isolated, almost uniquely friendless in a new world where the balance of power has relentlessly shifted in the last two-and-a-half decades. Proud of his Bedouin roots, Gaddafi claims to know the desert but the desert has taught him nothing about the shifting sands in politics.

However, all I can utter is, 'Hmm, well, they do it because they can. It's an opportunity for Cameron and Sarkozy to win an easy war…'

He interrupts me. 'Where are you from?'

'Bulgaria,' I say. I can see the cogs moving in his brain. Can I be on his side? Although I say that I'm now British having lived in the UK for the last twenty-five years, he still classifies me as a Bulgarian. And there is one Bulgarian story in Libya, which is an embarrassment for every intelligent person here. He doesn't mention it but I can feel that the thought of the Bulgarian nurses weighs heavily on his mind.

The case involves five Bulgarian nurses and a Palestinian doctor, known as the 'Benghazi six', arrested in 1999 for allegedly infecting more than four hundred children with HIV. Five years later, after allegations of torture and dubious confessions, and despite testimony in their favour from leading HIV experts, all six were convicted and sentenced to death. Prosecutors alleged that they intentionally infected the children with HIV as part of a secret experiment to find a cure for AIDS. Experts insisted that poor hygiene and contaminated blood, and not conspiracy, were behind the infections. The authorities found it impossible to admit that HIV infections existed in the 'pure and revolutionary' Libyan society and that they were looking for scapegoats. It is not clear what Gaddafi's personal role in the affair was but it is hard to believe that he did not provide any guidance about how the nurses should be dealt with.

In 2007, after a deal between the European Union and Libya, and personal intervention by Cecilia Sarkozy, the then wife of the French President, the six were freed. There were reports of their appalling treatment in jail, where one of the nurses attempted suicide. So it's best not to mention the nurses even though it's the only recent connection I can find between Bulgaria and Libya. When I was growing up in Bulgaria in the late 1960s and 1970s, it was a mark of real affluence if your parents were doctors working in Libya because they were paid in US dollars.

'Why don't you persuade Mr Saif to say exactly that in an interview with Simpson? Why is the West turning against Gaddafi's Libya after trying very hard to bring it into the fold? What has changed?'

Fuad leans back. 'Dr Saif is a very intelligent man. He can be very persuasive. But what good would that do if the West is determined to get rid of the regime?'

I notice that he's referring to Saif as 'Dr'. That PhD from the London School of Economics has come under the spotlight recently. It was revealed that the LSE had accepted a large donation from the Libyan government a year after Saif's doctorate was awarded. The authenticity of his thesis is now being investigated, and the LSE director, Howard Davies, resigned a couple of weeks before Simpson and I embarked on our trip to Libya.

'Dr Saif can handle the interview, I'm sure,' I continue. 'Mr Simpson asks tough questions but he is always very polite. The interview will not degenerate into a shouting match.'

Fuad is still sitting on the sofa, sipping his tea. He looks like a man in no hurry. I suddenly realise that the prospect of an interview with Saif is real. We are now in the realm of practical negotiations. On the one hand, I have to demonstrate to him that Saif and the authorities on the run can benefit from an interview with one of the most famous names in the world of international news. On the other, I have to be absolutely firm that I don't compromise the BBC's integrity by making promises which may affect our editorial independence.

I am now prepared to outline and discuss the questions. 'We can write down the areas of questioning so that Dr Saif will have a good idea about what Simpson will ask him. However, I can't guarantee that the questions will be formulated in the same way or, indeed, asked in the same order.' I give him a blank sheet of paper and start dictating questions. He writes them down in Arabic. The questions revolve around military and political strategy, possible talks with the opposition, and are deliberately broad and vague. But I also manage to get in things like: 'Has Dr Saif discussed with his father the possibility of surrender or leaving the country? Has he got enough money to sustain a prolonged campaign?'

As we are finalising the list of about seven or eight questions, Musa Ibrahim passes by. He is puzzled. He looks directly into my eyes without acknowledging my greetings. Fuad ignores him. Well, well, talking about shifting sands. I thought that Musa Ibrahim was a close friend of Saif's but he would never facilitate an interview with him. He doesn't like Simpson very much, he doesn't like me, and he prefers to give the interviews himself. He loves the limelight.

He knew that John was reporting from the rebel side in Benghazi last month and despite all that the Foreign Ministry gave him a visa. Simpson thinks that the issuing of the visa was a clerical mistake. They hadn't realised who he was. If they knew, he thought, they would never have issued it. But I thought they knew exactly what they were doing.

I still don't quite understand why Fuad is helping us. I think his efforts are genuine and the interview will happen but does he really think that an interview with Simpson will change public opinion in Britain?

On the morning of Saturday 26th March, an incident occurs in the restaurant during breakfast. I am sitting on my own at a big table for eight behind a pillar by the door. Breakfast is dull and I am bored of having the same things day after day but I suppose I should be grateful there's something to eat at all, bearing in mind the circumstances.

Suddenly, there is a commotion. A well-dressed woman rushes through the door and starts shouting and waving her arms in the air. She wears make-up and her hair is nicely done. Waiters and waitresses rush towards her but she runs around and starts taking off her clothes. I am ashamed to admit it, but I think she is a suicide bomber and hide behind the large pillar to get protection from the blast. Almost a minute passes, and there's no explosion. I can see that she is on the ground being wrestled by a female member of staff. Her hair is dishevelled, her make-up smudged. Journalists and photographers rush in and cameras start filming the aftermath. The hotel workers back off in the face of so many foreign journalists. She sits down at a table and is given a glass of water.

A reporter from one of our main competitors intervenes and starts asking her questions. I strain to hear the Arabic translator. She alleges that fifteen pro-Gaddafi militiamen raped her over three days after she was stopped at a checkpoint. Hence the reason for lifting her skirt to show the cuts and bruises on her legs. This goes on for a few minutes. Then plainclothes police and hotel security guards storm in and push the reporters aside. A man in a brown leather jacket and a trademark policeman's moustache gets to her and starts shouting. She looks frightened and shouts back: 'La! La! …La!' (No! No! No!) He tries to grab the woman by the arms. Journalists intervene but are being pushed back. A camera falls on the floor. It looks like it's been broken. A pistol has been brandished but I can't see the face of the man who holds it. Eventually a few plainclothes policemen drag the woman out of the restaurant into the hotel lobby. She fights back. Almost comically, they all fall on the marble floor. I am worried that we didn't get any footage but I have already noticed the Reuters cameraman there so at least we'll get some agency pictures.

This event will dominate the news out of Tripoli over the next few days. Some networks will go really big on it. In the absence of other news since we are under virtual house arrest, it's hardly surprising. Initially, we are sceptical about the story. How can an ordinary woman, without any inside knowledge or connections, be able to gain access to one of the most heavily guarded buildings in the city? Is it a ruse by Gaddafi to divert our attention from what's really going on in Tripoli? It is certainly a rich human-interest story, involving allegations of rape and out of control young militiamen, the collapse of security at the hotel for foreign media, and provides for almost open-ended coverage. But are they really so clever as to feed us a negative story like this?

At a press conference, Musa Ibrahim describes the woman, Iman al-Obeidi, 26, as a 'prostitute', as if this is some kind of excuse for fifteen people to rape her. He also says that the accused 'boys' have filed a counter claim for defamation. Does he realise how ridiculous this sounds?

We meet Fuad again when he comes to lunch at the hotel the following day. He gently raises the subject of the coverage of the story. He is far too clever to try to influence us but we can see that he's worried. The story must be genuine then. We tell him about our misgivings but say that we can't ignore a story that has happened on our doorstep. We are giving it an objective dispassionate treatment as we do with all other stories. That doesn't assuage his worry. We don't talk about the interview but just before he goes I remind him that John Simpson, one of the most well-known names in the world of broadcasting, is the right person to conduct the interview with Saif, just in case he's thinking of giving it to somebody else.

In the meantime, NATO bombardment of Bab al-Azizia next door continues relentlessly every night. Other buildings in the city are also being targeted but we are not allowed to see anything. It does cross my mind that we could be obliterated by a NATO bomber through a single error. We could die in vain without even sending a decent story to London. I casually ask our security adviser, an ex-SAS man who has been assigned to us by the BBC, about how NATO gathers information on the ground in order to target buildings with such precision. He thinks that there are British Special Forces operating undercover in Tripoli. He also suggests that it's not inconceivable that there are people masquerading as journalists at the hotel who slip out during the night and shine infrared lights on the buildings they've identified for destruction for the NATO pilots to see. I am not sure if I should believe that.

Over the last few days, I'm being harassed by frantic calls from London about the imminent fall of the regime. They think Gaddafi's hometown of Sirte is about to fall and that will spell the end of Gaddafi. I must do everything I can to get permission for a BBC satellite dish and engineers to arrive in Tripoli so that we can broadcast the fall live on air. The engineers and the dish are already waiting in Tunisia. I have prepared the necessary paperwork and have handed it to the man in charge at the Government Media Office. However, I tell London that I think the game is far from over. My judgement is that the regime will hold on for a while. There are quite a lot of people with vested interests and I have seen undiminished enthusiasm from these people to fight.

I am quite emphatic, adhering to the motto that an old hand at Broadcasting House once coined for me: 'Often wrong but never in doubt!' This was during the war in the Balkans in the 1990s. I was doing an attachment as a Foreign Duty Editor in the Radio Newsroom at the old Broadcasting House. Every time the old boy, a senior editor who was nearing retirement, came to me with a question about the contents of agency copy or for clarification about who was who in the panoply of factional players, or for a prediction about what was likely to happen to this besieged town or that, I would give him a definitive answer. I had sussed out that what they most wanted was certainty. Even at that early stage of my career, I realised that I could only be 50 per cent wrong and with my knowledge of the history and geography of the area, the odds would normally be in my favour.

I say to my direct boss in London that we'll have a few months to play with before we really need to report the fall of Tripoli. I tell Simpson about my conversation with London and he agrees with my assessment.

In the early morning of Monday 28th March, the piercing ring tone of my mobile phone wakes me up. This is the time when normally the foreign desk in London rings with an urgent request or to pass on a breaking news copy from the news agencies. I answer with a sleepy voice. It's my partner in London. I sit up in anticipation – there must be a good reason for such an early call. It is 5.30 in London. My mother in Bulgaria has been calling our home in London again, every few minutes for the last hour with garbled ranting in Bulgarian. Sadly, it's a familiar story. I promise to call her immediately, which normally makes her stop.

Since my father died more than 10 years ago, my mother has been coping well although she lives alone in our flat in Sofia. My brother, who lives in Holland, and I normally visit her once a year and she's been quite happy with that. She has been well and has enough money to enjoy an independent life. In the last year, though, disturbing symptoms of dementia have begun to appear. Neighbours complain that she rings their doorbells in the middle of the night with incoherent requests. A recurrent theme is that an imaginary woman wants to take over her flat and she has nowhere to go. When they don't answer the door, she rings them on the phone. She refuses to accept any live-in help and gets very angry when we suggest that she might be better off in a nursing home. Leaving her alone in Sofia is an unsatisfactory arrangement, which bears down hard on my conscience, but she's rejected every proposal we have made, including bringing her to live with us in London or in Holland. But to our neighbours in Sofia, it looks like we've abandoned her.

I call her immediately. Her firm and clear metallic voice cuts through the airwaves. That's a good sign and I relax.

'Where are you?' she says.

'In Tripoli, Libya.'

'Are you visiting Gaddafi?' She laughs loudly.

'Sort of,' I say, 'but I can't spend much time on the phone. I'm here for work.'

'I just wanted to check when you are coming to see me again. Not that I want to interrupt your work, but it would be nice to have something to look forward to.'

'Is this why you have been calling the flat in London all morning?'

'Have I?' she ponders. 'I can't remember. Anyway, I'm fine. So, when are you coming?'

'Well, it will be in a couple of months, as we agreed,' I say quietly.

We have abandoned her – I feel powerless and guilty – and we'll burn in hell for it. I wind up the conversation. It will be a few days before she starts calling London again. My brother says that he unplugs his landline before he goes to bed. We've told her never to call our mobile numbers and strangely she never does.

Today the government minders are organising a bus trip for us to Misratah. Misratah, a costal town about 120 miles east of Tripoli on the road to Benghazi, is very much the main battleground in the news. Since the rebellion began in February, pro- and anti-Gaddafi forces had been fighting for control of the city. The battle for Misratah will be well documented because of the amount of mobile phone footage that has been coming out from the rebel side. The previous week, NATO began airstrikes against loyalist forces in the city. People say that if Misratah falls to the rebels, the road from Benghazi to Tripoli will be open for rebel advances on the capital. That's why it is essential for the government to take us there and demonstrate that they are in control.

These trips are so stage-managed that it's worth going only for the amusement of witnessing the ineptitude of the government propaganda machine. A few days ago we were taken to the outskirts of Tripoli, a place called Tajoura, to be shown the aftermath of an alleged NATO strike on a residential compound, where civilians were allegedly killed. When a couple of busloads of experienced journalists arrived there, it was clear to everybody right from the start that this could not have been an airstrike. Whatever it was, it certainly wasn't a NATO bomb. And the inconsistencies in the witness statements were so glaring that at the end of it we all filed a story about 'incompetent government propaganda' rather than harrowing news of 'civilians killed by NATO'.

The journey to Misratah is fraught. I am worried about the skin eruption on the back of my leg and all sorts of grim thoughts go through my head. The big 'C' always comes to mind. I am also worried about how my transition from BBC staff to freelancer will take place. I am due to leave the BBC on the last day of March, which is in a couple of days, but my email to my boss that I had sent before we arrived in Libya still remains unanswered. I worry about whether I'll be covered by the BBC insurance, as well as how I'm going to get paid for the time I put in after my last day. Simpson is grumpy because a leading broadsheet in London has published a snide attack on him saying that he went soft on the Iman al-Obeidi story because he was hoping for 'a big interview'. This is totally untrue and thoroughly below the belt. It also smacks of a leak from our camp. There was another leak to the press a couple of months later referring to this very stint in Tripoli, according to which Simpson and I had fallen out here and that's why I had left the BBC. This could not be further from the truth.

My relationship with the cameraman has almost broken down. He doesn't tolerate any advice or suggestion from me. On the other hand, I think he's not very good, rather pedestrian in his work, a bit 'old school' in his approach to the job. But the BBC is very bad at giving objective feedback. I know it's hard to be critical of someone's work when you know that he's risked his life working in a dodgy place like Tripoli when NATO is bombing the hell out of everything around you. For that reason, some people think they are better than they actually are.

On arrival in the outskirts of Misratah, the government is putting on a display of popular support for Gaddafi, with crowds of mainly young people shouting support for the Colonel, kissing his portrait as a sign of unwavering love, and telling us how they will win in defiance of NATO bombing. There's not a lot to film after you've captured the fake popular enthusiasm and a bit of wreckage left after the bombing. I hope the cameraman has filmed the big plume of smoke in the distance. It looks like NATO has hit an oil installation or some fuel storage facility. I film it on my small handy cam but it can't zoom in sufficiently.

We are not allowed to leave the designated area in the suburbs of Misratah. The minders say it's for our own safety. The rebels control downtown Misratah. They also control the port. So much for the promises that we'd be taken to the port to demonstrate that Gaddafi forces are in charge there.

I dial London on my satellite phone and put Simpson through to record an on-the-scene descriptive audio piece for all outlets. Continuous news programmes line up in a queue to get their own two-ways with him. He does it with panache, surrounded by a crowd of young men who shout pro-Gaddafi slogans. Passions heat up and some in the crowd begin to get hostile. In a short interval between interviews, I look at him and say, 'The crowd is turning ugly…' He smiles. It's a reference to a story he likes to tell about an incident in Afghanistan in the 1990s. The vehicle, in which he and his crew were travelling, was surrounded by a crowd and it ground to a halt. The passengers found themselves surrounded by rugged unfriendly faces pressed to the windows to see who's in the car. Curiosity turned to hostility and the crowd started rocking the vehicle trying to overturn it. It was a hopeless situation. Then one of the members of the crew, a mild British academic travelling with them as a consultant, looked at the scary faces of the agitated people outside and said with a dry sense of humour, 'The crowd is turning ugly.' Everybody inside the car burst into laughter. When the crowd saw that the passengers were laughing, the mood changed and they started laughing, too. Anger suddenly turned into goodwill.

Our minders start rounding us up saying it's getting late – we have to board the buses if we want to be back in Tripoli before dark. Simpson is still doing two-ways on the satellite phone. I leave our security adviser with him and rush to our bus with the intention of holding it so that it doesn't leave without Simpson. Most of the journalists are already inside. I say to the minder that we have to wait for Simpson. There is uproar from the people on the bus. 'We can't wait for him! We need to get going. It's getting late.'

'He is a star, he wants to be a hero again, we can't risk our lives for him,' a female voice shouts.

I am shocked by the response. There is one particular middle-aged photographer with a thin bedraggled face and long hippie hair who is the most vociferous. 'We should leave without him. He has chosen to stay behind for his own glorification and should bear the consequences.' This is journalistic rivalry and bitchiness at its worst. The driver moves the bus very slowly. The minder looks worried because it's his responsibility to get everybody back to Tripoli. I stand in the door and block it from closing. There's howling inside the bus: 'Go! Go! Go!' I can't believe that this is happening. Suddenly, I notice that a Toyota pick-up truck is racing behind us trying to catch up with the bus. I recognise Simpson among the people in the back of the truck. A few minutes later, the pick-up pulls up alongside our bus. Simpson gets off and slowly climbs on board. There's hushed silence. No one dares say anything. He apologises and the driver steps on the accelerator towards Tripoli.

Unlike our outward journey to Misratah in the morning, very few people on the bus take pictures through the windows. I look around. Everybody looks tired. Our cameraman is sleeping. The ITV cameraman is editing his pictures on his laptop. The Editor of the Six O'Clock News is expecting a piece from us. Libya is only an hour ahead of London, so we don't have a substantial time difference in our favour. I calculate in my head that we'll probably have about fifty minutes between arrival at the hotel and the booking on the satellite at 5.50 pm London time. And that's without taking into account any possible delays on the road. I suggest to our cameraman that he should at least transfer the pictures from his camera to his laptop for editing so that we don't waste time when we get back at the hotel. He shrugs and does it.

There should be just enough time to edit a short two-minute piece. Some of the pictures we want to use are taken by mobile phone from the rebel-held part of Misratah and distributed on social networks. We've had them on the hard drive for a couple of days.

The bus driver is moving at a decent speed and there's no traffic. I'm sure the minders want to get back to the relative safety of the Rixos as soon as possible. The NATO bombardment normally starts after dark.

When we pass through small towns and villages, we can see pick-up trucks parked in the side streets with heavy machine guns and antiaircraft weapons mounted on the back. This is the new strategy designed to avoid weapons being destroyed by the air bombardment. They are mobile units with no fixed abode, so it's more difficult to pinpoint them. Most of the people manning these mobile units are young men who wear no uniforms.

Without any explanation the bus makes a long diversion, leaving the motorway and taking a secondary road through rural areas. I ring the Six O'Clock News to tell them that there's a delay on the journey back but hopefully we'll still make it. What happens next is every producer's nightmare. We get to the hotel with about forty-five minutes to spare. I try to suggest a structure for the piece but am chased out of the room by the cameraman who is in a flap. Simpson motions discreetly with his head telling me to get out.

I leave and go to the uplink control room from where we feed our pieces by satellite to warn the two British guys who run it that we'll be late with our tape. The room is on the first floor adjacent to a large terrace over the front lobby. There are several positions on the terrace from where we do our live injects into the programmes. I call London to tell them that there is a possibility we might miss our feed. I suggest it would be safer if they moved our piece down the running order to give us some breathing space. It's painful to remember the details of this event and I cringe at the memory because, whatever happened, ultimately the responsibility for planning and organising our work there fell to me.

The piece doesn't make it to London on time and misses its slot in the running order. The cameraman arrives with the tape about 10 minutes after the Six O'Clock News has gone on air and insists on feeding it. But we've missed our slot on the satellite, too, and the uplink engineers are busy with other clients. Simpson arrives a bit later to do a live inject for BBC World. He asks me if the piece has made it. I shake my head. He is visibly annoyed. The cameraman does not speak to me for the rest of the evening.

This is the second time in my career that I have missed a feed. I know that this time it's not my fault but I'll be blamed for it nonetheless. The first time was seven years ago in Baghdad in the aftermath of the war and I admit it was entirely my fault. I made the wrong call and I took responsibility for it. Everybody in London was so stunned by my public admission of guilt that no one made any comment. BBC middle managers never admit responsibility. The concept is alien to them. They always try to find someone else to blame.

Things, however, go from bad to worse. On the following day I get an email from somebody in the operations department of the BBC asking me whether I'll be ready to return my company mobile phone on 1st April, the day after my last day at the BBC. This is when I realise that very few people at the BBC know that I am in Libya. Obviously, my direct boss, the Foreign Editor, has failed to inform them. On top of all that, government convoys out of Tripoli down to the Tunisian border only run once a week now. I fire off an email, copying in several of my bosses. In it I explain that even with the best will in the world, I can't be back in London before the middle of the first week in April. But on the other hand, if they are prepared to keep me here I am happy to stay for as long as it takes. The day is then dominated by frantic calls between London and Tripoli, which prevents me from doing any work. I am told that if I stay on the payroll beyond 31st March, this may jeopardise my redundancy terms.

When I told Simpson about my decision to leave the BBC a couple of months earlier, he tried to persuade me not to do it. He took me for lunch at RIBA (Royal Institute of British Architects), a posh place at the back of the new BBC headquarters in Portland Place. Simpson offered champagne. There was going to be pressure on me to reconsider. It was quite flattering that he valued my work so highly.

I had always been an aggressive advocate of the Simpson product, pushing our stories high on the news agenda. That meant fierce battles with editors for a prominent place in the bulletins. Sometimes the stories imposed themselves as the natural lead of all bulletins across the BBC, sometimes the editors had to be persuaded of their value. There had been battles with Simpson himself, trying to convince him to do stories which, for various reasons, he was reluctant to do. But Simpson had always been box office success. I was propelled to the highest echelons in the discussions about newsworthiness of stories at the BBC, punching above my pay grade. And that felt good.

Towards the end of the main course he asked me why I wanted to leave the BBC. I wanted to tell him so much about the BBC, about myself, and my professional relationship with him but suddenly it all felt very trivial. All my anger against the 'system' suddenly became meaningless. I could only manage to say that the redundancy offer on the table was too good to be ignored and that if I didn't take it now it would never be available again. I summoned the courage, though, to tell him that I felt that our work as a team was becoming more difficult. I reminded him that just a couple of months previously I was comprehensively excluded from his trip to Burma to cover the release from house arrest of the pro-democracy leader, Aung San Suu Kiy. He gave me one of his looks that I had known for a very long time, lowering his chin and lifting his eyes as if he was peering over imaginary reading glasses. I knew that I had touched a nerve there.

'What are you going to do about money? Have you got another job?' he said.

'No I haven't. But you know me. I have taken reckless steps in my life before without thinking too much of the consequences. Defecting from Bulgaria in the 1980s without even telling my parents is an example…'

He smiled. He had shown incredible bravery on many occasions during our work together and in the past, long before I started working with him. This was, I thought, our strongest bond. Both of us liked taking risks.

Resigned that I was not going to change my mind, he downed another glass of red wine. For the rest of the meal, we discussed the vague possibilities of working together after I went freelance. I also reassured him that I would work with him until my very last day at the BBC, forgoing my accumulated holidays.

And that day, it's decided, is 31st March. I'll hand over my phone and responsibilities to the cameraman and get on the first convoy out of Tripoli. What a relief!

Fuad has gone quiet. Simpson thinks that he is out of the country. I'll be thoroughly pissed off if I can't get the interview with Saif before I leave. On the last day of March, I demonstratively hand over my local mobile phone to the cameraman and ask him to inform London that I no longer work for the BBC. That causes a lot of commotion on the desks in London, mostly out of curiosity. My direct boss has also gone quiet. It feels as if I don't exist.

On the morning of 1st April, we are offered a trip to Sabratah, a city with Roman ruins about 40 miles west of Tripoli. It's basically a day out with very little prospect of newsgathering. Simpson and the cameraman decide to stay at the hotel and I go on my own. It feels like being on holiday. I notice in the mirror while I shave that I have put on weight. Food has been good, although very samey, and I've had no exercise. Sitting all day in the hotel lobby drinking tea and coffee is not really conducive to keeping fit. I am looking forward to getting back into shape when I'm in London. Riding my mountain bike on Hampstead Heath, close to my home, always does wonders for my fitness. At the thought, my mouth fills with the taste of damp cold north London air mixed with the smell of wet brown leaves on the ground. But here in Tripoli, the early April morning is hot and dry. Another uncertain scorching day lies ahead of me.

As I get on the bus with other journalists, a sudden thought comes to my head. *Wouldn't it be ironic if our convoy gets bombed on my last day while on a day out to Roman ruins?* But I don't dwell on it for too long and expunge it from my mind. I take my small Sony camera with me, just in case. We are going to drive through Al-Zawiya, after all, where the uprising earlier this month was crushed with utmost brutality. Once on the bus, I look around and realise that I haven't made any friends on this trip. The members of the ITV crew are the closest I've had to friends in the last week or so, even though they are the main competition. I'm told that their cameraman had even suggested that the restaurant make a cake for my leaving the BBC but that they didn't have the ingredients. Food comes from Tunisia but more and more irregularly and we have noticed slimmed down choice in the restaurant offerings. I know the ITV crew will be leaving with me on the next convoy out of Tripoli; however, they are not on this trip.

Just after leaving Tripoli on the main road west, we see a white building on the right nestled behind a row of leafy trees. Some of the journalists who've been here longer begin talking about the building and I understand that this is a compound of Libyan military intelligence where a three-member crew from the BBC Arabic TV were held before the re-capture of Al-Zawiya by Gaddafi's forces. The three were beaten up, tortured and subjected to mock executions. The ordeal lasted three days. In their accounts, they said that the man who interrogated them on the last day before their release spoke perfect English with an Oxbridge accent.

We see a bit of Al-Zawiya, the scene of bitter fighting only a few weeks ago. Shops are closed and boarded up. Houses have been shelled and most walls bear the scars of gunfire. There are the usual pick-up trucks with heavy machine guns mounted on them. We look for mercenaries as rumour has it that the regular army has dissipated. Saif has already boasted in an earlier interview that he's got enough money to pay for the war but we are keen to see what the mercenaries look like. Locals suggest that they are people from sub-Saharan Africa, therefore not Arabs or Berbers. We can see a few black faces among the militiamen roaming the streets but they could be African Libyans. No one is wearing a uniform. Most of them look like ordinary teenagers.

My mood is lousy. I am fed up with everything: the lesion on my leg, the likelihood that I'll miss Simpson's interview with Saif, the BBC management for mismanaging my departure, but above all myself for creating the whole unsettled situation. I never pursued clarity about how to conduct my departure from the BBC. I should have discussed with my boss the precise details of what would happen if I was still in Libya after 31st March. But I didn't. The only thing I insisted on was that there should not be any official announcement, i.e. the usual hagiographic email to staff. I wanted to go quietly. But now everybody knows because of the gossip swirling in the News Department in London.

Sabratah is an ugly town but the Roman amphitheatre on the Mediterranean coast is one of the wonders of the world. It's a piece of architecture on a grandiose scale. I could've stayed here for hours meditating on my own. The yellow stone changes colour depending on the time of the day, from bright almost-white to gold and red. There are two gaps in the middle of the colonnade like two big windows through which you can see the Mediterranean Sea from almost every seat in the theatre. They give you the illusion of two enormous oil canvases – seascapes, hanging in the middle behind the stage, except that the pictures are alive. The serenity of the location and the permanence of the structure calms me down. *Everything will be fine*, I think. *It always is*. I have jumped into the unknown many times before and it always works out all right. I'll come through to the other side.

The bus journey back to Tripoli is uneventful. But when I get back, I am faced with messages to call various people in London who want to speak with me. My direct boss, the Foreign Editor, has called several times on my local mobile, which I have left with the cameraman. I don't feel like speaking to anybody. I am ratty and unintentionally I have sharp exchanges with Simpson. He is not happy that he'll be left without a producer for the rest of his stint there and is making arrangements to leave soon after me. Deep down I know that the Saif interview will happen after I leave.

After rejecting several calls from my boss on the grounds that I am busy, I finally speak with him. He is uneasy. He knows that the situation is unsatisfactory and my rushed departure is partly due to the fact that we had not discussed in advance what would happen after my last day with the BBC if I had been held back in Tripoli. He keeps repeating how grateful he is for everything that I have done, as if I have done it for him personally. I loved working for the BBC and I loved working in dodgy places. I loved working with Simpson and I'm proud of the stuff I've done during my years with him.

I insist on no official announcements. My boss is pissed off with that because I deprive him of one of his greatest pleasures, which is to write hero grams. These emails are never an honest account of a person's work and character. How many times have you seen a departure or retirement announcement like: 'He was an incompetent plodder with no imagination, but stuck with the BBC for 25 years because no one had the courage to sack him'?

I go into Simpson's room to tell him about my conversation. He's working on his laptop. I offer to make tea. His eyes light up. There are a couple of dry biscuits by the kettle. I am in one of my belligerent moods. I hope I'll calm down while making the tea but there's wave after wave of anger in my chest.

'I said goodbye to the Foreign Editor. I wonder if I'll ever see him again,' I say. 'And do you know what? All he said was how grateful he was for everything I'd done at the BBC.'

Simpson closes down the eBay page on his laptop and reads me an email in which the editor explains to him that it should be possible to find a way for us to work together again, but not immediately. There are strict terms in my redundancy offer.

'But if he knows the terms of my departure why on earth did he let me come with you to Tripoli on an open-ended ticket?'

'Oggy!' Simpson raises his voice. I know that when he calls my name like that, he's irritated. He doesn't offer any further explanation. There's an uneasy silence but I won't let it go.

'How about the interview with Netanyahu that I've been working on? Do you think I should hand it to another producer after so much time and effort?' I say acerbically.

This is unnecessary. Bringing that up now is designed to pick a fight.

'I can't ask you to do that. It's your baby. It's up to you,' he says pensively.

I have been working on this interview through a well-connected friend of mine who has helped me before. He arranged a Simpson interview with a previous prime minister of Israel, Ehud Olmert, a few years previously, which surprised the top BBC bosses and annoyed many BBC reporters, especially those who specialised in the Middle East.

I deliver my intended *coup de grâce*. 'Well, if the BBC doesn't want me to work with you I might as well give the interview to Sky News.'

What follows next is unclear in my memory but there were raised voices on both sides, followed by prolonged silences and sulking for the rest of the evening. After a restless night of self-criticism, I rush to Simpson's room immediately after breakfast on the following morning to apologise.

'We all say things in the heat of the moment, which we regret afterwards,' I start.

He gives a little smile but avoids my eyes.

'After all these years working together, you should know by now that I'll never do anything to dent your reputation,' I say quietly but firmly, in a rehearsed manner. 'And I'll never give that interview to Sky…'

'I know,' he says. 'Maybe this will be an opportunity for your first freelance project for the BBC. I'll be very happy to work on the interview with you.'

The interview never happened, but that's another story.

Two days later I am on my way out. Luckily, I travel in a minibus with the ITV crew. There is a lot of banter. We talk about stock market tips and how it's better to invest in silver rather than gold because silver, in addition to being a precious metal, has proper industrial use, which hedges against market fluctuations. Before we know it, we are at the border post with Tunisia. We wait in a Soviet-era roadside restaurant for the incoming crews who swap with us. When they arrive, I see an old friend of mine who is a producer with the American network, ABC. He says, 'I tried to email you when I learned that you were leaving the BBC but the email bounced back. They must have cut off your email account.' I only laugh uneasily.

So this is the end really. I reach home after a night in a hotel on the Tunisian island of Jarbah, and an airport transfer in Nice, exactly a fortnight since we first set off on our journey to Tripoli. Two days later, on 5th April, I see the interview with Saif al-Islam headlined in the early evening promo for the Ten O'Clock News but am too angry to watch it later in the bulletin. A neighbour of mine tells me that he thought Simpson came across as too soft on Gaddafi's son. When I decide to see it two days later on BBC iPlayer, my first impression is how beautifully it has been shot. The lighting is perfect and the images crystal clear. It's been shot on two cameras. The olive skin on Saif's shaved head glistens gently under the HMI light. He is wearing a black knitted jumper with a big open collar and rimless glasses with gold temples, which he frequently re-adjusts during the interview. Simpson looks tired. He asks barbed questions with politeness but there's a perceptible irony in his tone. It's a brave thing to do. Saif is defiant. With an arrogant smile, he dismisses suggestions of abandoning the fight and fleeing abroad.

'It's my country,' he repeats several times. 'I'm not going anywhere, I'm staying here.'

The close-ups on his face and his predatory white teeth are magnificent. His defiance, however, is the defiance of the condemned. It's a scoop in the best tradition of the BBC. But instead of feeling gratified that I have played a part in it, I am angry that I wasn't there.

The fall of Tripoli in August the same year provokes an intense debate about why it was a Sky News crew and not the BBC who were the first to report from 'liberated' Tripoli. The nature of our industry dictates that the only real measure of success is whether you are the first with the news. That will not change.

Gaddafi is killed in his hometown of Sirte in October as he comes out of a sewage pipe where he's been hiding from a NATO aerial bombardment.

After leaving Tripoli at the end of August, Gaddafi stayed at a different location every four nights before making his way to Sirte. Others suggested that he managed to get into Sirte in a small inconspicuous convoy the day Tripoli fell to the rebels. From Sirte he tried to mobilise loyal tribes in the southern desert to fight the rebellion. When Sirte eventually fell to the rebels after a month of fierce fighting, Gaddafi with about two hundred and fifty loyal fighters, including his son Mutassim and his Defence Minister, Abu Bakr Younis, tried to escape into the desert. Witnesses say that his convoy was headed to the village of his birth in the Jarref Valley, Jahannam ('Hell' in Arabic) outside Sirte. Two NATO missiles hit the convoy. Gaddafi, Younis and a bodyguard ran on foot to hide in a drainage pipe. When surrounded by rebels, the bodyguard rather comically threw a grenade which accidentally bounced back and exploded between Gaddafi and Younis. It all ended like a pantomime. Younis died while Gaddafi suffered severe shrapnel wounds to the head. Disoriented, like a drunk, he was captured by angry rebel fighters. Gaddafi's last words were incoherent: 'What's wrong? What's wrong? What's going on?' After forty-two years as undisputed ruler of Libya he died an ignominious death, captured by the rebels, stripped naked and with a bayonet up his backside, the ultimate humiliation. A young man in a baseball cap brandished a golden pistol he claimed he'd taken from the Colonel while Gaddafi's limp, naked body was loaded into an ambulance.

Like Ceausescu, the vast bunkers and tunnels he built to provide an escape route for himself and his family in case of war or rebellion proved useless and didn't save his life. Like Ceausescu, he left a rich country in ruins, and a fractured nation deeply scarred. And like Ceausescu, he deluded himself until the last minute that the people loved him and that by some miracle he'd pull it off; that he would ride a wave of popular support back to Tripoli. There's no other explanation for the bizarre circumstances of his last days.

In November, a few months after his 39th birthday, Saif al-Islam Gaddafi was captured by rebel fighters in the desert of southern Libya. He lived up to his word to stay in his country until the bitter end. He was taken by plane to the town of Zintan in the north-western Nafusa Mountains, a stronghold of the rebellion. He was held there while fierce debate ensued about where he should be tried, in Libya or at the International Criminal Court in The Hague. He denied all charges of murdering and torturing civilians.

Claims by Saif, made just before the fall of the regime, that his father subsidised Nicolas Sarkozy's election campaign in 2007 to the tune of €50 million were given a fresh boost by a Lebanese-born businessman. Ziad Takieddine, an arms dealer under investigation for bribery and known as Mr Fix It, told a French judge in January 2013 that he had documentary evidence that Sarkozy's campaign in 2006-2007 was 'abundantly' financed by Tripoli. He also said that the payments had continued after Sarkozy became president.

Four journalists had died by the end of the war: documentary maker Tim Hetherington and photographer Chris Hondros, killed in Misratah; Al Jazeera cameraman, Ali Hassan al-Jaber, shot dead in Benghazi, as well as Libyan journalist Mohammed Nabbous. Others were held prisoner for long periods of time.

My main question about the coverage of Libya in the summer and the autumn of 2011 by the British media is not why Sky News were the first to broadcast live from the streets of liberated Tripoli, but why after that it was left to researchers from Human Rights Watch to discover documents with unsavoury details of links between the British secret service and the Gaddafi regime. And why it was an American network, CNN, which first tracked down and interviewed the man convicted of the Lockerbie bombing, Abdelbaset al-Megrahi, before he died.

I took part in a discussion in London about coverage of armed conflicts. I told the participants that it requires meticulous preparation but also a little bit of recklessness – recklessness, because despite all your knowledge and experience you can never predict what might happen next.

The skin eruption on the back of my leg turned out to be an allergic reaction to painkillers, which I had been taking liberally to combat tiredness and headaches. The allergy mimics skin disease and that can be really scary.

Tripoli was my last assignment with John Simpson. A bizarre little article appeared in the *Guardian* a couple of months later. It said that the talk among the foreign correspondents was that Simpson was not best pleased about my decision to leave at short notice. When I read it I thought that it was trying to suggest that I had left the BBC because we had an argument in Tripoli. The paper quoted him as saying that despite my speedy departure there was no rancour on either side. No one at the *Guardian* bothered to contact me. Irritatingly, to prove that the whole thing was based on unsubstantiated rumour, the article ended on a farcical note. It said that Simpson had married an earlier producer (his present wife, Dee), so I, perhaps, had had a lucky escape. Many people found that funny. I didn't. I wonder if he did.

My memory of Tripoli is ambivalent. It was hardly a personal success. But it wasn't always like that.

HARARE, ZIMBABWE, JANUARY 2008

7th January, 10 pm. The Zimbabwean side of the Beitbridge border crossing. It's distinctly darker than the South African side, with only a couple of yellowish light bulbs hanging on the brick building of Zimbabwe Passport Control. Behind a flimsy wire fence, a patient crowd of desperately tired people wait to cross into South Africa. They are nervous and wary of causing any trouble, which might prevent them from getting out of the country. It's eerily quiet. Even the babies and small children in the queue don't utter a sound.

John Simpson and I wait in the car. It's my first time in Zimbabwe. Our South African cameraman, Nigel, has gone into the building with our passports. We'll try to get them stamped with Zimbabwean entry visas without being there in person. After a while Nigel's large silhouette fills in the doorframe of the single-storey building, blocking the light. He approaches the car and says: 'The officer wants to see you before you get the visas.'

Silence. We shuffle out of the car. John adjusts his baseball cap to cover all that's visible of his distinctive white hair. I unnecessarily tidy up my crumpled shirt. In the empty waiting room, a young, well-dressed female officer throws a cursory look at us and tells another clerk to issue the visas. John is travelling on an Irish passport, I – on a British. While the clerk is counting the money for the visas, we both look at the floor, pretending we've just woken up after a long road journey. We couldn't be more alert.

Our first trip into the heart of the Mugabe regime, flouting a ban on the BBC, lasted a week. Reporting from Zimbabwe without accreditation carries a two-year prison sentence. The spectre of what might lie in store for us in the notorious Chikurubi prison in Harare had informed our decision making process during the first stages of our journey.

Our preparations started the previous year. In the winter of 2007 there were some developments in Zimbabwe which were interpreted as a sign that Mugabe's power might be challenged. He suddenly reshuffled his cabinet without explanation and several long-serving ministers were ousted. This sparked rumours that Mugabe might have been challenged from within the ruling elite. The economy had tanked and inflation reached stratospheric levels. Elections were scheduled for the following year, 2008. At the end of March 2007, the opposition leader, Morgan Tsvangirai, was arrested and badly beaten up for attending a banned demonstration. This is when Simpson first put the thought of going undercover to Zimbabwe firmly in my mind. We both knew that it would take a huge effort to achieve this, not only finding the right people to help us on the ground but also winning the battle with BBC bureaucracy to get approval for an undercover trip.

Throughout 2007, Simpson and I were busy covering the Iraq story. Saddam Hussein had been executed on 30th December, 2006, and we spent the New Year in Baghdad. However, we found time for other stories, too, like going to South Africa to highlight the inordinately high levels of crime, spending time in Buenos Aires for the 25th anniversary of the Falklands war and, of course, Afghanistan. While in Kabul in the summer of 2007, we met a South African man who said he had just come back from a holiday in Victoria Falls, Zimbabwe. We found out from him details about how easy it was to cross the Zimbabwean border by road from Zambia, and how the border controls and immigration worked. He told us that there were no identity checks and that the immigration officers on the border did not have access to computers. Their main preoccupation was to collect the money for the visas, which are normally issued very easily on arrival. That was a good starting point.

The next step was to find a cameraman who was prepared to film undercover in Zimbabwe and some local fixers who would organise a safe house, transport and help with the filming schedule. When we presented our plan to our big boss, the Head of Newsgathering, we were disappointed to find out that a freelance reporter for the flagship current affairs programme, *Newsnight*, had already been given approval and was about to go into Zimbabwe on an undercover mission herself. She eventually produced a valuable but entirely predictable film, which focused on empty shelves in the shops and children scavenging for food. We knew we could do better than that but we also knew that there had to be a gap of at least a few months before we would be allowed to go. The then Head of News reportedly had said that the BBC had had a perfectly good film out of Zimbabwe so it was unnecessary for Simpson to go. While we were battling it out with BBC bureaucracy, our main competitors, ITV News, put out an undercover film from Zimbabwe along the same predictable lines as the *Newsnight* story. But that wasn't the point. The point was that they had beaten us on the main domestic news bulletins, with large viewing figures, and not on a current affairs programme like *Newsnight*, which traditionally has a very small audience. We were very disappointed. It was time to employ an undercover strategy in our dealings with the BBC management.

Simpson approached the Editor of the Ten O'Clock News on BBC1, a young ambitious chap who had just joined from our main competitor, ITV News. We had worked very well with him on the Iraq story and had managed to by-pass the sclerotic layers of middle management, which separated us from the direct consumers of our product, the programme editors. He agreed that this was a project worth pursuing and came up with an ingenious idea. He would persuade the top brass that Team Simpson should go to Zimbabwe undercover, produce a film but also deliver a live broadcast from there into the Ten O'Clock News on the night that ITV was to re-launch their main news bulletin. The plan for a revamped News at Ten on ITV was the worst kept secret in the industry. The idea was to bring back from retirement an old presenter, a familiar avuncular face, the darling of the housewives, in order to improve the ratings. In addition, ITV were to have a high-profile investigative story with popular appeal to grab as many viewers as possible. Simpson's live broadcast from Zimbabwe would scoop all that.

'Can you deliver it?' the Editor of the Ten asked me.

We were in his glass office, with the door shut, a sign to everybody in the newsroom outside that something confidential was being discussed. 'We need to start planning immediately although no one knows for certain on which date ITV will re-launch. I reckon it will be soon after the New Year.'

I stared at him in silence. He was a young man, younger than me, with a fresh face and steely eyes. His reputation for being clever and ruthless had preceded him. I was shocked by his next words because I thought he had read my mind.

'I know that you will be risking your lives there. I know what you are thinking. Why bother with this if Simpson is going to get all the glory, whatever happens, and you won't get a mention?'

But this is how it goes.

'Well, you will have a story either way. If we get arrested, this will scoop any ITV story. If we succeed, you'll get the first live undercover broadcast out of Zimbabwe,' I said.

'So, you'll do it, is that what you're saying?'

'Of course, I'll do it. And I'll do my best to make it a success,' I continued. 'But I need something from you.'

His eyes focused on me as he leaned forward attentively.

'I need a guarantee of absolute secrecy,' I said. 'I mean absolute secrecy within the BBC. Only you, me, and Simpson know about it, and a few of the top brass, of course, but no assignment editors, and absolutely no one in the Johannesburg Bureau, especially not the Bureau Chief.'

I paused for reaction but he remained silent.

'The BBC leaks like a sieve. If this is to be a success, it will have to come as a surprise to everybody.'

I saw a sign of approval on his face.

'You will be my point of contact,' I stressed. 'Not the Foreign Editor, and certainly no one from Newsgathering. I'll tell you what I need after I've identified a cameraman. Simpson has mentioned Nigel to you as a possible candidate and I think it will probably be him.'

Nigel is a South African cameraman who used to live in London. I worked with him during the Kosovo crisis in 1999 and found him very reliable. He is ex-South African army and is fully trained as an army medic. He is also a friend of Simpson's – they go back a long way and the South African connection has strengthened their relationship because Simpson's wife, Dee, is South African. Nigel is unflappable in the face of danger. He knows southern Africa very well. But also, having a South African with us in Zimbabwe will reduce any suspicion.

The Editor of the Ten guaranteed me total secrecy. His bosses agreed that keeping very few people in the know was a good idea. Even the new Johannesburg Bureau Chief with direct responsibility for coverage of Zimbabwe was excluded from the project completely. In fact, she only found out about our undercover trip after we were in.

Once on Zimbabwean territory, we drive in our four-by-four in the dark about fifty miles to a small game lodge where the owner is expecting us. It is shocking how dark and deserted the road is. Nigel has already been here during the initial planning. He told the owner that he was going to bring some European tourists on an exotic safari. Simpson is supposed to be Nigel's Irish uncle and I'm his Bulgarian butler. This is our cover story, in case we get in trouble by the police. But Simpson and I have made a pact that this will only be used if nobody recognises him first. Otherwise there is no point in pretending. It will be to our benefit if we actually emphasise how famous he is as this might give us preferential treatment in prison and make it easier for us to get access to senior officials. It's the juniors in every totalitarian regime who are always the most difficult to deal with. They could keep us in detention for days before somebody higher up the food chain realises who we are. We have also put in place a procedure that if we miss three consecutive check calls to London, the Editor of the Ten would alert the Irish Foreign Minister through an intermediary – a journalist friend of Simpson's – and the Dutch Ambassador in Harare. Knowing Mugabe's anti-British sentiment, keeping the Foreign Office out of it seems to be for the best, at least initially.

There is dinner waiting for us on the veranda of the game lodge despite the late hour. It's salad and cold meats, quite elaborate bearing in mind that Zimbabweans are starving. We find later that there is plenty of food around but never in the shops. The situation reminds me of the days in the Soviet Union, which I visited as a teenager in the 1970s, and later in the 1990s after its break up – no food in the shops but most people able to make ends meet.

We sit on the veranda drinking beer and listening to the sound of the bush. I feel we've entered a different world, slow and forgotten, away from the madding crowd. Mugabe's oppressive regime seems a million miles away. It's the beginning of summer in the southern hemisphere. This is a small piece of paradise.

I inhale the warm evening air permeated by unknown scents but there is a knot in my chest, which tightens every time I think about whether we'll succeed. It's the same feeling I experienced on my first day at school in a godforsaken, little provincial town in Eastern Europe many years ago. I had spent the hot summer playing with the other boys barefoot in the thick warm dust of the unpaved streets. We ate ripe tomatoes, white cheese and freshly baked bread. We caught fireflies in the balmy evenings and kept them in matchboxes overnight, only to find them dead in the morning. And suddenly school was upon us and for the first time in my life I had that piercing thought – 'Would I succeed?' – which has re-visited me time and time again during the course of my life.

I want this moment on the veranda to last longer, maybe not forever, but to be extended beyond the short night ahead of us. I want to delay the drive to Harare tomorrow morning and all the uncertainties which go with it. It's not personal safety that I am worried about. If we get arrested, we'll become the story and our faces will be splashed all over the newspapers in Britain and around the world. We shall survive any detention and we won't have to do any work. No. The worst possible scenario is being unable to do any meaningful story and fail to do the live broadcast, and still be able to slip out of Zimbabwe undetected.

We get up early in the morning and set off on the perilous road to Harare. The weather is wretched. Heavy tropical rain is beating down on the car windows. The windscreen wipers can't cope. The road surface is unpredictable because the potholes are full of water and I can't see them. I drive by intuition.

'You are doing well,' Nigel says, which annoys me.

My head is cocked over the steering wheel and my eyes are fixed on the narrow road. On a couple of occasions, big lorries loaded with mining equipment appear out of the blue from the opposite direction at threatening speed and I swerve instinctively to avoid a head on collision. But generally, there's hardly any traffic. Disturbingly, we spot a lot of disembowelled corpses of donkeys and dogs killed by motorists and left strewn across the road. I navigate around them.

I stop by a crashed old Nissan loaded with food. Tins of cooking oil lie scattered around, some of them with open lids. Puddles of oil have gathered. Several sacks of potatoes, rice and fruit have been torn and their contents spilled on the road. There is blood on the seats inside but we can't find anybody. Hopefully, the passengers have been saved by whoever hit them, possibly one of the big lorries with mining equipment shuttling between Zimbabwe and South Africa. It dawns on me that the biggest threat to us in Zimbabwe is not going to be the secret police but the treacherous road conditions. It will be a great shame if we die ignominiously on the road. But I don't share these thoughts with John and Nigel.

A few miles further, after the rain has stopped, we notice an old man in tattered clothes filling in a pothole on the road.

'He works for tips,' Nigel says. 'He earns small change from people like us, mainly South African visitors. We have to give him something.'

Nigel looks at me. I am the producer. I hold the purse. I pull a five US dollar note from my pocket and give it to the old man. His lined face lights up, eyes sparkling. He takes the money and makes a gesture of thanks but doesn't say anything. His mouth opens in a big smile revealing few yellow teeth. Poor diet and lack of vitamins, I think to myself. As we get in the car and drive off, he takes off his red woolly hat and waves it in the air.

The weather clears up and we see the lush vegetation on either side of the road in its full glory. It is wild and lovely. As the sun peers from behind the dark clouds our mood improves. We arrive in Masvingo, a major town on the road to Harare, formerly Fort Victoria. During the brief stop in the centre, Simpson and I visit the only supermarket to the consternation of the locals who are hanging around aimlessly in the main square. The shelves are empty except for a few tins of beans arranged symmetrically high up beyond the reach of any human being. When outside, we see that Nigel is talking to someone. He is a young, reasonably well-dressed man. Nigel is the quintessential South African – big, fat, with a ginger beard, enormous belly and fleshy red face. He is wearing what I can best describe as baggy boxer shorts, quite low cut so that his enormous thighs are visible to the world. He is trying to get away but the other man follows him.

Simpson and I discreetly move closer to our vehicle. I have the keys so we get in and wait. Eventually, Nigel gives the man some South African money and he moves away.

'I thought he was a spy, because he wanted to know where we were going and whether he could help us with directions. But then I realised he was only after some money. I gave him a couple of South African rand,' says Nigel as he gets in the car.

'Let's go. We don't want to get in trouble before we've even arrived at our destination,' I murmur and start the car.

As we approach Harare, Nigel and I change seats. He sets up his satellite navigation system and types the address of our host. An irritating female voice with an American accent starts to guide us to the address. The Harare skyline appears in front of us without warning. From a distance it looks remarkably modern and affluent. The Sat Nav takes us through the industrial southern suburbs into the centre and then into the leafy northern parts. The roads are clean. People are well dressed, especially the school children in their pristine uniforms congregating in little groups for their morning classes. The amazing thing is that they look so happy, quite the opposite of what I expected.

As we approach the house of our host, I wonder why Simpson and I haven't had any big discussions in the car as we normally do. No arguments, no big political debates, no talk about the books we either love or hate, no old jokes and no endless repeats of stories we both know by heart. These conversations are our usual way of passing the time but also of disguising any nervousness. But not this time.

I feel exhausted and slightly unsettled by the fact that everything around me looks so normal. A black gardener opens the gate and we drive in. The mature garden looks delightful. It's one of the less opulent houses in the street, but it looks lovely nonetheless. It's on one level and the interior is very 1970s, all in brown and autumnal colours but pleasant and homely. At the far end of the sitting room there's a big dining table behind which is the serving counter of the kitchen. I see all this before I see our hosts. Nigel's voice is booming outside talking to someone with a gentle Irish accent. And this is when Simpson and I see a Dickensian gentleman with bushy sideboards and bad yellow teeth – a smoker and a drinker – probably a lot younger than Simpson but with the air of an old man. This is our host. Nigel hasn't said very much about him in advance, probably because he doesn't know very much about him.

Nigel had made a trip to Harare before Christmas in order to smuggle in our broadcasting equipment, a satellite phone, a computer and a camera. I had managed to get the BBC to give me a complete kit for recording and live broadcasting, including a small satellite phone, on the pretext that we were going to use it for the coverage of the ANC conference in Polokwane, Limpopo province, close to the Zimbabwean border. It was held 16th-20th December 2007, just three weeks before our intended trip to Harare. I didn't want to take any chances of compromising our secret plan by requesting a technical kit through the official channels for an undercover operation in Zimbabwe. For that, I needed to bring on board a trusted cameraman who was going to work with us in Polokwane. Simpson was not even due to cover this story but the Foreign Editor agreed to send us there so that we could take the equipment in without suspicion. The cameraman eventually told the Head of Operations what the kit was needed for and that it might never come back if we were caught. It was decided at a very high level that the risk of losing several expensive pieces of equipment was worth it.

When it was announced to Newsgathering that Team Simpson, which normally meant John, myself and a cameraman, was due to go to Polokwane for the ANC conference, a middle manager with not very much to do but attend vacuous meetings all day said to me, 'But what about the resident correspondent? You can't simply go and big-foot her.'

'Yes, we can, and this is exactly what we are going to do.'

To big-foot someone is a horrible expression, which means that a more senior correspondent arrives on the patch of another one who is based in the field and takes the story over. It's a dreaded scenario for any foreign reporter, especially if the person you are being big-footed by is Simpson. In practical terms it means that the local reporter will not appear on the Ten O'Clock News on that rare occasion when there is a big story on his or her patch, in this case South Africa where Jacob Zuma was due to be elected leader of the ANC, which in turn meant that he would become the next president of South Africa.

A member of the so-called High Risk Team, a department which provides security advisers or, in lay terms, bodyguards for reporting teams in dangerous zones, had overheard something about equipment being ear-marked for a Simpson undercover operation in Zimbabwe and told me that he knew about it. The reason for telling me was just to demonstrate that he was in the loop since being excluded from your bread and butter operations is the death knell of any department. The Editor of the Ten O'Clock News dealt with the matter swiftly and ruthlessly. He simply told the security adviser in question to shut up and that if the story leaked any further he would hold him personally responsible for any failure of the operation. I applauded his decisiveness but nonetheless feared that our secret had been compromised.

It wouldn't be truthful to say that I didn't think through the possible nightmare scenarios of being caught by Mugabe's notorious secret police, the CIO (Central Intelligence Organisation). Every time I started thinking about it, I ended up with a nasty thought of being kept in a small confined space with no air to breathe. A reporter from *Time* magazine had been caught a few months previously while trying to talk to some striking miners. He was betrayed by one of the people he was due to interview about worker grievances. His vivid report of being held for a week with more than a dozen semi-naked prisoners in a small cell designed for two people produced an image in my head, which made me choke and suffocate every time I thought of it. Fear of confined spaces has always been an anxiety which could shatter me into a panic attack. As we were planning our assignment, this particular image became so powerful that it invaded my thoughts before going to bed, during my sleep, after getting up, when exercising in the gym, even when getting into my car – to the point where I thought I was going to lose my mind. This is when I discovered Rachmaninoff's Piano Concerto No.2. The melody is simple and soothing and I would put the CD on and lie in bed until I fell asleep. My appreciation of this piece was even more acute after I found out that the composer wrote it at the age of 28 after receiving psychological treatment to overcome writer's block. Listening to the music time and time again, I felt Rachmaninoff's suppressed talent bursting out and spilling generously in the big bad world. What a relief it must have been for him after years of artistic sterility.

Another way to purge my grim thoughts was to carry on with detailed planning of the operation.

The cameraman and I arrived in Johannesburg a couple of days before the start of the ANC conference. Simpson was due to arrive on the first day of the conference and we planned to drive to Polokwane together. The reason for our early arrival was that the cameraman was to give Nigel some training on how to operate the equipment. In the meantime, I wanted to forge some contacts with South Africa-based NGOs which had presence in Zimbabwe. The plan was to try to get some film footage from them. I was particularly interested in any pictures illustrating the AIDS epidemic in Zimbabwe. With 15 per cent of the population living with HIV, this was a ticking time bomb waiting to explode.

With a bit of luck I managed to find out that UNICEF in Johannesburg had some footage filmed legally in Zimbabwe of children living with HIV. Most of the HIV epidemic was fuelled by heterosexual transmission and passing the virus from mother to child. The footage that I obtained was heartbreaking. It showed young kids orphaned by AIDS, some of them HIV positive themselves, studying and playing at a residential school sponsored by the UN. Most AIDS orphans, however, live with their grandparents. A plan was already forming in my head that we must find a local cameraman to do some undercover filming at a hospital in Harare where women die of AIDS. Little did I know at the time that the footage we would eventually manage to film secretly at a hospital in Harare during our undercover assignment would spark complaints by viewers in the UK for allegedly breaching the privacy of dying women. One complaint forcefully stated that the BBC would never dream of filming victims of AIDS without their consent in the UK. The difference was that patients in Zimbabwe would have given us permission to be filmed in order to highlight their plight and the lack of medication. This was what AIDS activists told us. It was the oppressive government which wouldn't have given us permission to film at the hospital. Did we ask for permission? No, because that would have blown our cover and exposed us to great danger. Anyway, this was how I explained our motives when I wrote my response to the BBC complaints department.

Our Polokwane trip served another purpose, too. We wanted to research unofficial exit routes from Zimbabwe. While the other BBC crews were covering the boring and predictable conference proceedings (it was a foregone conclusion that Jacob Zuma would be elected leader of the ANC), Team Simpson jetted off to the Zimbabwean border and checked into a lodge within a wilderness reserve north-west of the town of Louis Trichardt. The owners of the lodge were a retired Dutch couple who had put their hearts and souls into making the house a delightful place to relax. The main building was refurbished to a high standard in Dutch colonial style while the outbuildings were basic wooden structures but very cosy and with all modern amenities.

It was the rainy season so we couldn't stay on the veranda for long, but on the occasions when the sky cleared the views were unparalleled. The husband had recently retired from the Dutch Foreign Ministry and was very well connected in diplomatic circles in this part of the world. We disclosed to them that we were planning to go on an undercover trip to Harare and they offered assistance. The Dutch Ambassador to Zimbabwe was a personal friend of theirs and before we knew it we had his contact details and a promise that by the time we left he would be informed about our secret mission. This is how Mr Jos Weterings, Dutch Ambassador in Harare, ended up as one of our main emergency contacts on my risk assessment form for Zimbabwe.

We spent two nights at the lodge. Our Dutch hosts served us dinner in an exquisite way. We were the only guests because it was off-season. They didn't use servants to attend to our table, serving us themselves. It was touching to see this elderly Dutch diplomat pouring wine and bringing food. They had been to enough diplomatic receptions to know how to do it properly. Every little detail of the service was really well thought through, which didn't escape Simpson's attention. He is a great connoisseur of food, wine and service. And in the end, it was cheaper than staying at a hotel in Polokwane. In fact, the BBC Southern Africa Bureau hadn't booked us any rooms saying that everything was booked months in advance and we (Team Simpson) had only decided to come at the last moment. So it was our problem to solve. The team consisted of Simpson, our cameraman from London, a Zulu fixer-producer, who we'd worked with before, and me. Mbuso, our South African fixer, was a clever and ambitious young man who lived with his mother in Soweto. He loved it at the lodge.

When we thought that the retired Dutch diplomats were living the dream in this picturesque corner of South Africa, they dropped a bombshell while Simpson was offering cigars to go with the brandy after dinner. The farm had been at the centre of some idiosyncratic South African land dispute. They had bought it in good faith from the previous owners and had legal title deeds. However, the local community was invoking some ancient rights over it, which had thrown a dark cloud on their happy retirement. The uncertainty and the prospect of a long drawn out legal battle frightened them.

On the second day, Nigel arrived from Johannesburg on his way to Harare. The broadcasting equipment was in his car. He was to smuggle it into Zimbabwe. A single South African man pretending to be visiting relatives in Harare for Christmas was less suspicious and less likely to be searched on the border. And border officials were likely to be less vigilant ahead of the long holidays. Nigel, Simpson and I had a brief meeting with our Dutch host. Poring over some border maps, the former diplomat suggested that it would be a mistake to seek unofficial exit routes into South Africa if we went on the run in Zimbabwe. The South African border was mostly fenced off to prevent illegal immigration except for some impassable stretches. He thought that if we were to make an illegal exit we were better off going into Mozambique to the east. The border there is very porous and some of the checkpoints are not staffed at all.

The people who helped us in Zimbabwe wish to remain anonymous. I shall not be divulging any big secrets if I say that all of them were white except for a competent and reliable black cameraman who we hired through our host for some of the most daring missions.

We sit on the brown sofas and drink pale tea. Paul, the owner of the house, introduces us to various people who live under his wing. Nigel has met Paul only once before when he came here before Christmas to smuggle our broadcasting gear. The equipment is not in the house, we are told, it's been stored somewhere else. Simpson and I are not going to stay the night in the house – we have lodgings elsewhere – but Nigel will. It becomes our main base and an office.

I am keen to agree a plan of action immediately. But Simpson is less keen on that. He prefers to get a feel for the place first and then form an opinion about what to do. His instinct is that we should aim to do a strong political story and he prefers to wait a few days so that ideas can crystallise. I am hyperactive and want to start filming immediately. That, of course, will increase the risk of being found out.

But Simpson is the quintessential newsman, he wants to do things at the last minute. While I agree that it's preferable to find a news story rather than just say, hey, we're here in Zimbabwe and here is what it's like to work secretly under the nose of the police, I would like to gather as much footage as possible because I want our films to be visually strong. Some people call this type of footage 'wallpaper' but it is essential for television. You can't have a brilliant script over blank shots. My instinct tells me that we may be discovered by the secret police sooner than we expect and that would amount to failure. Simpson has always been sanguine about that. We often joke that if we were arrested that would be the biggest news story we could ever engineer, short of having a chance interview with Mugabe himself.

'Can we investigate where Mugabe is likely to be in the next few days?' Simpson says, 'for example, at church or a cricket match this Sunday, and doorstep him?'

Doorstepping is when a journalist asks a question without prior warning at a venue, which is not a press conference.

'You'll be arrested immediately,' Paul replies.

'I am not sure,' Simpson continues. 'Mugabe loves media attention. I'm sure he'll answer. What will happen after that is less clear.'

'What would you ask him if you had time for only one question?' I say.

'I'll have to think about that,' Simpson says pensively and sips his tea. 'You see,' Simpson continues, 'these leaders not only love media attention but they also appreciate bravery.'

I can see another of his stories coming on.

'Nigel and I were in Havana some years ago,' he continues. 'No one could get an interview with Fidel Castro but we camped outside a venue where he was delivering a speech. There were other crews with us and we were told that he normally ignores doorstep questions. I was told that he liked to be addressed as "Comandante" so I shouted: "Comandante Fidel" and his answer to me lasted forty minutes. Nigel couldn't hold the camera on his shoulder any longer…' Nigel smiles approvingly.

We only have seven days on the ground to prepare at least two short films and do a live broadcast. We need to decide where we do the live from, Harare or the farm on the border. My view is that we should do it from Harare for maximum impact: undercover live broadcast from the heart of the regime, just under the noses of the notorious secret police. Paul and Simpson are less convinced. They point out that doing the live on the border gives us the chance to drive back into South Africa immediately after the event thus minimising the chances of getting caught. Nigel says he's happy with either location.

Presidential elections are due to be held here in a couple of months. There are strong indications that the opposition leader, Morgan Tsvangirai, from the Movement for Democratic Change might win. The unthinkable might happen. Mugabe might lose power through the ballot box. I outline to Paul what we would like to achieve: not only looking ahead to the elections but also giving the viewer a representative picture of life in Harare. I understand that filming outside Harare in rural areas is out of the question. Mugabe's thugs, the so-called war veterans, some not old enough to remember the struggle for independence, are roaming the countryside intimidating the voters. We'll be exposed to far higher danger there than in urban Harare. Paul thinks that Mugabe will do whatever it takes to stay in power because the alternative is unpalatable not only for him but also for his closet cronies. The current political joke here is: what did the thieves find when they broke into Mugabe's house last night? Answer: the results of next month's presidential elections.

I am gagging to outline to Paul what we want to achieve but I see in Simpson's eyes that now is not the time. And we've just been told that the takeaway lunch has arrived. They have ordered a Chinese. For people with money, life in Harare can be quite agreeable, as we are to find out in the next few days. We sit at the dining table in the dark musty end of the sitting room and eat our meal. It's actually rather good.

We don't see anybody else in the house except Paul, but we can hear people moving about and doing things. They are, however, somewhat invisible. Despite my hyperactive frame of mind, I decide that it's better to let things go. There's no point alienating Paul at this early stage. But I feel that things might come to a head at some point. We have a general chat about life, food supplies, inflation, white farmers and so on. Paul tells us that the president of the Commercial Farmers' Union is offering himself for an interview tomorrow. I'm not very enthusiastic. I tell Paul that if we manage to make a film without empty shelves in shops and without complaints from white farmers about land seizures, I shall consider it a job well done. I even use the phrase 'whinging white farmers' which doesn't go down well with Paul and a couple of people who have somehow found their way into the sitting room without saying hallo or introducing themselves.

'Almost every story that has come out of Zimbabwe in the last five years,' I say, 'is about land seizures by war veterans and food shortages. Ah, and inflation but no one has illustrated inflation on television in a sufficiently interesting way.'

Nigel then says: 'Why don't we go to an expensive restaurant for lunch tomorrow and pay with a big bundle of cash? I'll film a sequence when we pay the bill.'

We all look at each other with approval. So it's decided, Paul will go to an approved money changer to get cash in pristine bundles, machine wrapped with paper straps. He'll then take us to one of the most expensive and desirable restaurants in Harare, Amanzi, on the Enterprise Road in Highlands, north-west of the centre. But there is a catch. In return, I shall have to go with Nigel and interview the president of the Commercial Farmers' Union. It will be a gesture of goodwill even if we don't use the interview. Simpson prefers to stay out of the limelight for the time being.

After supper, Simpson and I are taken by car to our sleeping abode, a large house situated on beautifully tended grounds. The big wrought-iron gate opens onto a palatial pebbled driveway at the end of which there is a sprawling white building on one level. The owner is a small middle-aged cockney man, an estate agent in his current incarnation. The main door leads into a large old-fashioned dining room with dark furniture. There are lots of framed pictures of yachts on the walls, obviously, a passion of his. His demeanour is a bit reserved, a sign of shyness, I think. He looks at Simpson with evident awe. We are led to our rooms, comfortable albeit a bit chintzy. The house has a smell of cleanliness, which nostalgically reminds me of a reputable bed and breakfast in the English countryside.

We are tired and retire to our rooms immediately. I fall asleep, instantaneously oblivious to the dangers lurking beyond the walls of the house. We have put our trust in these people and our only hope is that no one will betray us.

In the morning, I look at my watch with disbelief. I have slept uninterrupted for more than 10 hours. I rush into the bathroom. The bath is luxuriantly big, old-fashioned English solid cast iron, which they stopped manufacturing in Britain about 50 years ago. Hurriedly, I start to fill it up and I am keen to jump in it straight away. However, I discover there is no hot water, so I take a cold shower.

Simpson is already sitting in the garden reading a book. We both feel like we're in a time warp. The housekeeper, a slightly camp middle-aged black man, brings out two glasses of orange juice. Simpson has already asked for fried eggs. I order mine scrambled. The tea is delicious. We are both going to enjoy all this. There is no rush, no deadlines to meet, no conversations with the news bulletins in London. It makes a great deal of difference from our normal assignments. In the privacy of the quiet garden, overlooking the lush grounds in front of us, we begin to discuss in earnest what we want to achieve. We both agree that there must be a groundbreaking long piece-to-camera in the centre of Harare, no better way of demonstrating presence! We should have lots of general scenes from Harare to show what life is like: interviews with ordinary people, slum dwellers, at least one dissenting voice. Is it totally out of the question to have an official voice, someone who speaks on behalf of the government?

I find these short brainstorming sessions with Simpson most productive. If we are both on the same wavelength, then everything else seems very easy.

I suggest that we should do a second news film on the AIDS epidemic. 'We already have some UNICEF footage,' I remind him. All we need to do is find some AIDS sufferers for interviews and organise secret filming in a government hospital where mothers and children are dying of AIDS.

The morning air is damp. Although it's too early for mosquitoes, we both spray our arms, hands and around the neck with mosquito repellent. The smell is unpleasant and will remain an abiding memory of this trip for me but there is no better way of protection. I don't take the anti-malaria drug Malarone because it gives me nightmares. Also, my hair moults when I take it. I often joke with Simpson that I would prefer to die with a good mane of hair rather than live longer with a bald head. Chloroquine, the choice of anti-malarial drug for sub-Saharan Africa doesn't agree with me, either. So I wear long sleeves and douse myself in mosquito repellent containing DEET (N,N-diethyl-meta-toluamide), not a totally harmless substance developed by the American army after the Second World War following its experience of jungle warfare.

By 11 am, a young man appears and says that he's been sent by Paul to drive us back to his house. This driver will become one of our most trusted assistants during our assignment here. He is a relative of Paul's, who's dropped out of school and has some family problems. He doesn't get on with his father, we are told, and he is temporarily staying with Paul.

We drive back to Paul's house in a vintage green Mercedes with pale leather seats. I am dispatched to interview the head of the Commercial Farmers' Union. Thus our work schedule begins to roll out. At lunch we spruce ourselves up and drive to the Amanzi. Paul holds a plastic bag full of freshly acquired cash, the most amazing prop I have ever used in my career as a television producer. We pretend we are tourists from South Africa, a cover story I hope we never have to use if questioned by the police. I want to enjoy the experience but anxiety prevents me from doing so.

The Amanzi, which means water in Zulu, is a lavish place by anybody's standards. A waiter in starched white livery leads us through the main dining room to a table on the veranda overlooking the garden. I notice lots of raised heads and eyes following us as we make our way between the tables, which is not very reassuring if you are trying to be inconspicuous. We are the only white guests in the restaurant. It might be our casual clothes that make heads turn. The other male diners are all in immaculate suits and the women incredibly well turned out, with beautifully coiffured hair, elegant dresses and expensive jewellery. Amanzi is definitely the place to be seen in Harare. It's probably the last place the police will be looking for undercover journalists from the BBC.

We sit down and pretend to admire the scenery. We have two small tourist video cameras befitting any self-respecting South African tourist party. Nigel grabs one of them and rushes into the garden to film the fantastic flower bushes. In fact, he is discreetly pointing the camera at us and gets a few wide shots of the restaurant and of our table. When he comes back the drinks are already served. He films every course the waiter brings. The generous gin and tonic portions have relaxed me and I feel less anxious. I am tempted between the prime sirloin steak and the ostrich medallions but decide in favour of the Zimbabwean beef. My steak is deliciously undercooked. Generally the food is excellent and exquisitely presented. The service is good although the waiter is a bit unctuous. His oily smile is no doubt deployed to elicit a large tip.

Then we come to the money shot, literally. The bill arrives and we say we would like to pay in Zimbabwean dollars. There's panic on the waiter's face. Paul assuages his fears by saying that we shall pay at the unofficial rate, meaning the black market rate, which is 3,000 times higher than the official bank rate. We have purchased the Zimbabwean dollars at the unofficial rate, anyway. But by the time the waiter goes to the money changer to convert it back into US dollars, the rate will have fallen even further. Top government officials and Mugabe's cronies have access to US dollars at the fixed low official rate. They can acquire certain amounts at the low rate every month, which they then sell at the black market rate and enrich themselves enormously. After a bit of faffing about the exchange rate, Paul gets his plastic bag out and lays the bundles of cash on the table. Nigel is filming. Simpson begins to count deliberately: '10 million, 20 million… 100 million, 200… 450 million dollars!' he pronounces, looking directly at the camera.

The waiter gives another of his oily smiles.

'And 50 million for your tip,' continues Simpson. '500 million dollars altogether. Wow, I'm a billionaire!'

This is a meal for four people worth about US$75 plus a generous tip of under US$10. It even falls within the BBC daily allowance. Only six months later, in July 2008, after the second round of the presidential election, a hundred billion Zimbabwean dollars was worth just US$2! I kept a hundred billion dollar note as a souvenir. And our footage from the Amanzi went into our most memorable television piece from this secret mission to Zimbabwe.

On the way out, I see that Simpson is trying to avoid a man who is attempting to say something to him. But Simpson escapes to the toilets. I noticed that the man, a youngish bloke with a round face dressed in a sharp suit, had made a beeline for him as Simpson was approaching the exit. The man hangs around outside the toilets for a few minutes and when there's no sign of Simpson he goes back to his table. A few minutes later, Simpson emerges from the gents and hurriedly gets into the car, which is waiting outside in the driveway.

'I tried to avoid this bore who's recognised me,' Simpson says anxiously, 'says he is a journalist from Zambia.'

I begrudgingly admit to myself that the word is probably beginning to get around Harare about a BBC team working undercover but I don't say anything. I wonder how long before we get stopped or get the proverbial knock on the door.

In the afternoon, I want to meet our local cameraman. Paul is reluctant to let me discuss things with him alone for fear I may find out how much he pays him per day. I know I am being overcharged by Paul but this goes with the territory. Farai, a youthful lean black man, arrives in a battered old car. He wears baggy basketball shorts and an old T-shirt. I want to test his technical abilities and very soon he impresses me. He also shows initiative when I tell him what we want to achieve. Paul is monitoring our conversation but doesn't interfere. I am satisfied and he is hired. I warn him not to tell anybody about working with us. Paul says he is totally trustworthy.

We already have in the bag an interview with an academic from Harare University who is highly critical of Mugabe. The interview was recorded by Farai before our arrival. When I ask about why our professor is allowed to be so critical of Mugabe, I'm given one of the most bizarre explanations, which may offer a clue about how things work here: 'Because Mugabe is afraid of him. He is an albino and Mugabe is scared of doing anything to him for fear that he might cast a spell on him.'

Both John and I feel that we are making progress and we decide to go sightseeing. I suggest that we might as well use our trip to downtown Harare to record some GVs (general view shots). These are usually film shots of the environment in which you want to place your story – streets, buildings, crowds of people, traffic, etc. – which help you tell the story but also with the transition from one location to another. And I would like to have Simpson in some of these shots. There's no point in getting Farai to do them because it will only arouse suspicion. It's better if Nigel does them.

We drive into downtown Harare. Nigel films POV (point of view) shots from the car. These allow the viewer to see exactly what we see when driving in Harare. I love driving shots because they edit very well but also because of their immediacy. They give the viewer the illusion that he or she is in the car with you. We film Simpson looking at shop windows, crossing the street, and asking passers-by for directions. He is wearing a baseball cap as his only disguise. It's amazing how much you can change someone's appearance simply by wearing a hat. Before we left London, he toyed with the idea of wearing a false moustache or dying his recognisable white hair dark. But that would have been ridiculous and he would've been subjected to brutal sarcasm by the newspapers in the UK. So he decided against it.

We are tempted to walk in to the Meikles Hotel for coffee but Paul advises against it because he thinks Simpson will be recognised there even with his baseball cap. We drive deliberately in front of the hotel, though. The Meikle family is the closest Zimbabwe has to aristocracy. In the second half of the 19th century, John Meikle emigrated from Scotland to Natal, South Africa. He had three sons, John, Stewart and Thomas, who started a trading business in Fort Victoria (now Masvingo) in what was then Rhodesia. Their fortune grew to comprise department stores, hotels, farming and tea production. Thomas built the eponymous hotel in Salisbury, now Harare, in 1915. Then it was considered to be one of the most desirable hotels in Africa. The original hotel was demolished in the 1970s. The new structure was re-built several times with new additions, the most notable of which is the Meikles tower, a high rise of 12 floors, completed in 1980. Over the years, the Meikles Hotel has been in the centre of political events, a venue where momentous developments in the history of the country have taken place, from the first Rhodesian parliament in 1924 to the power-sharing agreement between Robert Mugabe and Morgan Tsvangirai in the summer of 2008.

But for Simpson there is another landmark that holds some dear memories, the iconic Harare shop, Fereday's – specialists in safari apparel. He says he is very sentimental about it. And that goes back to the time when he was a BBC reporter in South Africa in the 1970s. Unfortunately, the old shop in the centre of Harare has closed down. We drive past the distinctive Edwardian building with its white painted wrought-iron ornaments but don't get out because the area looks a bit rough. The new owners have moved to a new location in one of the wealthy predominantly white suburbs, Borrowdale, in the north-west of Harare. A day later, Simpson and I venture out to Borrowdale on our own. Our usual driver drops us off outside Fereday's and says that he'll be back in an hour.

'Don't worry,' he says. 'Even if anybody recognises you no one here will shop you to the police.'

And, indeed, the place looks like any British suburban shopping centre with plenty of parking in front of every shop. Disguised in his baseball cap Simpson walks into Fereday's. I follow. The shop is empty. The shop assistant takes a cursory look at us and goes back to his newspaper. There are fantastic green canvas bags and holdalls, all handmade in Zimbabwe, lovely little wallets, which make perfect presents, and of course caps and hats of various proportions. Simpson is interested in some walking boots with special anti-slip rubber soles. There are all sorts of hunting knives; it's a little treasure trove for little boys who never grow up.

We move deeper into the far end of the shop to look at the serious hunting gear, when a short man with glasses jumps up from his desk and says, 'Hello, Mr Simpson! Welcome to Harare!'

John coughs nervously and touches the peak of his cap as if to re-adjust it a bit lower to cover his face. 'Would you do me a great favour, please?' he mumbles so that the shop assistant at the front won't be able to catch it. 'I am not supposed to be here…'

'Well, of course, silly me…' It is now the manager who coughs nervously. 'Do you want me to take off the poster from the front window while you're in town?'

'What poster?' Simpson and I look at each other.

By that time, not only the shop assistant at the front knows who the customer in the baseball cap is, but another of his colleagues has popped out of the store room to have good look. The manager, Simpson and I walk out of the shop and look back at the shop window. Here we see an enlarged framed page of the *Sunday Telegraph* from eight years ago with a picture of John and his wife, under a banner headline: 'Fereday's bag travels the world with BBC editor.'

'This is rather sweet,' says Simpson as we walk back into the shop.'There is no need to take it down. We are here undercover so we'd be grateful if you keep it quiet.'

'That goes without saying,' the manager says and tells the shop assistant behind the counter that we are to receive a 10 per cent discount.

As we take another look at the display at the back of the shop, Simpson notices a copy of the *Zimbabwean Independent*, a leading privately owned business weekly newspaper, on the manager's desk. On the front page there is banner headline: 'Makoni to challenge Mugabe in election.'

To be perfectly honest, at that time I didn't know who Simba Makoni was. We ask the manager. He is a bit dismissive of the significance of such a move but acknowledges that it might be a symptom of a split within the ruling ZANU-PF party. Simpson and I look at each other.

'Could we have this newspaper, please?' Simpson asks.

The manager obliges with a smile.

'Are we missing something here?' I ask, still looking at Simpson. 'Why is no one reporting this in the West? Is this a red herring?'

But Simpson sees this as our salvation. 'Why, finally we may have a serious story!'

I am not so sure, perhaps because I don't know enough about the ins and outs of Zimbabwean politics and the intricacies of the ruling party elite.

Our driver is waiting outside in the green Mercedes. We load our purchases into the boot. Simpson needs to come back for a pair of his favourite boots because they don't have the right size. Back at Paul's house we begin our investigation into Simba Makoni.

It turns out that once he was the darling of the revolutionary establishment. Qualified as a chemist in Britain, with a PhD from Leicester Polytechnic, he was appointed Deputy Minister of Agriculture in the first Mugabe government after the elections in February 1980. Makoni was just 30. Since then he had held ministerial posts, including Finance Minister in 2000-2002 when he presided over the devaluation of the Zimbabwean dollar. His 11-year spell (1983-1994) as an Executive Secretary of SADC (Southern Africa Development Community) was marred by financial scandal, although he denied any personal wrongdoing. After the 2002 presidential elections, in which Mugabe's power was seriously challenged for the first time by MDC's Morgan Tsvangirai, Simba Makoni's name surfaced as a possible replacement for Mugabe, supported not only by elements within the ruling ZANU-PF (Zimbabwe African National Union – Patriotic Front), but also by MDC and some African leaders. That makes him a credible player for the next presidential elections in a couple of months. But how can we confirm it, short of meeting Simba Makoni himself?

Over a beer in a small internal courtyard at Paul's house, Simpson and I talk to Paul about Simba Makoni. Paul is not sure about the significance of Makoni's possible nomination as an independent candidate.

'It could be a ploy to split the MDC vote,' suggests Paul. 'I think Makoni is too much of an insider.'

But Simpson is determined. 'It doesn't matter. The question is whether he will stand against Mugabe or not. If he does, this will give us a strong news angle, and our piece will not be just a feature about us being here undercover.'

I can't agree more with such logic. Then I remember that Paul has mentioned a close friend, a lawyer, who is quite high up in the ruling party. Paul had previously suggested that his friend could be very useful if we got into trouble with the police. He could get us bail, if nothing else. I suggest we meet him.

Jonathan is a young Shona man (Shona is Mugabe's tribe, the majority in Zimbabwe) dressed in a very English tweed jacket and red tie. A big gold watch glistens on his wrist, a display of affluence. For some obscure reason, which I never manage to unravel, Paul had supported him through school and university, a story reminiscent of Jack Nicholson supporting Matt Damon through school in *The Departed*, but with less gruesome consequences.

I ask Jonathan if the CIO knows that we are here. He thinks they don't.

'They are more preoccupied with internal enemies,' he says enigmatically.

We talk about London, which Jonathan visits regularly, South Africa and Namibia, where he has an office.

What will happen in the presidential elections at the end of March?

'Mugabe will win,' says Jonathan emphatically.

Does he have any presidential ambitions?

'Not yet! I'm biding my time. The situation is very complicated but I am still young. I can wait.'

We understand that he is a protégé of the second most powerful man in Zimbabwe after Robert Mugabe, Emmesron Mnangagwa, who holds the bizarre post of Minister of Rural Housing.

How about Simba Makoni?

'He is nobody, but I understand that he will be announcing his candidature for the presidential elections in March,' says Jonathan. 'I've heard it as a rumour.'

Well, this is what we needed. We can now go ahead with this story angle. Simpson looks pleased. I have another worry on my mind: how do we get footage of Simba Makoni to put in our piece?

But before that we have something else to do, perhaps the most important job, the centrepiece of our Zimbabwe film, the piece-to-camera in the centre of Harare without being noticed. We bring together Farai, our local cameraman, Paul and our driver. The discussion centres on location, technical capabilities and security.

Simpson wants it to be among lots of people. This is his trademark, walking and talking, surrounded by unsuspecting crowds. We have done plenty of those in Baghdad and Kabul. I would like it to be in a recognisable Harare location, somewhere where people will say, 'This is without a doubt Harare!' Can we have both?

Farai suggests downtown, in the main shopping street. But where shall we put the camera? If it's openly visible to anyone, it will only be a matter of time before the police spot us, especially if Simpson has to do a second take. We all agree that in an ideal world it will have to be just one take. If the camera is concealed and far away from Simpson, we shall have the problem with the range of the radio microphone. We agree that Farai will go alone and research the area. He is to report back in the evening.

Nigel has spent all day trying to work out how to operate the satellite technology for our live transmission. We also need to make it work for sending our two films plus a few promotional clips to be used on the big day to whet the appetite of the viewing public. He's been on the phone to the BBC technical department, which sort of blows our cover internally within the BBC.

Farai comes back in the evening while we are eating supper. He is not offered any food, which makes me uneasy. He's found a vantage point on the second floor of an office block above a pharmacy.

'There's a toilet which can be locked and its window overlooks the main shopping street,' he says.

He's confident it will work. Our driver confirms that there's hardly any danger of Farai being discovered in the toilet. He has to smuggle the camera and the tri-pod in a bag so that it doesn't arouse any suspicion. I can't be sure that this is going to work but only ask if the radio microphone will be within range. Farai nods.

'Can we do it tomorrow at the busiest time of the day?' I ask, and then, looking at Simpson, add, 'And can we do it in one take, please?'

He nods, too.

On the following morning I try not to divulge my nervousness. This is going to be the biggest test of our planning so far and the risk of being caught is very high. We set off in the green Mercedes – Paul, Simpson and I. Farai will be getting there in his own car. We meet outside the chemist's shop. Farai points with a nod of his head to a small window on the second floor. The window is open. The tri-pod is already there. Farai is holding a black gym bag. The camera and the microphone are in the bag. Simpson has already been wired up at the house. The radio transmitter is in his pocket from where you can see a thin black wire disappearing under his shirt. The black head of a small lapel microphone is discreetly positioned at the neck of the shirt. It's almost like a little black button. In the lunchtime crowds of downtown Harare, Simpson looks like any white farmer or a businessman going about his own business. He is wearing chinos, a pale beige shirt and a baseball cap.

The plan is that as soon as Farai sees Simpson in position at the bottom of the street he should start recording. We don't have any means to provide communication between the two of them. Once Simpson is finished he should get into the green Mercedes, which will be parked in a side street nearby. Farai should come down to find out from us if a second take is required. The only person who will decide if there's to be a repeat is Simpson because he has to be happy with the contents and the delivery of what he has said. If a second take is required, we will go through exactly the same process again.

The green Mercedes is parked in such a way that I can see Simpson's every movement. I have decided that if he gets in trouble, I shall rush out and make sure I am arrested with him. But Paul and the driver are to stay in the car and try to get away. Farai will see what's going on and will disappear from the building as soon as possible. Simpson and I are to deny that we have any accomplices.

What happens in practice is very close to the plan. Simpson gets out of the car, walks slowly to the designated starting point at the bottom of the street, and looks up at the open window to establish contact. Then he makes his way through the crowd up to the junction in front of the chemist's shop and crosses the street. The whole thing lasts only about four minutes but it seems like ages to me. Then he is back at the green Mercedes and we drive around the block to allow Farai time to come down. As we drive past the chemist's shop for a second time, Farai's car pulls up next to ours at the traffic lights and he stretches his arm through the window handing Paul a small tape hidden in his fist. This wasn't in the plan but is an excellent idea. Paul passes the tape to me. Farai gives us his thumbs up.

Simpson says he wants to do a second take because he was not sure if he started on time and if the delivery was as smooth as he wanted it. Paul is a bit nervous of repeating the whole performance and looks at me for support. As a producer I am in charge of the operation and will hate myself if I deny Simpson a second take only to find out the one we have is not usable. As the lights change, I say to Farai that we have to do it again.

The second time around we all feel more relaxed. The whole thing goes like clockwork. Once we've finished, we drive to the car park of the Holiday Inn. It's less conspicuous for white Zimbabweans to hang out at the car park of an international hotel than in the street. Farai pulls up next to us. We play the tape on his camera. Simpson is there in frame among the crowds of downtown Zimbabwe. The video is excellent. The audio, however, is a bit patchy. Farai starts to make excuses about the range of the radio microphone. I listen to it again, this time on headphones. It's not ideal but it's something I can live with. I tell Simpson that I'm happy with it and he defers to me. Paul is relieved when we finally decide to drive back to his house.

We already have the elements of a strong piece but we're missing archive footage of Simba Makoni. This is when Paul introduces us to an elderly gentleman who had worked as a journalist for the BBC World Service in London forty years ago. He takes it upon himself to procure the footage for a certain fee. The circle of people who know about us is getting bigger and bigger. I am just wondering how long we can rely on the incompetence of the Zimbabwean intelligence service before the bubble we're living in bursts.

Over the following couple of days we move our attention to the topic of our second piece, AIDS. In one of the outbuildings on the grounds of Paul's house lives a young woman who is dying of the disease. She is also an activist promoting education among women in the slums of Harare. She puts us in touch with other activists who in turn take us to a small village just outside Harare to interview families coping with AIDS. In the village, we pretend we are aid workers. We'll only tell the people we film that the interviews will go out on the BBC. Do they want their faces obscured or do they want to be seen? All of them are happy to be seen. Farai films the interviews with John. Paul is there, too, looking after them. Nigel and I stay in the four-by-four on the main road.

On the way back I say to Paul that we want to drive through Mbare, the notoriously crime-ridden suburb of Harare, which is a no-go area even for government forces. Mbare was the first high-density township established a hundred years ago by migrant workers from neighbouring countries. They arrived during the construction boom, when white settlers began the expansion of Fort Salisbury, which then became the city of Salisbury, present day Harare. Parts of the township were demolished by the army and the police in 2005 in an effort by Mugabe to regain control of the slums of the capital. Operation Murambatsvina (Drive out Rubbish) was designed to clear the illegal dwellings in the slums but only antagonised the local population. Mbare is iconic in many ways: it's the home of one of Zimbabwe's best-known football clubs, the Dynamos, a famous arts and crafts market, and one of the oldest theatres in Harare. It also has the best fresh vegetable market. But driving through Mbare in a four-by-four with South African number plates is asking for trouble. Paul is not happy and is getting grumpy. Simpson is irritable, too. That's very unusual for him because he's normally up for such adventures. Both of them think it's unnecessary. But I think it's essential for our piece. I also want to see it for myself. I don't want to rely on Paul's descriptions any more. I feel he is beginning to ration our exposure to anything that might give us first-hand knowledge of Zimbabwe. That diminishes his value as a fixer.

Nigel, however, is very enthusiastic. As a South African, he knows the value of claiming first-hand experience from Mbare. I tell him quietly that the more pictures he gets of demolished houses the better. I also want him to film Simpson looking through the window while we drive through. It's another way of demonstrating presence. Paul tells us we can't stop. We just have to get driving shots. I don't mind because they are just as powerful. My only regret is that we won't be able to talk to anybody there.

We make a few loops through Mbare's ramshackle but picturesque parts. Some purpose-built tenements look half-destroyed – piles of rubble on one side, hollow walls and windows on the other. Other parts look like a mosaic of allotments: little green gardens with shacks built of corrugated metal sheets and scraps of wood. Poorly dressed people hang out on the unpaved streets. I was expecting to see a Brazilian favela but this is much more sprawling and surprisingly green. On a couple of occasions we get some angry looks from local people standing outside their shacks, especially when they spot the camera.

We all feel that it's a job well done for the day. The gin and tonic tastes better under the clear night sky, which envelops Paul's garden like a warm blanket. We watch the stars in silence. Then my satellite phone rings. This means trouble. Only selected people in London know this number. We have made our check calls for the day so it must be something more important.

It's the Head of Newsgathering, our overall boss, only a notch down from the Head of News. She is very direct. After a few seconds of pleasantries, she says that she's been informed that the news of our presence in Harare, including our names, is being widely circulated among the opposition here. I want to know who has told her that. She is reluctant but I know she can't hold back the name because this concerns our safety. I tell her that without knowing her source we shall be unable to make a judgement. Simpson overhears the conversation and would like to speak to her directly. I make an instant decision and tell her, 'It's better if we discuss it here between ourselves and with our fixers first. Perhaps we can talk in about an hour or, even better, in two hours.' She agrees and suggests that we should have a conference call. Oh, no, we can't escape the BBC conference calls even here in Harare.

Paul is worried because he thinks we are going to blame him. Simpson is annoyed when I tell him who has informed the Head of Newsgathering about the possibility that our names are now known among the opposition. It comes from someone who works on a freelance basis for the BBC in Harare and the information has been channelled through the BBC Bureau Chief in Johannesburg. We had chosen to exclude this person from the planning and the preparations for this trip and we chose not to meet face to face while here. Both Simpson and I felt very strongly that this person has a vested interest in preventing us from coming to Zimbabwe.

Half our battles are with people within the BBC who are trying to scupper what we are doing. In this case, Simpson has destabilised this person's position as the ONLY person who can report officially from Zimbabwe. A myth was cultivated that it's so extraordinarily dangerous to report undercover from here that no one could do it. However, we've already been happily filming away for nearly a week. This is the tenor of the conversation we have been having among ourselves when the phone rings again. This time it is the Editor of the Ten. He's been made aware of the rumours. He agrees with us that there are vested interests at play but he'll defer the decision about what we're to do next to us.

I suggest we get a second opinion. Paul calls a close friend, a British resident of Harare, closely linked to the opposition. She arrives almost instantly. L is a no-nonsense woman who speaks briskly and listens to our case attentively. She knows all the people involved and is aware of the competitive nature of our line of business together with the rivalries between journalists in principle. However, her summing up is chilling: 'The opposition is heavily infiltrated by government agents. In my opinion you have 48 hours before the secret police comes after you.' We have to reassess our plans.

Our initial plan was to do a live transmission from Harare but that may no longer be wise. We've got to edit two short news films and record three promotional clips in the next two days before heading for the border with South Africa.

We decide that we'll stay on regardless of instructions from London. We'll keep a low profile and do the live from the same farm where we stayed on the way in. With this plan in our heads we wait for the conference call. The Head of Newsgathering rings exactly at the agreed time. Simpson wants to handle the call himself so I pass the phone to him. He is very polite but firm. We understand the risks but we have taken advice from here and we shall stay on. Leaving prematurely without doing the live programme is out of the question. In the meantime, we'll keep our heads down. We won't attempt to do the live from Harare. The idea is to do it from the South African border and drive into the safety of South Africa immediately after that.

The call ends amicably. I am curious to know the details. Simpson tells me that the Head of the High Risk Team was on the call, too. He is another person we had successfully excluded from the planning of this assignment and he won't forgive us for that. We've just demonstrated how irrelevant his team is on certain assignments. I wouldn't dream of going into Baghdad without his team's help. But to Zimbabwe? There is no meaningful role they can play here. However, we're forced to take them with us on another trip to Zimbabwe later in the year. And what a palaver that turned out to be.

I am determined to film the promotional clips at a high point in Harare so that the camera can give the viewer a bird's eye view of the city. Nigel, Paul and I research a few high-rise buildings in the centre but access to their roofs is difficult. Caretakers and security people are paranoid of letting you climb onto the roof let alone film from there. It's too risky. Then Nigel suggests the Kopje, a granite hill in the south-western corner of central Harare. It's arranged as a public park and although not very high the views are spectacular. We set off in two cars mid morning. Paul's wife parks her car at the bottom of the Kopje to watch the entrance. If police or any suspicious vehicles enter the park she will call Paul on his mobile. Hopefully, the mobile phone network will not be congested. Nigel holds a small camera. In his big arms, it looks even smaller. The top of the Kopje is deserted at this time of the day. We spot a single woman taking a walk there. She looks curiously at us but Paul thinks there is nothing.

The views of the Harare skyline are spectacular. The city looks surprisingly modern because from here you can't see the details of dilapidation of the big buildings. I breathe in like I do on every occasion when I want to enjoy a transient moment of excitement. I know that this moment here on the top of the Kopje looking down on Harare's skyline will not last very long and I may never be able to come back to this spot again. And deep down in my soul I am grateful to Simpson for making it possible for me to be here. Despite the creative, often painful, friction in our relationship I still feel very lucky to be able to work with him. And I know that the promo clips that we're going to record at this spot will be a big hit.

Nigel records a few takes of every version of the promotional clips, each with a duration of 10 to 15 seconds. As we are making our way to the car park at the top of the Kopje, Paul's mobile rings. It's his wife. She says that a suspicious car is heading towards the top. We quickly jump in Nigel's South African four-by-four and drive down. We see the suspicious car. There are three men in identical grey suits and black shirts in it. We don't make eye contact with them, choosing to talk animatedly between ourselves like any normal tourists excited by the trip to the top of the Kopje. We look with baited breath to see whether the car turns back and follows us. It doesn't.

Elated by the experience on the Kopje, we begin to plan our last assignment: an undercover visit to an AIDS ward at the Harare General Hospital where we plan to film with a concealed camera. Farai cuts out a round hole in the side of his black gym bag and positions the camera inside. After a few tests he is confident he can perform the secret recording either clutching the bag under his arm or dropping it low and holding it by its handles.

The cover story is that Simpson is looking for his injured gardener and accidentally strays into the AIDS ward. Farai is supposed to be his driver. Paul drives his green Mercedes into the hospital grounds. Simpson and I are in the back seat, Farai is sitting in the front. I am tempted to ask him to film a driving shot as we enter under the lifted barrier, but hold back because the tension in the car is very high. Paul thinks it's very risky and quite unnecessary to expose ourselves to such danger. The hospital reminds me of one of those Soviet-style establishments I was all too familiar with in my childhood in Eastern Europe, from the smells to the look of the building.

I quietly repeat my instructions to Farai: 'Make sure you get shots of Simpson walking in the hospital corridors and talking to some of the women and children suffering from AIDS. Try to get close-ups of their faces and especially the eyes.'

Paul looks grumpily at me.

As Simpson and Farai disappear into the hospital main door, I close my eyes and slump back into the leather seat to avoid talking with Paul.

I can feel tension in the air. I look intently at my watch every few minutes. The agreement is that they will only spend twenty minutes there. It's the famous twenty-minute rule we've inherited from Baghdad and Afghanistan – experience teaches that it normally takes twenty minutes to be spotted and reported to the enemy. So if you are doing undercover work or if you film in a hostile environment, don't hang around for more than twenty minutes in one place! However, I see the hands of my watch moving painfully to the twenty-minute mark and Simpson is still inside. Thirty minutes pass, and still no sign of them. I begin to worry but don't say anything fearing the 'I told you so' response from Paul. I surreptitiously dial Simpson's mobile but it's switched off. The only consolation is that there is no commotion at the hospital. Everything seems normal and quiet.

Eventually, Simpson and Farai emerge from the main door and start walking hurriedly towards us. They jump in the car without saying anything and Paul drives off. I have regained my confidence and tell them that we must get some exterior shots of the hospital to use as an establishing sequence in the edit. Simpson nods in agreement. Paul is positively angry but stops the car on the main road outside the hospital. I instruct Farai that we need at least two different shots: a wide and a medium.

'If you get a close-up of the hospital sign, that will be a bonus,' I add.

He opens the passenger door and films from the car, holding his camera in his lap. Very inconspicuous.

Back at the house, Farai's pictures from inside the AIDS ward are beyond my expectations. The hole in the bag is not big enough for the camera lens and the shots are framed by a rough outline, which gives them a spooky atmospheric feel. It cries out 'hidden camera'. Simpson is walking through the ward. Then he stops and talks to some of the women. There are nice shots of children with big, sad teary eyes. This sequence is one of the most powerful in our material from Zimbabwe but provokes viewers' complaints in the UK about filming sick people without their consent.

We are now coming to the end of our week in Zimbabwe. The two pieces have been edited and sent by satellite technology to London, together with the promo clips. I am now more relaxed because if all else fails, at least they have two films to run on the night when the BBC goes head to head with ITV's revamped News at Ten. But there's still the icing on the cake to be done – our live transmission from an undisclosed location in Zimbabwe. We've ditched the idea of doing it from Harare after our bosses in London were spooked by reports that our presence was an open secret among opposition members.

Before we left London, I had a curious conversation on the phone with the Head of Newsgathering. She asked me if I was comfortable about going undercover to Zimbabwe. A bit late, I thought, as we were about to get on a plane to Johannesburg. After going through the alert procedure in case we get in trouble, she suggested that Simpson might stretch the boundaries of our assignment even to the extent that he may want to get arrested. This would guarantee enormous publicity for him but would not necessarily be good for the BBC. She was concerned about a possible diplomatic incident. I tried to assuage her fears by saying that from our research we had learned that the courts in Zimbabwe still have a great degree of independence and made many rulings against the government. This meant that if we had a good lawyer on stand by, as we did, we could at least get bail. I didn't share this conversation with Simpson until our last day in Harare.

'Did she really say that? I have a two-year-old son, who's the light of my eyes. I would like to get back to London as soon as possible instead of lingering in a prison cell or under house arrest. Sod the publicity.'

There is one more thing we want to do before we leave Harare, a shopping expedition to the main arts and crafts market. Simpson feels safe enough to brave a walkabout in the market. Our usual driver takes us there. He is a fresh-faced young man of about twenty. There are no jobs for people like him so he, like most of his school friends, works occasionally in the safari industry. A few months earlier during the dry season he worked for the father of a friend of his. They took a group of Italians on a hunting expedition in the bush. He recalls the traumatic events when one of the Italians was impaled on an elephant tusk and died. 'The animal crept quietly behind him. He turned back and saw it in horror. He panicked and tried to run but elephants are unusually fast for their body mass and the poor chap was pierced through the chest.' The boy is still traumatised by the experience.

The arts and crafts market is on the roof of an underground car park. We are the only white people here and everybody competes for our attention. Most of the stuff is quite ordinary and mundane but behind someone's stall I notice a few head sculptures carved out of leopard stone. They look unfinished. I express interest and the shopkeeper, a woman with a large face and even larger hips, moves a few things around so that she can get the carvings out and then carefully cleans them with a damp cloth. The leopard stone faces look sad. I choose one, which is not too big to put in my suitcase and start negotiating the price. I say I'll pay in South African rand and her face lights up. Eventually, I pay the equivalent of $10. This face, carved by an unknown Zimbabwean artist, stares at me from the top of a bookshelf as I write these lines. It will always remind me of my first trip to Zimbabwe.

Simpson buys a couple of wooden toys for Rafe, his two-year-old son. The toys are made of wood painted in bright colours, and look charmingly old-fashioned. One of the toys represents a little brightly painted man who moves his arms and legs when you squeeze the handles of the contraption.

We walk around aimlessly enjoying the freedom of being on our own among the friendly shopkeepers. Our cover is perfect – we are tourists from South Africa. And luckily, no one recognises Simpson from the telly.

In the evening, we have a farewell meal at Paul's. I pay Paul his fee for helping us, rent for the accommodation, rent for our safe house, food and drink, wages for the cameraman and the driver, the cost of the Makoni archive footage, and all sorts of small expenses. I want to reward our driver with a separate tip because I know he'll get paid a fraction of what we pay Paul as driver's wages. I choose my moment and slip a 50-dollar note into his hand. He's embarrassed and protests. This is a lot of money here but he's been with us on every filming assignment and we like him. Eventually, he looks around and when he's confident that no one is looking folds the note several times into a very small square and puts it in his sock.

At the safe house, the owner is waiting for us. He offers gin and tonic and we sit inside on the dark leather sofas in the drawing room. The room looks very grand in the dark. He talks about his life in the UK and his obsession with boats. He has owned different boats at different times. He proudly shows a photograph of a swanky yacht he used to keep at Southampton. But the conversation stalls. I feel he's a bit self-conscious. We thank him for his hospitality and for putting himself in danger by hosting us. He says it's a pleasure for him and that he hopes we can come back again.

The house is situated on one of the main roads leading into the centre of Harare. We were told that the road was part of the official route for the Mugabe motorcade when he travels from his residence to parliament or the ZANU-PF headquarters. We saw the black limousines a few times through the big iron gates in the morning. Normally, there's hardly any traffic on that road. And it's so quiet day and night. We feel safe in the house after the gate is locked behind us every night. And I sleep deeply despite the worries that we might be caught. But several times during our stay I wake up wondering, 'Where am I, and what is the story I'm doing?' It takes me a good few seconds to place myself in Zimbabwe. Then I strain my hearing to find out if any of the passing cars are stopping outside the house. My heart sinks in trepidation with every noise. Have we been betrayed? Is that the secret police coming to get us?

Sometimes during those confused nights in Harare, a niggling thought about my mother in Bulgaria lodges into my brain. It burrows itself relentlessly in my mind and won't leave me alone. A hazy slumber is the only escape but it only makes me even more exhausted than staying awake. Just before I left for Zimbabwe my brother told me that my mother had confessed to him of having a 10-year affair, which had been kept secret from both of us. But after telling him, she swore him to secrecy because she didn't want me to know. The story she told my brother was bittersweet. A few weeks after my father's funeral back in 1997, she was travelling on the tram in Sofia. There were no vacant seats so she stood on her feet when the tram was brought to an abrupt stop. She swung and fell onto the lap of a distinguished, white-haired gentleman in the seat nearby. He smiled and said, 'Fate has sent a woman into my life.' He turned out to be a retired surgeon with an unhappy family life. They began a passionate affair, spending most of their time together except for the few days in the year when we visited her.

What bothered me was not the affair itself but the fact that she concealed it from us. And what was even more hurtful was that she preferred to tell my brother but didn't want me to know. Why would she do that? Am I perceived as domineering and autocratic as my father? Does she think of it as a sordid diversion, which besmirched his memory? Is she ashamed of it? Does she think I wouldn't understand? When my brother told me, I felt like a fool. Or worse, I felt the bond with my mother had been broken. I didn't understand her any more.

My mother was never a glamorous woman. She only bought clothes when she needed them. The austerity under communism had made her very frugal. Some things suddenly made sense. I was baffled when she started spending money on what she would normally consider to be nonsense while my dad was still alive. No one can bear the thought of his parents' private lives but had she been happy with my dad? Was the affair a race to happiness before it was too late? Did she rush to make up for what she had lost in her youth? Grim thoughts. But in the morning I purge them from my head and focus on the jobs for the day.

Months of planning have gone into our Zimbabwe project. We researched exit routes through Mozambique, Zambia and Botswana, we commissioned interviews and material before we arrived, we rehearsed how to conduct ourselves if we got arrested, but nothing has prepared us for our last day, the day of the live transmission.

We set off early in the morning from Harare to the South African border. The aim is to set up base at the same game lodge we stayed at on our first night. The owners have been warned about our arrival by phone. The drive back is uneventful. Does it feel that way because we've become more confident? We even attempt to film police roadblocks.

Nigel is driving. I hold the small camera covered with a baseball cap supported on the plastic box by the gear stick. The first attempt is unsuccessful. Perhaps I am too nervous. By the time I switch the camera on, the policeman has waved us through. The second time, just before Masvingo, a policewoman stops us. Her face looms large in the open window on the driver's side. Nigel deliberately leans backwards so that the lens can have a full view of the policewoman's face. The red light of the camera blinks indicating it is recording. Nigel is chatting away. She asks where we are heading. Then she asks for some South African rand. Nigel gives her some small notes and a bottle of water. She waves us through. The weather is dry and we can see the potholes on the road clearly.

I tell Simpson that I would like to stop at the next baobab tree. I just want to touch it. When I was a kid in Bulgaria I had a book with illustrations of exotic plants, trees and animals. The baobab tree caught my imagination and I was obsessed with it. It would be a shame if after all these years I miss the chance to touch and hug the enormous tree of my childhood imagination.

Simpson thinks the story is very moving and we stop at a lay-by with a solitary baobab. As we get out of the car, we notice an old man sitting under the tree. There is a basket in front of him full of black bits, which look to me like enormous dried mulberries.

'Mopane worms,' says Nigel. 'The best source of protein in Africa.'

I look at them and squirm. Nigel grabs one from the basket and quickly puts it in his mouth, chewing loudly. I learn that Mopane worms are not worms at all but the caterpillars of a particular species of moth, indigenous to southern Africa. They are found on the Mopane tree, also known as the Butterfly tree because of its butterfly-shaped leaves. I am tempted to buy some to take back to London but change my mind. Nigel slips a couple of South African rand into the old man's hand and he smiles broadly. His friendly rugged face looks sad and his watery eyes swim in tears as if he is mourning the death of a dear friend.

Our last day in Zimbabwe. We arrive at the lodge just before lunch. I am keen to start setting up the equipment so that we can test it but am overruled and we decide to have lunch first. Then Nigel sets up our portable BGAN (Broadband Global Area Network) terminal and easily locates the satellite. That's a success. However, when the camera is connected to the laptop, it can't see it. BGAN is the first mobile communication service which delivers data and voice from anywhere on the internet. The network is provided by a company called Inmarsat, which uses stationary satellites for global coverage.

We change the camera and the picture goes through to the London control room. However, after a minute the signal from the camera switches off. It is frustrating. Nigel's face is getting redder and redder as if it's going to explode. He's bent over the equipment in the back of his car and shuffles the notes he took during his crash training session in Johannesburg. Although I'm not highly proficient in the technical department, I start asking questions, which might alert him to an aspect of the set up he might've forgotten. This irritates him even more and he shouts, 'Stop hovering above my head. I know I can do it. Just go away! I'll let you know when it's done.'

I sheepishly go back to my room. Simpson, who has wisely stepped away so that his presence doesn't add to the tension, asks me how it's going.

I say, 'Not well. We may not be able to do our prized live transmission…'

He looks at me anxiously. 'Well, Nigel is good at these things. Let him play with it and see how it goes. I'm going to put my head down for a while, and I suggest you do the same and stay out of his way.'

I nod and go into my room. It's clean and smells of freshly ironed bed linen. I snuggle on the bed in my clothes and make sure there's no opening in the mosquito net that drops from a hook on the ceiling around me. Surprisingly, despite the anxiety, I sleep for about an hour.

When I get up, Nigel is not at the vehicle. The equipment is packed in the back of his four-by-four. I go to his room and peer through the window. He is snoring happily under the mosquito net. It's mid afternoon. The weather is pleasantly hot. With Simpson and Nigel sleeping, it feels like the calm before the storm. I feel I have to do something but can't think what. When you don't know what to do, don't do anything! This was the advice I was given when I first arrived in the UK more than two decades previously. The person who gave me this advice is no longer alive. My thoughts drift back to the days when I was alone and unemployed in London. But I knew then that things would turn out for the better. And they did. Will they turn out for the better now? I go out on the veranda overlooking spectacular scenery and order a pot of tea. It takes ages for the tea to arrive but, when it does, Simpson turns up almost simultaneously. He asks about the equipment and I say that Nigel is taking a nap.

'If he's not up by 4.30, we should wake him up,' Simpson says.

'Nigel was pretty pissed off, quite angry. I thought he was going to thump me in the face so I backed off,' I say.

We drink our tea in silence. Simpson asks for some biscuits and I go down to the kitchen to fetch them.

At 4.30 I brave myself and go to Nigel's room to wake him up. He's already in the shower, so I quickly go back to the veranda and sit with Simpson.

'Do you think we should tell London about our problems?' Simpson broaches the subject.

'Not yet,' I say. 'Let's see whether he'll be able to make it work this time.'

'I think they should know,' Simpson insists.

I can't bear the thought of telling the Ten O'Clock News that we've let them down.

Nigel is huffing and puffing by the vehicle. It's obvious even from a distance that it's not working.

'We need another camera,' Nigel says. 'I'm not doing anything wrong. The picture from the camera goes through but then drops off.'

I despair and walk away to make the phone call to London in private. Normal mobile phones don't work here. I try my satellite phone and the call goes through to the Ten O'Clock desk straight away. The Deputy Editor picks it up. I tell him that our camera has broken down, that we are in the middle of nowhere, that it'll be almost impossible to find another camera and that the live transmission into the programme may not happen. We are trying to sort it out but they have to be prepared for the worst. He is disappointed, um-ing and ah-ing, and doesn't know what to say. I tell him I have to go and hang up.

The manager of the lodge tells me that she doesn't have a camera but there is a farm down the road and the owner there might have one. I go back to Nigel and Simpson by the car and tell them about the farm next door. Nigel has already called his wife in Johannesburg and asked her to get in her car and drive down here with a reliable camera. The drive will take about six hours, depending on traffic. Even if she makes it, she will be here just a few minutes before the Ten O'Clock News goes on air.

I suggest we drive down the dirt track to the neighbouring farm. It takes us about twenty minutes to get there. The house looks deserted but after we knock on the door a middle-aged woman opens up. She looks bewildered because she is not expecting anybody. Nigel's ginger looks and big frame, together with his South African accent, have a calming effect. She's friendly and listens attentively. 'Video camera? I think we have one somewhere.' And she disappears back into the house. Two minutes later she produces a black plastic box covered in dust. There is a Sony Handycam, complete with power supply and batteries in it. 'Not sure if it works,' she says, 'but you can try it.' Nigel turns it on but there's no power.

We take it anyway and drive back hectically to our hunting lodge. We plug it to the mains and hurray it works. It also has a night vision switch, obviously bought to film hunting animals at night. After the battery is fully charged, Nigel connects it to the laptop of the BGAN and… the pictures go through to London. We leave it for a few minutes and the picture doesn't drop off. I can't contain my excitement and run off to my special spot from where I can make a satellite call to London. The Editor of the Ten O'clock picks it up. I can hear him but he can't hear me. The line goes dead. My chest is heaving. I can't get enough oxygen to fill my lungs. An overwhelming sense of well-being suffocates me. My satellite phone rings and it's the Editor of the Ten. He says that his office phone registered my number so he just rang it back without knowing whose number it was.

He is expecting bad news and I am quick to placate him. 'We found a camera. The test is successful and we can do the live transmission.'

He passes the news to the people on the desk and I can hear a big cheer in the background. He also suggests that we should come up fifteen minutes before the start of the bulletin to record 'as live' headlines. 'As live' means pre-recorded material done quite close to airtime. The benefit of it is that it can incorporate the latest news but also avoid the technical glitches normally associated with live broadcasts. It gives the programme immediacy but also a smooth and polished look by allowing you to record two or three different shots, giving the illusion that you are using multiple cameras.

The live transmission is a tremendous success. Nigel and I point hand-held torches at Simpson to shine light on his face. The background is completely dark. Simpson tells the audience that he can't reveal our precise location but we are on Zimbabwean territory. This adds to the Boy's Own feel of our adventure. I know we've done it.

As we are packing up the satellite equipment, the generator and the cables, a South African four-by-four pulls up. It's Nigel's wife with a camera from Johannesburg. In the excitement after the successful programme, we had forgotten all about her. It's getting on to one in the morning. We leave the Sony camera, which saved our professional lives and our reputations, with the manager of our hunting lodge and drive towards the South African border. I don't care if we are arrested now or not. Our job has been done.

A sleepy official lazily places a stamp in my passport. The others are already in the car. We are out of Zimbabwe. I ring the Duty Editor in London to tell him that. Behind us, we leave a queue of desperate people clutching small bundles of possessions waiting to be allowed to enter the prosperous world of Zimbabwe's neighbour.

During the six-hour drive to Johannesburg I am in a state of euphoria fuelled by endless cans of Red Bull. I tell Simpson that I feel reckless, like a Russian soldier throwing himself into battle having drunk a bottle of vodka. This is how the Red Army motivated soldiers during the Second World War. We talk about Russian literature. His favourite author is Turgenev. '*Fathers and Sons*,' he says, 'is one of the greatest novels ever written.'

I remember Turgenev from my school curriculum in Bulgaria but *Fathers and Sons* is not a novel that touched my soul, perhaps because it was hijacked by Soviet propaganda. We were led to believe that the main character, Bazarov, was the precursor to the Bolsheviks, a man who in the spirit of the then fashionable 'nihilism' rejects everything that cannot be proven scientifically, most of all human emotion.

Simpson, however, sees in the novel the enduring power of love between fathers and sons, the bond which exists between them despite their opposing political views. This is the relationship he hopes to achieve with his son, Rafe, when he grows up. I can see the endearing value of this interpretation, which I couldn't be bothered to spot thirty years ago when I took a cursory look at the novel. *Fathers and Sons* was the first Russian novel to become widely known in the Western world not only because of its literary merits but because Turgenev lived in Paris, spoke French fluently having been brought up in an aristocratic Russian household, and mixed in Parisian literary circles. I say to Simpson that the Russian title of the novel is 'Fathers and Children' but was translated in English as *Fathers and Sons* because it sounded better. But Simpson already knows that. He can even pronounce the original title in Russian.

The motorway to Johannesburg is clear and I break every speed limit. Nigel and his wife drive in the vehicle in front of us. Occasionally, my phone rings and Simpson answers to take the messages of congratulations. The sense of achievement is overwhelming and I revel in it. I know, though, that this will not last for very long.

To kill time, I start a conversation about my favourite Russian novel, Bulgakov's *The Master and Margarita*. Simpson sees it in predominantly political terms. The Devil, who comes to town, is Stalin and everything's a high-powered political allegory. I think it's much more than that – it's a triumph of human imagination, it's literary thought unbound. It empowered me to believe that despotism cannot poison the human mind, and that even all-pervasive propaganda cannot prevail over the free human spirit. But its most enduring feature for me is its detailed portrait of Moscow, which will transcend generations. What James Joyce is to Dublin, Bulgakov is to Moscow.

Engrossed in such conversations, we approach Johannesburg. We hit the morning rush hour. Nigel drives like a maniac, overtaking recklessly and jumping red lights. I follow suit not wanting to lose him. When we finally arrive at his house, I receive the ultimate compliment from him: 'You drive like a true South African.' I'm not sure I want to receive this compliment again. Simpson didn't try to stop me when I charged through red lights and raced over the speed limit. We both wanted to get back as soon as possible and get some rest.

My mobile phone rings soon after we've had our breakfast in Nigel's garden. The Editor of the Ten tells me what a fantastic response our piece and live transmission have had not only within the BBC, but also from the newspapers. He is wondering if we have enough material to do a piece on the theme 'How did they do it?' Everybody wants to know as much as possible about the hidden, background details.

'We can easily do two-and-a-half up to three minutes,' I say. 'We've got fantastic footage from one of the most expensive restaurants in Harare where we paid millions of dollars for our meal.'

All he says is, 'I'm looking forward to seeing it.'

This is what a producer wants to hear from his editor. It's his total trust.

Simpson is in his element when writing the script. The pictures are more powerful than I expected, particularly the driving shots during the night as we approached the Zimbabwean border, the filling up at the last petrol station before the border and the extra cans of fuel we loaded in the back of the vehicle. During the edit I feel like a zombie. We haven't slept for 36 hours but I still have a sizeable reserve of energy.

The piece provokes more interest than any of us expected. Every BBC programme wants to talk to Simpson not so much about the political story in Zimbabwe but about how we managed to accomplish our undercover trip. After the piece is played on the Ten O'Clock News, Simpson does another live inject, this time from the safety of the BBC roof in Johannesburg.

The feedback from the BBC was glorious. However, the reaction from the press was mixed. Although on the first night, Monday 14th, the BBC's Ten O'Clock News pulled 4.9 million viewers, considerably more than ITV's re-launched News at Ten, which stood at 3.8 million, the critics were a bit cold about our performance. Some said the BBC's lead story of Simpson undercover in Zimbabwe was self-generated and 'baffling'. Our Simba Makoni angle was interpreted as woolly evidence of plans to topple Mugabe from within the ruling party. One said that if a coup occurred in Harare in the next few months, the BBC would be vindicated. If not, ours was a 'funny sort of lead', which had left viewers worried about Simpson's personal safety more than anything else. One newspaper even had a poke at Simpson's disguise, the baseball cap in the piece-to-camera, and created cartoons of what kind of disguise he might use on other undercover stories, including a housing estate and hospital. Thank God he didn't use the false moustache prepared for him by a makeover artist!

ITV News, fronted by Trevor McDonald, returning from retirement, and glamorous Julie Etchingham, had a 'self-generated' lead, too, an exclusive interview with Hasnat Khan, the Pakistani heart surgeon who Princess Diana described as Mr Wonderful. They were lovers for two years before the affair ended in the early summer of 1997. This was more in keeping with ITV's tradition of being royalty mad.

The two things that people asked me most often since our return were, first, 'Did it feel more dangerous than Iraq?' I had been going to Iraq repeatedly since February 2003, when John and I were based in the Kurdish north. In Iraq, we always had the whole of the BBC local infrastructure at our disposal: security advisors, trusted drivers, reliable fixers. In Zimbabwe, we were on our own and the dangers were very different. The three of us planned the trip in utmost secrecy and the people we worked with were complete strangers to us. And yes, at times it did feel dangerous.

The second was, 'Was this just a ratings spoiler for the re-launch of ITN's News at Ten?' Journalism is a ferociously competitive activity. If on a night when our main rival re-launched its prime time news bulletin we were able to demonstrate our strength in solid, first-hand, interesting reporting, even if at times it felt that we were the story, I couldn't be embarrassed for playing a part in it.

I normally measure my success on any particular story by the depth of silence that greets me when I enter our office, the World Affairs Unit, on the second floor at the old Television Centre in White City. On this occasion, the silence was deafening. When I came in, all stopped talking and looked down at their computer screens. No one even said 'Hello'. This was the final confirmation that the undercover trip to Zimbabwe had been a resounding success.

The middle managers in our department, Newsgathering, had been kept at bay so they couldn't claim a slice of the success this time. The Editor of the Ten O'Clock News let us have the full glory. He took just Simpson and me to The Ivy for lunch, a big treat for me since I had never been able to book a table there. By coincidence, when we got there we found the Editor of ITN's News at Ten with Julie Etchingham and some others celebrating the success of their re-launched flagship bulletin. In this game there are no losers.

A few weeks after our trip to Harare, the Zimbabwean government mouthpiece, *The Herald*, printed an article which stated that the Mugabe administration knew all along about our presence in Harare. The article went even further to suggest that the CIO was keeping an eye on us to make sure that we were safe. But the fact that Simpson and I made three more undercover journeys into Zimbabwe without permission from the authorities still bugs them. I tried unsuccessfully to get an interview with the Great Dictator himself despite getting close to some people, who saw him regularly. But the answer was always negative. One man who I trust told me that we wouldn't be allowed to film an interview with Mugabe because due to old age he loses concentration pretty quickly and at times becomes incoherent.

As late as February 2011, three years after our first undercover journey, *The Herald* still harped on about Simpson even when they wrote about somebody else, in this instance a professor at SOAS at the University of London who had travelled to Zimbabwe undercover to assess if sanctions against the regime had worked.

> *18 Feb 2011, The Herald, Bankrupting Europe's Moral Stock, … The authorities here know the man very well, watch him closely even. They even allow him, nay, encourage him to make contacts here, including with and in ZANU-PF itself. The same way John Simpson is tolerated when he 'visits' the country – again surreptitiously – thinking his success owes to his impeccable credentials as an undercover*

'fireman'. Of course all this goes to show paradoxical moments in the life of interstate conflict: often hostile visits are allowed – suffered – so your enemy realises the futility of his endeavours. It's not war, war, war all the time. That is the name of the high game.

TEHRAN, IRAN, JUNE 2009

An extraordinary sequence of events after the presidential election on 12th June 2009 made it a punishable offence to use a camera in the streets of Tehran. Iran's intelligence minister, Gholam-Hossein Mohseni-Ejei, warned people like me, on a journalist visa, that the government regarded newsgathering as a crime. Thus, gradually the big Sony camera of our cameraman was replaced by a smaller PD150. It in turn was downsized to a tourist digital device, which fitted in the palm of your hand or in a box of tissue paper. And finally, I used my Nokia 95 mobile phone to film the violence and Simpson's piece-to-camera during the anti-government protests on our last day in Tehran.

It wasn't just us who risked arrest. Ordinary people posted breathtaking videos of police brutality on social networking sites. Some of them sent their material directly to the BBC. Hundreds of thousands of people defied the strong-armed tactics of the authorities and a number of them were killed. Others risked arrest and torture simply by helping us produce our news reports. But our most daring escapade was leaving Iran with expired journalist visas. Outstaying your welcome in the Islamic Republic of Iran, especially if you are a journalist, can have unpredictable consequences.

It takes at least an hour from Tehran's new Imam Khomeini airport to the centre of the city. With cameraman Nick, Simpson and I use the time to get to know our translator. He has been supplied to us by an organisation linked to the government. It's a facilities house offering assistance to foreign journalists run by former members of Iran's Revolutionary Guard. The Revs, as they are known, are the pillars of repression. They ensure that the theocratic regime survives. Individually, the people who run this outfit are very pleasant albeit with a questionable past. I prefer to keep the identity of our translator hidden for reasons that will become apparent later. But I can reveal that he wanted to be known under his ancient Persian name rather than its Islamic equivalent.

We spotted further evidence of this type of rebellion by young people here. Frequently, during the demonstrations in the following week against what many in Iran saw as rigged election results, I noticed policemen yanking away medallions of the ancient Zoroastrian Supreme God, Ahura Mazda ('Lord Wisdom'), from the necks of youngsters. The Ahura Mazda medallions are normally cast in silver and depict the image of the Supreme God as a bearded man with long horizontal wings, wearing a hat and a skirt. Turning to their ancient Persian roots is a demonstration of dissent by the young.

As we approach the city limits along the Tehran-Qom freeway, the golden dome of the Tomb of Imam Khomeini looms on the right-hand side, surrounded by four minaret spears. Sadly, I haven't been able to visit the compound before and there will be no time during this visit either.

Driving in Tehran is a nightmare. Although the city has a modern metro system, public transport is insufficient and most people use their cars. As a rule, you see one person per car. Despite recent cuts in fuel subsidies, petrol is still incredibly cheap. At rush hour Tehran grinds to a standstill.

Our translator is a young man in his late twenties. He speaks English with an unmistakable Persian accent. He is wearing a short-sleeved purple shirt, grey trousers and a black leather belt, and that symbol of Iranian, or is it Near Eastern fashion, pointy black shoes. His demeanour is friendly and he's very keen to tell us about all the landmarks as we pass them in the car. He says he works full time for the Oil Ministry but moonlights as a translator whenever freelance work comes along. 'But this is the first time I am working with such a famous person,' he says looking at Simpson with his big almond-shaped black eyes.

Simpson looks pleased.

The flight from London arrived into Tehran in the morning, so all three of us are tired and looking forward to a nice comfortable hotel bed. We politely nod our heads when our translator talks.

'Mr Simpson has been to Tehran many times before,' I say. 'He was on Ayatollah Khomeini's plane when the Imam arrived back in Tehran in February 1979.'

I know that this impresses everybody in Iran, including liberal middle-class boys like him.

As a 30-something foreign correspondent, a dashing youthful Simpson was dispatched to Paris to cover Ayatollah Khomeini's daily press conferences in the dying days of the Shah's regime. Khomeini was based in a modest house in the village of Neauphle le Chateau, an hour's drive from Paris, just west of Versailles. Khomeini spent about four months in the village before chartering an Air France plane to return to Tehran on 1st February 1979. His entourage invited journalists to travel with him and started selling tickets for the limited seats on the plane. The BBC warned Simpson not to get on that plane because there were wide speculations that remnants of the Shah's air force would shoot it down. But Simpson, together with a group of international journalists, including the late presenter Peter Jennings of the American network ABC, got on the plane, and the rest was, as they say, history.

The anatomy of revolutions has always fascinated me. There is something fatally irreversible in the inability of an old dying regime to get a grip on events. The Shah had left Iran two weeks before Khomeini's arrival. The interim prime minister, the leftist Dr Shapour Bakhtiar, thought he could do a deal with Khomeini and preserve the secular state. Barely a month later, Bakhtiar was no longer prime minister and by April 1979 he was exiled. A decade later, Khomeini's agents brutally murdered him at his home in Paris with a kitchen knife. Arguably as much as 10 per cent of the Iranian population participated in the revolution, as opposed to barely one per cent in the Russian revolution of 1917. Most of these people were prepared to perpetrate despicable violence on their countrymen. How do you build so much anger? And how do you channel it for a particular cause? You simply brainwash impressionable youngsters with promises of a great clean cause, which in practice never materialises.

I was lucky enough, on a previous occasion, to meet one of these people, who in 1979 as a weedy 16-year-old boy volunteered to be one of Khomeini's bodyguards, then survived the Iran-Iraq war to apply his experience as a fighter in Bosnia, Chechnya and Lebanon. When Simpson and I met him he was already a doting 45-year-old father and his greatest wish was to be able to send his young son to school in Britain.

I am trying to discuss with Simpson the mechanics of revolutions.

'The vicious cycle of violence as I remember it,' he says, 'started with demonstrations by Islamist students at the end of 1977. The army was sent in and a number of them were killed. Forty days later, memorial services (Arbaeen) would be held according to Shiite Islamic tradition for those who died. These memorial services would turn into anti-Shah demonstrations in which more students would be killed. Their memorial services after another forty days would become demonstrations... and thus the cycle of violence was perpetuated.'

Our translator is looking at Simpson with wide open eyes and nods his head in agreement although he is too young to remember any of this. In fact, he was born in the early 1980s.

The three of us had been here in Tehran only a few months earlier, staying at the same hotel, the Laleh, in the centre of the city. Simpson loves it because this is where he stayed during the revolution and later during the Iran-Iraq war, when Tehran came under attack by Saddam Hussein's rockets. In February, we were allowed to come for the celebrations commemorating the 30th anniversary of the Iranian revolution. The visas were issued months in advance and I clearly remember that the news reached me when we were in Chicago on the day after Obama's election victory. In preparation for the story, we travelled to Paris where we interviewed Abolhasan Banisadr, the first president of Iran, elected with an overwhelming majority in January 1980. He was in the post for just over a year when he fell out with Khomeini in June 1981. He was a delightful old boy, living in an even more delightful grand old house in Versailles, where he received us in style. He fled Iran on board an Iranian air force plane, which he and his friends piloted out of Iranian air space first to Turkey and then to France, where he was granted political asylum. His friends in Iran were ruthlessly executed, the presidency suspended, political parties banned and Khomeini reclaimed the title Commander-in-Chief.

We've already reached the city limits. The old Mehrabad airport is to our left. The driver, very skilful at showing tourists around the sights of Tehran, makes a left turn and the full glory of the Azadi Tower, the symbol of Tehran, is revealed in front of us. I have seen it before but nonetheless the view makes my heartbeat quicken. 'It was built by the Shah, you know…' our translator continues with his tour guide duties. Built as part of the profligate commemorations of the 2,500th anniversary of the Persian Empire in 1971, it was designed to perpetuate the glory of the last Shah of Iran, Mohamed Reza Pahlavi, and was appropriately named Shahyad Tower, the Royal Tower. However, after the 1979 revolution it was re-named Azadi (Freedom) Tower.

It's amazing how things have changed. Young liberal people like our translator were at the forefront of the revolution against the Shah before it was hijacked by the Islamic fundamentalists led by Imam Khomeini. And how things have gone full circle now – people like him, fed up with the restrictive theocratic regime, look back on the Shah's time as some kind of a golden age.

The Azadi Tower is impressive, not only because of its sheer scale but because of its clean design, too. From a distance, it looks as if it has been carved out of a single piece of white marble. The concept is similar to the Eiffel Tower and gives the impression of lightness. Its four foundation pillars are as delicate as birds' wings and they elegantly evolve into an octagonal tower. The octagon is a universal symbol of balance, harmony and cosmic order. The eight-point star or the two overlapping squares are used in Islamic art as the seal of the prophets.

Our dark blue Toyota minibus advances through the increasingly dense traffic of downtown Tehran. We are moving north and past the Tehran University campus the driver turns right and follows the one-way loop before he pulls up in the forecourt of the Laleh Hotel, one of the city's landmarks. The old boys at the door recognise Simpson and exchange pleasantries with him. He is treated here as a celebrity. Most of the hotel members of staff have worked here all their lives, some of them since before the 1979 revolution.

The building is a 1960s structure, which was cutting edge at the time and has some references to Le Corbusier's functional designs. It was originally built as the Intercontinental Hotel. From a distance it looks like an elegant cigarette box placed on the ground on its longer side. However, its glory is fading. The swimming pool hasn't worked for years, the smell is musty and the paint is peeling. It's in need of a good dust off, like the uniforms of the ageing bellboys. On the positive side, the huge crystal chandeliers in the lobby still sparkle. So do the eyes of the shopkeeper of the antiques shop next to the main door. He is standing by the glass door of the shop, which opens into the foyer, and watches as the bellboys unload our baggage. Men in black suits lounge around on the big sofas in the café scanning the visitors from their vantage points. A group of underwhelmed Japanese tourists makes its way silently towards the minibus parked outside.

We check in and as valued guests we are told we've been given rooms on the eighth floor overlooking the north of the city and the Alborz Mountains, always an awe-inspiring view for me. I leave a substantial deposit in cash in US dollars and the receptionist takes our passports. We won't be able to have them back until our departure.

A few years ago I worked here with some other BBC people and I had to pay their bills because they only brought credit cards with them, and no cash. It's easy to forget that Iran under international sanctions does not have any clearing deals with Western banks and payment by Visa or Mastercard is impossible, apart from the antiques shop at the Laleh, which has a direct link to a Dubai bank.

The corridor on the eighth floor smells of cigarette smoke, which has permeated the old carpets, mixed with a whiff of blocked drains. The room has seen better days, the tiles in the bathroom have been painted over with white acrylic paint and there is a stain in the corner of the ceiling, but the bed linen smells fresh. This mixture of smells makes me conscious that I am in Tehran again. It's always a unique experience to be here. As foreign journalists, our every step will be monitored closely by the secret service. Our translator might be informing on us. And yet, like on previous occasions, we shall find people to help us gather pictures and information behind the backs of the authorities. This time the atmosphere will be different, more sinister and fraught with danger, which will make the help we receive from local people even more exciting and rewarding. At this particular moment, despite the hype and hysteria surrounding the pre-election television debates, I cannot anticipate the rapidly unfolding events of the next 10 days and my judgement at the moment is that we're in for routine, quite boring, election coverage.

I have been to Iran several times before but every time I come here I fear it might be my last. The authorities are so fickle that there's no rhyme or reason in the way they issue journalist visas, especially if you work for the BBC. Simpson and I came here together for the first time in 2008, after he'd been banned from Iran for many years. He didn't believe me when I said that I could get visas for both of us through an outfit I had been introduced to by some Iranian friends on a previous visit. I came to Iran for the first time in 2005 for the presidential election, which brought Mahmoud Ahmadinejad to power. As it happened, the vote went to a second round, as the first was inconclusive, and I was given an extension to my visa. I spent more than two weeks in Tehran and had a great time. This was the end of the Khatami's tenure as president, generally considered as a more liberal and reformist stage in Iran's recent history. I was invited to parties in north Tehran, the wealthy middle-class liberal part of the city, to rival the wild parties in north London, where I live. Ahmadinejad turned the clock back.

It was at that time that I had a brush with the treacherous nature of the regime's secret service. It taught me a lesson to be on my guard and not to take anything at face value. I was enjoying a rare moment of calm in the BBC office at the time, which was located in a nice house in Farmaniye, a well-to-do suburb in the northern part of the city. It was the time after the first, inconclusive, round of the presidential elections when most liberal residents of Tehran hoped that the venerable former president, Ali Akbar Hashemi Rafsanjani, would win against Ahmadinejad, who they considered to be a nasty upstart. One of our translators said he'd taken a call from somebody who claimed to be a member of an underground resistance group.

'The caller said that his group was planning a bomb attack on a target in central Tehran and was wondering if the BBC would send a crew to film it,' our translator told us.

There had been minor bomb explosions in Tehran before, usually blamed by the authorities on the militant group MKO (Mojadedin e-Khalq Organisation), closely linked with Saddam Hussein before his downfall in 2003.

'Did he say what the target was?' I asked.

'No, he didn't.'

'Did it not occur to you to ask this question?' I continued, well aware that the house was thoroughly bugged and this conversation would be listened to. The resident correspondent was listening anxiously to our conversation. She had already warned me about listening devices in the house and that all the local staff, including translators and drivers, would be required to report our activities to the police.

I deliberately paused and then said in a clear and loud voice, 'Please, call the local police and inform them in detail about your telephone conversation. The BBC does not approve of any terrorist activities, and we are not prepared to encourage any such activities by promising to give them air time. You didn't do your job properly, you didn't ask the right questions, therefore we can't help avert it.'

Everybody in the house stopped doing what they were doing and listened in silence. There was a light smirk on the correspondent's face. She knew where this was going. She knew exactly what I was trying to achieve and approved of it.

'Also,' I said, 'please inform all staff in the house not to accept any packages addressed to the BBC. If any such package is received, you must not open it and should inform the police immediately.'

That had the desired effect.

A few hours later, after returning to the house from lunch, the translator said to me proudly, 'A guy from the secret police came around. He was a proper secret agent equipped with a walkie-talkie and dark shades. I told him about the conversation and he said we had done the right thing.'

For a second, I thought how desirable it might seem to our translator to be a plainclothes agent. He spoke with such admiration about the walkie-talkie and the sunshades. He didn't mention any gun, though.

Having grown up in a totalitarian state, I knew the appeal of joining the secret service: good money, good food, and most of all power, power over your peers. Every totalitarian regime encourages that sort of appeal. Otherwise, there won't be any volunteers to perpetrate the oppression. Well, maybe one day our translator would fulfil his dream and become a secret policeman, I thought.

'And by the way,' he said casually, 'your visa extension has been approved. It can be stamped in your passport as soon as you want.'

Needless to say, there was no explosion in Tehran in the following days and weeks. I was pretty certain this was a hoax designed to entrap the BBC office and me in particular.

I am sitting on one of the large sofas in the lobby with our translator, waiting for Simpson and Nick. We have ordered tea and biscuits but it takes ages for the surly waiter to bring the stuff. As soon as Simpson arrives, our tea turns up. He immediately says, 'Can I have tea and an English cake, please?'

The waiter looks at Simpson as if he is intruding on his important business and leaves without saying anything. Simpson has been having English cake at the Laleh intermittently for the last 30 years. When it arrives, it's a normal fruitcake with raisins and dried cranberries. Simpson doesn't like it. He prefers it plain. It looks quite dry, too. Sometimes, when you ask for English cake it arrives plain, without the fruit, just yellow cake baked in a tin, made of butter, sugar, flour and eggs. My grandmother in Bulgaria used to bake a similar cake with a dash of chocolate in it – marble cake – which she called English cake. We talk about how everything English is synonymous with sophistication here but also with treachery and duplicity.

The United Kingdom and Persia, or Iran as it's been known since 1935, have had a turbulent relationship. Most Iranian nationalists blame the British for a series of acts which undermined Iranian sovereignty and strength. Even young people like our translator quote the 1953 *coup d'état* as such an example. The elected government of the then leader Mohammad Mossadegh was overthrown with the help of the British and American foreign intelligence services in favour of a puppet government, effectively transforming the constitutional monarchy into authoritarian rule by the Shah, Mohammad Reza Pahlavi. It was the CIA's first big success in overthrowing a democratically elected foreign government, which the US considered unfriendly. It put the CIA on the political map and in the following five decades it became an integral part of American foreign policy making. The replacement of the popular left-leaning Mossadegh with the heavy-handed right-wing dictatorship of the Shah was seen as a historical inevitability dictated by the rules of the Cold War. The Americans and the British could not leave Iran, with its vast oil wealth and strategic geopolitical position, to lurch into the orbit of the Soviet Union. Mossadegh had nationalised the oil industry, music to the ears of the Russians who were fighting for influence around the world under the banner of anti-imperialism and anti-colonialism.

Like many other examples, what we see in Iran today is a direct albeit unintended consequence of the battles of the Cold War. More examples are Afghanistan, Somalia, DR Congo, Angola, and countless others. There isn't a single country in the world whose history hasn't been shaped by that great partition of the globe.

On the next day, Friday 12th June, Election Day, we turn up unannounced at the polling station in President Ahmadinejad's neighbourhood, Narmak, in the north-east of the capital, known as the Shoreditch of Tehran. Although he now lives at the presidential palace, he still keeps a house there, which he used when he was the city's mayor. I have obtained some footage showing the interior of Ahmadinejad's modest house, which demonstrates that he is a man of the people and explains his popularity among the uneducated poor. 'He is an idealist,' I have heard people say. Unfortunately, it's too complicated for me to remind them of a quote by Bertrand Russell: 'Much that passes for idealism is a disguised love of power.'

As we unload the camera and the tri-pod from the van, a plainclothes policeman approaches us and asks for our permits. Our translator duly produces the document from his leather bag. The agent, a rough-looking youngish man with a severe five o'clock shadow, reads it carefully and then exchanges some words with our translator. I shall learn later from him that what the secret agent said was something along the lines of, 'Be careful not to allow them to film anything that portrays the Islamic Republic in a bad light.'

Our translator puts the permit carefully in a plastic folder and then locks it in his leather bag. It's a valuable document. In Iran, you have to have a 'city permit' if you want to film in the streets, 'an office permit', if you want to work from a bureau, and for some areas, like the hills above Tehran from where you get a breathtaking view of the sprawling city, you need a very special permit, a 'strategic permit'. Despite our best efforts, we still haven't been able to obtain such a document.

The polling station is situated in some sort of a government office on the ground floor of a residential block of flats. We are allowed to film freely and to interview anyone we want, but I feel we are being watched constantly. Some of the local residents recognise John from their TV screens and approach him directly. Satellite dishes are banned in Iran but everybody watches satellite television. The rooftops of Tehran are littered with home-made satellite dishes. Every now and then, the police launch a crack down and confiscate many of them only to find that they sprout like mushrooms after rain. Those who understand English watch BBC World News or CNN. The authorities, however, fear Persian language channels a lot more. BBC Persian TV has been the main source of friction between the corporation and the Iranian government which accuses the BBC of employing Iranian dissidents to broadcast anti-Iranian propaganda.

I remember a meeting at the Iranian embassy with the Iranian Charge D'affaires after they had pulled out the ambassador from London. He started with the usual accusations about anti-government bias of dissidents at BBC Persian TV.

'Well,' I said, 'one way of avoiding this perceived bias is to allow BBC Persian TV to recruit openly in Iran. Thus, the BBC will be able to employ Iranian journalists who actually live in Iran. The field will be open not just for émigrés and dissidents, but for hard-working Iranian journalists, too.'

He looked at me in disbelief. His face changed and anger turned into total bewilderment. He thought that I was taking the piss.

'This is what happened during the Cold War when I was working for the Bulgaria Section of the World Service,' I continued. 'The governments in Eastern Europe had exactly the same complaints. They said that the BBC employed dissidents who broadcast anti-government propaganda. The BBC replied that it should be allowed to recruit in the so-called target countries. However, this was only allowed after the fall of communism.'

He smiled at me. The penny finally dropped. He was far too clever not to understand what I was getting at.

I have always been impressed by the calibre of some of the people the Islamic Republic can produce, even if this man looked like a hard line Revolutionary Guard: thin angular features, no tie and an ill-fitting grey suit. We parted on good terms. He even gave me his email address.

An old man with thick spectacles and dishevelled grey hair approaches Simpson and starts talking in a very animated way. I nudge the cameraman to take a wide shot of the conversation while I'm switching the external microphone on. We both approach them and start recording the conversation. The man speaks broken but understandable English.

'All politicians in Iran are corrupt,' he repeats. 'There is no real choice. No one cares about the people. They are all here to line their own pockets. Prices are going up every day, and what do they do? Nothing.'

While the man continues with his animated monologue, a group of young people gather around us. Some of the youngsters have the most outlandish hairstyles. Girls with big hair and Gucci sunshades giggle about. They refuse to be interviewed and self-consciously adjust the token silk scarves at the back of their necks. Under Islamic law their hair should be entirely covered. But this is a middle-class neighbourhood and these rules don't apply here. The rules are for the poor and uneducated. Weedy boys with coiffed jet-black hair, open-neck shirts showing silver medallions of Ahura Mazda, the Zoroastrian Supreme God, mill around the girls. They, too, refuse to be interviewed.

Outside the polling station, Iranian state television, IRIB, is broadcasting live from a specially built stage. The atmosphere is festive. The young presenter spots Simpson in the crowd and rushes towards him. He speaks excellent English and invites Simpson on stage to be interviewed. Simpson climbs on the stage, his imposing figure in white suit towering head and shoulders over the tiny Iranian presenter. The two could not be more different – a short olive-skinned young man with dark stubble and a big grey-haired clean-shaven Englishman. Both exude confidence in different ways. The Iranian presenter steps away from Simpson so that the camera can't get a two-shot, i.e. both of them in the same frame, so that the viewers won't be able to compare their height.

The young man is a professional. He announces immediately that they will be going live on air in 30 seconds. He is comfortable in front of the camera. He feels relaxed and in control. He asks the questions in English, then waits for the answer and translates back into Farsi live on air. The translations always seem to be longer and more explanatory than Simpson's answers in English. Simpson is praising the organisation at this polling station but then surreptitiously smuggles a paragraph about how difficult it is to obtain reporting visas for Iran, which makes it even more difficult for foreign journalists to paint an objective picture of what's happening in the country. The presenter takes it in his stride. He doesn't flinch. Smoothly, he continues with the translation and then moves on to another question:

'How long have you been reporting from Iran?'

'Well, since before the Revolution,' Simpson says. 'I was here during the demonstrations against the Shah and then flew on Imam Khomeini's plane from Paris to Tehran in 1979.'

What follows is an elaborate and very long translation. The presenter revels in it.

We learn from our translator later that the answer about how difficult it is to obtain visas for Iran was skilfully brushed aside and not translated at all. Only the English speaking part of the audience was privileged enough to enjoy Simpson's mild dig at the regime on the main IRIB television channel.

When back in London I reviewed the pictures in my camera. I noticed our translator featuring prominently in the shots from Simpson's live interview for Iranian television outside the polling station. Then realised that he'd been in the shot of the IRIB camera throughout the live broadcast. His mum must have been very proud. I wonder if he had phoned to alert her before IRIB went live on air.

We do a piece for the main BBC television bulletins later that day showing a young lady in big sunshades and elegant pink scarf drawn half-heartedly over the back of her head, ignoring Islamic rule. She says that she wants more freedom, more economic prosperity and better relations with other countries. Unfortunately, the old man's rant is not usable at all.

The day ends with a violent thunderstorm, perhaps a divine prophecy of the social unrest to come. To escape the rain we do a piece-to-camera inside the Hosseiniye-ye Ershad Mosque in north Tehran, an opulently decorated building, which always doubles up as a polling station. Voting hours have been extended to accommodate the enormous turn out. As the storm ebbs away, the main challenger to President Ahmadinejad, Mir Hossein Mousavi, claims victory.

That was short-lived. But the young embraced him as a beacon of democracy, disregarding his past. The so-called Green Movement, taking the colour of Mousavi's election campaign, became a driving force for change. Behind the scenes, a vicious power struggle within the regime unfolded. It was invisible to the demonstrators in the street.

Saturday, 13th June 2009. I get up late wondering what are we going to do for the next 10 days. When we applied for visas a couple of months earlier, we asked to arrive in Iran a few days before the elections to do some previews for radio and TV. We planned to leave two days after Election Day. An invisible hand, however, granted us 10-day visas starting on the day before the elections. Little did we know at the time that this would give us a competitive advantage not only over other broadcasters but also over other BBC teams, which had swarmed on Tehran. In practice, we would be the only BBC team left here in addition to the resident correspondent after everybody's visa had expired.

It's a lovely sunny day with not a single cloud in the sky. I open the window and admire the view over Tehran's rooftops towards the South Alborz Mountains. The air is dry. It will be a very hot day.

Breakfast at the Laleh is an appalling experience. The middle-aged waiters in black suits of questionable hygiene – on closer inspection I can notice oily spots on the front of their coats – carry a whiff of unwashed armpits as they swan around the tables without urgency, begrudgingly clearing the dirty plates. I normally have a piece of soft Iranian cheese, a few slices of fresh tomatoes and cucumber, and vast amounts of tea. I always envy Simpson's appetite, which is undiminished even in the face of utmost danger.

The breakfast table is our usual place for the morning editorial meeting. We quickly discount the idea of lunch in Darband, a lovely village in the northern outskirts of the city nestled in the foothills of Mount Tochal, part of the Alborz Mountains. The village has now become an integral part of Tehran. The fresh air and the gentle sound of mountain streams make Darband a very desirable place for eating. Reluctantly, Simpson agrees that we should go to the BBC office to find out what's going on. After months of negotiations, the BBC has been allowed to install a broadband connection in the office. Not always reliable, it's nonetheless become a vital lifeline to the outside world.

The office is situated in a large apartment in a residential part of north Tehran. It's not easy to find it even if you know the address. I have been there a few times before but can't give the driver precise directions. We need to phone someone at the office to guide the driver to the address.

The building is new with a large marble foyer and a lift. It looks like any other apartment building in the area. The location is very inconspicuous. There is nothing on the outside of the building to indicate its connection with the BBC. People inside the flat greet us politely but there's a frosty air of unfriendliness. It emanates from the 'producer in charge', a relatively new title given to a producer who manages any big BBC field operation, a de facto office manager sent from London for the duration of the election coverage. She is a cantankerous woman with very little creative talent but to give her dues, she has very good organisational skills. We are each given a small Nokia mobile phone with a local pay-as-you-go SIM card. This is a great help because roaming foreign SIM cards do not work properly in Iran, perhaps because of the international sanctions and poor infrastructure.

The resident correspondent is busy doing live injects into various programmes – it's Saturday and there's not enough news in the UK to fill the airtime of the continuous news channels. And doing a live from Tehran is an exotic thing to do, regardless of the merits of the story. The incumbent, Mahmoud Ahmadinejad, has been declared winner of the presidential elections with a landslide majority, contrary to the expectations of a great number of people. If his victory commanded a slim majority, it would have been more believable. But a suspiciously hasty declaration of the final results and the overwhelming majority in favour of Ahmadinejad seems like an insult to people's intelligence.

This doesn't come as a surprise to us. We decide to stay in the office and order takeaway lunch. I choose the Chelo kebab – lamb neck fillet, steamed basmati rice with crispy saffron crust and grilled tomato. I am the only one who orders doogh, a yogurt drink seasoned with salt and mint. The others order coca cola. Simpson decides on the chicken kebab. The food is so delicious that we gorge ourselves on the vast quantities delivered. As we are contemplating settling down with a glass of Persian tea, our local fixers suddenly get agitated. Postings on Facebook, which surprisingly hasn't been blocked, suggest that there are disturbances in downtown Tehran, close to the Interior Ministry where votes are still being counted. Some of the news agencies report smoke coming from the vicinity of the ministry building. Incidentally, the Interior Ministry is about half a mile from the Laleh Hotel. Simpson ignores the producer 'in charge', who's come to give him the latest briefing on the reported disturbances and looks at me.

'Oggy, we've got to go!'

Our translator is still eating his lunch. I sit next to him and say quietly, 'Do you know where exactly this is happening?'

'Yes,' he says, 'I've just had a text telling me all about it.' He doesn't say who's sent him the text. I don't ask. 'It's quite serious,' he continues matter-of-factly. 'There is a lot of riot police there. The demonstrators have burnt a police motorbike. This is where the smoke comes from.'

'Can you explain to the driver where it is? Do you think he'll agree to take us there?'

'It's OK,' he says. 'We can park in one of the side streets.'

I scramble Nick and start helping him with his gear. I think that taking the big camera is not a good idea and he agrees with me. He takes a smaller Sony PD150. It's easier to run with it. Before we get out of the flat, I ask Nick if he is happy to come with us into an unpredictable civil disturbance situation. He smiles and nods in acceptance. The BBC health and safety rules and the so-called 'risk assessment' process requires that Simpson as the correspondent or I as the producer get the consent of everybody else before venturing into any dangerous environment.

Nick smiles because he knows that there is no BBC security advisor with us. This was deemed unnecessary but also it would have been impossible to get a visa for an ex-SAS man to come with us to Iran. The Iranian authorities think we are all spies and that the BBC is a front for MI6. The driver is a bit anxious and our translator explains that this is because he doesn't want to lose his licence if we get in trouble with the police. The translator himself is very relaxed, almost enthusiastic about going to the scene of the disturbance.

Surprisingly, we reach downtown Tehran very quickly. As we approach the area of the Interior Ministry, we can hear the sound of hundreds, maybe thousands of people shouting. Smoke is rising in the distance and there's the smell of burnt rubber. Groups of young people hurry towards Fatemi Square from where we can hear the roar of the masses. The driver is getting a bit tetchy. He's worried that something might happen to his vehicle. I give him assurances that we'll pay for any repairs if the van gets damaged.

We park in a small street perpendicular to Assad Abadi Boulevard, not very far from Fatemi Square. The driver receives instructions to stay with his vehicle and not to move it until we come back.

'You stay here until we call you or we come back.' Our translator makes the instructions even more explicit. 'If the police force you to move, call me immediately.'

I realise that we've struck gold with our translator but I'm not so sure about the driver.

The four of us quickly rush on to Assad Abadi Boulevard, a wide tree-lined street. Nick is a big bloke, taller than Simpson, and his Yorkshire frame and fair complexion make him stand out in the crowd. The Sony PD150 looks very small in his hands. The translator is visibly excited. I instruct him to stay with Simpson, come what may. I grab Nick's T-shirt at the back so that I don't lose him.

What we see next is beyond any expectation. A police motorcycle is burning to our right. Throngs of young men sweep along the street shouting in exhilaration, some of them wearing green bandanas, others surgical face masks. Green is the colour of the opposition candidate Mir Hossein Mousavi, surgical masks prevent you from inhaling the fumes of burning objects but also makes it difficult for the authorities to identify you.

When the crowd sees us the volume of chanting goes up and the Farsi slogans turn into English: 'We want freedom, we want freedom, we want freedom…'

These boys have just dislodged a couple of policemen from their bikes, chased them away and set fire to the motorcycles. It's not what you expect to see in the heart of an authoritarian state. This would have been unthinkable in the streets of Bulgaria when I was growing up although we had more or less the same grievances. But I feel that their anger goes beyond a forged election result. They are fed up with the social restrictions imposed by a backward theocratic regime. Apart from political freedom, they want the freedom to hold hands in public, to have a drink in a bar, to wear what they want, to listen to any music they want. I am not sure if Mir Hossein Mousavi would be able to deliver these things even if he were elected. The young men and women in the street are prepared to ignore the fact that Mousavi has been at the heart of the Islamic regime since 1979. Although on the left of the Islamic movement – it's often been said that his early hero was Che Guevara – he was appointed prime minister by Ayatollah Khomeini in 1981. During the eight years of his premiership there were accusations that he was involved in the mass murder of dissidents and ethnic minorities. After the end of the Iran-Iraq war in 1988 he opposed the idea promoted by Rafsanjani that Iran accepted Western aid to help with post-war reconstruction. However, he is the best the young have got today.

At this minute, I can feel that their patience has finally snapped and anger is pouring out in the streets – anger at the election results which they see as an insult to their intelligence, anger at the lack of personal freedom, anger at the government's economic incompetence.

The authorities are stunned and clearly don't know how to handle this demonstration. Riot police in their Star Wars helmets charge from time to time on their motorcycles into the crowd, wielding menacing truncheons. The place is swarming with secret police, armed with handguns, but they too are at a loss about how to handle the crowd.

A secret policeman – a youngish man with beard dressed in what Simpson and I call a 'wanker' jacket, a sleeveless vest with lots of pockets worn mainly by photographers who like to feel important – approaches us and asks for our permit. Our translator tries a conversation with him without reaching for his bag to get the permit out. In the meantime, equally well-fed young men with body builder frames surround us. I sense trouble but the young men turn on the secret policeman and start pushing him violently towards the curb. He is confused and starts running. The 'wanker' jacket flaps open in the wind and we all notice the handgun tucked into his belt at the back.

Who are these young men? I anxiously think. *Are they part of a secret organisation? They don't look like the average emaciated angst-ridden Tehrani teenager who's fed up with the restrictive Islamic regime. Who pays them to be here?* Such thoughts are buzzing in my head but the subject is too complicated for this intoxicating moment. Amid the shouting, the pushing and shoving in the crowd I can't discuss it with the translator who is clinging on to Simpson as instructed. It's nice to think that a plainclothes policeman was chased away by a spontaneous crowd but I have the uneasy feeling that these well-fed well-built young men are not part of it. We shall see more of them during the demonstrations in the following days. They will discreetly act as stewards ushering the crowds in one direction or another. Whoever they are, I sense that something fundamental is changing around me. I sense that ordinary people are losing their fear.

We've collected enough material, including a piece-to-camera in the crowd in which Simpson says: 'Nothing like this has been seen in the streets of Tehran since the revolution of 1979.'

Afterwards, a young man tells him in English that: 'This government will not allow us to say what we want.'

This is followed by more chants: 'We want freedom; we want freedom…'

As we walk out of the crowd and towards the side street where our van is parked, we suddenly find ourselves strangely isolated and vulnerable without the protection of the demonstrators. This is when, out of nowhere, a police motorcycle sweeps towards us. He stops at the corner of the street, props his machine on the stand and walks towards us waving his truncheon in a menacing way.

We are only fifty yards from the van, faced with a choice – do we run towards the car and hope that we'll get there quickly and drive away before he reaches us, or stop and try to reason with him? We stop. He is a middle-aged man, quite portly and with grey hair. He shouts in Farsi. Our translator tells him we are from the BBC. He looks at Simpson, then at the translator and can't decide what to do. There is anger in his eyes.

Simpson says loudly in a very firm voice, 'What do you want?'

The man is startled. He is not used to his authority being challenged in the street. He looks at Simpson again, moves his eyes to the translator and whacks him with the truncheon on the leg. The boy drops instantaneously on the pavement with excruciating pain in his eyes but without uttering a sound, I think with a broken leg.

The uniformed policeman raises his truncheon again and looks into Simpson's face. Simpson doesn't flinch, whether out of bravery or because if he shakes his balance on the steep street he'll roll down even without receiving a blow. However, the truncheon treacherously moves towards me. I am standing on Simpson's other side and I feel it's my turn to be whacked because I look Iranian. I hide instinctively behind Simpson. The next thing I see is the policeman walking up to his bike. He's given up.

'It's all over,' I rejoice.

The translator is standing up on his feet looking shaken but able to hobble towards the van. The blood has drained from Simpson's face and he looks ashen. Nick is already in the car.

'Did you see that?' I say when we finally drive away. 'He only whacks people who look Iranian. He didn't dare hit an Englishman.'

Simpson gives a faint smile. We are all shaken but we've got good material. I am concerned about what our translator will do because I don't want to lose him. He's behaved marvellously on the first day of the troubles. He admits he's never been in a situation like this but doesn't have any intention of giving up.

The journey back to the office is tortuous. Traffic has been disrupted by the demonstrations and at times the roads are gridlocked. Once in the office, the translator becomes a hero. Everybody wants to know what happened and whether it hurt. We order another Persian takeaway, the usual kebab with saffron rice, and then review the pictures. What happens next is the worst part of my job as a producer.

It's already getting dark and we are receiving reports of fires burning and big crowds gathering in Vanak Square, a bastion of young middle-class Iranians. It was there, four years earlier, that I filmed with another BBC crew one of the most amazing candle-lit demonstrations in anticipation of Ahmadinejad's defeat in the presidential election against the veteran politician, Rafsanjani. Vanak Square is equidistant between the office and the Laleh. Simpson and I think we should go there immediately. Both the cantankerous 'producer in charge' in the office and the editor of the Saturday Teatime news bulletin in

London feel very strongly that we should stay in the office and edit a piece based on our afternoon pictures from around the Interior Ministry. Simpson suggests that the team in London edits a piece based on agency pictures and we go down to Vanak Square and do a live inject on the satellite phone with the latest news. Seems like a no brainer but no, the London editor digs his heels and wants a Simpson piece in his bulletins. No rational discussion can be held. I have a suspicion that people in London still don't realise the significance of the momentous events taking place here, treating the story as yet another demonstration against rigged election results.

Simpson forbids me to take any calls from London and we get ready to go. The driver is reluctant but we tell him we only need to drive to Vanak Square and no further. It's the downtown that scares him. As we approach the square, we see the red glow of a big fire burning to the north-east of it. The translator tells us that there is a gas depot there. We park at a safe distance from the square and again instruct the driver to stay with the car no matter what. Our aim is to get closer to the fire and film it. The danger, of course, is that if it really is the gas depot on fire we might get caught by a big explosion.

At this point we don't even think that the place is covered with police. We move quickly towards the fenced-off area of the gas works but the fire still looks far away. Nick is preparing to film when a passer-by looks at the camera and shakes his finger to say, 'It's forbidden to film.' The translator ignores him and tells us that he is nobody. However, as we advance further into the dark street, both the translator and I turn back and see the same passer-by talking to two riot policemen kitted out in helmets and truncheons. At this point we both know what is going to happen.

I shout at Simpson and Nick to stop. We haven't filmed anything yet so we arc not worried about hiding the tape. The two riot policemen are already very near. They look scary and rough – their dark sunburnt skin suggests they are not from Tehran. Their eyes are bloodshot, perhaps from staying awake during a long journey. They definitely look scarier than the avuncular policeman who whacked our translator earlier in the day. There is something unflinching and uncompromising in their demeanour. I think they have been drafted from the provinces. They don't have much time for the namby-pamby middle-class Tehranis.

One of them tries to grab the camera. Simpson and I remonstrate in vain. Nick holds on to the camera as we are escorted to the edge of the square where we see a temporary police station situated in what I can only describe as a portacabin. We have to go through the crowd in order to reach the makeshift police station. At that point, I push our translator into the crowd, which swallows him.

The three of us are ushered into the cabin. There is a small desk in the far corner and a wooden bench stretches along the opposite side of the cabin, where we are made to sit. Various people in suits and uniforms come and go through a door into an adjacent room, which I suspect is the interrogation chamber.

Eventually, a small weedy man in a dark grey suit presents himself to us. He's clean-shaven, which to me suggests trouble: a counter-intelligence officer. I look at my watch worried that we'll miss our live slot into the Teatime television bulletin on BBC1. The man speaks good English. He asks why we are filming here.

Simpson stands up and says, 'I've been invited here by your government to report on the presidential election. We have valid accreditations issued by the Ershad (the Ministry of Islamic Guidance, which looks after the foreign press). Why don't you let us do our job?'

'Well, Mister Simpson,' says the man, looking at Simpson's accreditation card, 'how would you feel if I came to your country and start reporting from an anti-government demonstration?'

'You are more than welcome to come to Britain and you'll see that you'll be free to report from anywhere you want. This is how things work in my country,' continues Simpson in an exaggerated angry voice.

'There have been anti-capitalist demonstrations in London recently and reporters from all over the world, including China and Russia were free to report from them,' I say, firmly, looking into the secret agent's eyes.

Simpson hates it when I interrupt, so I get an even more thunderous look from him.

The man looks embarrassed. 'But what are you doing in a dark street filming a fire?' he goes on. 'You were not filming the demonstration.'

'That is correct,' Simpson says. 'We thought that there was a public safety problem in the centre of your capital and we decided to investigate.'

'But this is not reporting the election. Your accreditation is for the election, not for burning fires.'

'I have been reporting from Iran for more than 30 years,' thunders Simpson. 'I have been beaten up by the SAVAK (the Shah's feared secret service), I reported on Imam Khomeini's return to Iran. In fact, I travelled on his plane from Paris to Tehran in 1979. Don't you tell me how to do my job! I am a guest of your government and look how you treat me.'

The little man squirms.

Simpson opens his leather-bound notebook, carefully unscrews the top of his Mont Blanc fountain pen and says, 'What is your name? I shall report you to your superiors.'

The little man ignores him. There's uneasy silence. At that moment the door of the cabin bursts open and the body of a beaten up demonstrator is hurled onto the floor. There's blood all over his face and his shirt is ripped. He is a gaunt young man with longish hair. We all look at the body sprawled on the floor. He doesn't utter a sound. I think he might be dead but a uniformed policeman helps him up to his feet and takes him to the interrogation chamber next door. This is a perfect opportunity for our interrogator to abandon us.

'You must give me your tape and you are free to go,' he says.

We look at each other and the tacit agreement in our eyes is: 'Give him the tape and let's get out of here.'

Nick surrenders the tape from the camera and we file out of the little door. I immediately spot our translator standing not far from the police cabin and nonchalantly watching the crowd. I think that we are going to develop a good working relationship with this young man.

There's only fifteen minutes to spare before the Teatime bulletin goes on air. Simpson has been energised by the arrest. He's got exciting things to say in the live inject. We hurriedly leave the square and sit down on the kerb of a side street from where we can just about see the crowds in the square. At the other end of the street, a dustbin has been set on fire, which illuminates the dark summer sky. It's a balmy evening and I breathe in deeply to savour the moment: I am in Iran and I am witnessing history in the making.

My old-fashioned satellite phone looks like a black brick in my hand. I pull out the aerial and dial the number for the Teatime bulletin in London. To my great surprise, I get through immediately. The editor is already in the studio gallery, the control room separated from the presenter studio by a thick glass pane, from where the programme is being directed.

He sounds very surly. 'What's Simpson going to say?'

'Well, the protests have stepped up a notch: there are fires burning in front of us in a middle-class area of town, mainly tyres and rubbish containers. The place is swarming with armed riot police in special protective gear. We think they have been drafted from the provinces so that they don't have any connections to the local residents here. The authorities are preparing a crackdown. In addition to the huge crowd, we've noticed that ordinary residents are now getting in their cars and by driving very slowly block the roads to restrict the movements of the security forces. And on top of all that, we were detained, interrogated and our tapes confiscated. We were released just a few minutes ago.'

'Wow,' comes back from the other end of the line. I am not sure if this is meant to be sarcastic or not. 'We'll come to Simpson in just a couple of minutes after the main package. You are the lead.'

I pass the sat phone to Simpson. He listens for a few seconds and then patronisingly says, 'Hello, my dear. How nice to hear your voice.' Then a prolonged silence. He nods at me and gives me a thumbs up. This means we won't be investigated for insubordination. Middle managers love investigating any clash between London and people in the field. A vivid example comes to mind in the balmy night while waiting for Simpson to finish his live two-way.

It was the morning after Saddam Hussein's first appearance in court in Baghdad in June 2004. I was running the Baghdad Bureau. After an exhausting day in which the BBC Baghdad team was firing on all cylinders in the appalling heat of the Mesopotamian summer, instead of thanks or at least acknowledgement of our hard work, a surly Newsgathering middle manager called me to complain that Simpson had missed one two-way and the programme in question 'wasn't best pleased'. I was so incensed about his temerity that I, in turn, complained to his boss. The matter was swiftly forgotten as it was very trivial but the said manager was duly promoted.

Simpson taps me on the shoulder to get me out of my stupor. It's become obvious that we can't film openly any more. The camera needs to be concealed. The translator has an overnight bag in the car, just in case he doesn't go home at night. He empties the contents and Nick places the camera inside. He zips it up leaving an opening for the lens. There is no street lighting tonight, the only light comes from car headlights and burning dustbins. It's very difficult to notice the camera lens in the corner of the bag. We walk past a cordon of riot police and Nick films it with the hidden camera. We don't look suspicious in this part of town because there are thousands of people dressed like us out in the streets tonight. The security forces are keeping their distance at present. Intermittently, their commanders move a single platoon at a time from one location to another alongside the edges of the square to intimidate the crowd with the clanking noise of shields and batons. The policemen run close together keeping their shields at breast level. If the danger to us hadn't been so real I'd have thought that we were on a film set.

I am worried about time and suggest to Simpson that we should try and do a piece-to-camera as soon as possible and go back to the office to edit and feed our late news piece. We are feeding the package on the office broadband which can be precarious. My other worry is that the authorities might cut off all broadband services, in which case we shall have to feed via satellite telephone. That is also unreliable and can take ages. Simpson starts to sketch the wording in his head. When he's ready we try to record it as he passes in front of a line of riot police. It doesn't work because the policemen stare at us, following every step we make. The crowd has been broken into smaller groups by lines of police. The numbers are still there but there is no demonstration to speak of, apart from individuals and small groups of youngsters pretending that they are going about their own business. We need to speed up our pace so that we don't look like we're loitering suspiciously.

Having missed the moment of doing a piece-to-camera in the crowd, we move away from the square and to the south-west into a main road called Brazil, which feeds into the main roundabout of Vanak Square. Nick and I hide in the entrance of an apartment building from where he films Simpson delivering the piece from the kerb of the pavement, thus letting passers-by move between the camera and Simpson. The translator stands a few feet away from Simpson and watches out for police. It's dark and spooky. Simpson is tired and has to do a few takes before we get a usable segment. Some of the passers-by throw knowing glances at us and at Simpson but no one betrays us to the police like when we attempted to film the fire.

Job done, the translator calls our driver on the mobile phone to summon him. The van is on the northern side. The driver says all roads are blocked and it may take a long time to get to us. I look at my watch and realise we are going to be late. Simpson suggests we get a taxi but there are no taxis around. In desperation, I float the idea that we might pay a private individual to take us back in his car. The translator starts working on it. We see a few men in a small street nearby sitting outside on small chairs on the pavement. Most of them are in their vests suggesting that their homes are just there. One of them engages in a lengthy chat with the translator. I butt in and say we'll pay him handsomely if he takes us to Farmaniye in his car.

'How much?' he wants to know.

'Twenty dollars,' I say.

'It's not enough. There are police around and the roads are blocked.'

'Thirty.' I move quickly.

'Fifty,' he says.

'Done. Where is your car?'

He moves towards an old banger parked on the opposite side of the street. It quickly becomes clear that the car, an old sedan of undetermined brand, is too small for all of us to get in. I suggest that Simpson, Nick and the translator go with the driver, while I wait for our driver at the agreed corner. As the translator starts dialling the driver's number we see our dark blue van pulling up at the end of the street. I look at the face of our disappointed partner in crime and push a five-dollar note into his hand.

When we get back to the office, the driver tells our translator that the police had checked his papers while he was waiting for us and asked searching questions about why he was in the vicinity of Vanak Square. He is worried about losing his license and has decided to quit. I pay him off. We start looking for another driver the next day.

This evening's experience has taught us that it's becoming more and more difficult to move around Tehran, especially after dark. After sending our piece to London, we drive back to the centre of the city, where our hotel is. It's a long drive at the best of times but the security presence and the escalation of violence make it even more difficult for us. Also, it eats into our rest time, which will become a more and more valuable commodity. This is the point when we decide that we should change hotels and I suggest the Esteghlal, the former Hilton, which is situated in north Tehran and is very convenient for the office. It's my favourite hotel in Tehran.

Sunday, 14th June. The morning brings another clear sky and views of unparalleled beauty from my hotel window. The rooftops and white façades of downtown buildings reflect the shimmering light coming down on the city from the Alborz Mountains. I take a few landscape photos from my window before I go down to breakfast. We are checking out of the hotel today and moving to the Esteghlal. The staff at the Laleh think we're leaving Iran altogether, scared of the street violence and tell us approvingly that we are doing the right thing.

We have a new driver with a new van, this time a dark grey Toyota. Simpson and Nick are already in the back of the van. The translator is in the front passenger seat. I am late because I had to sort out the bill and get the receipt. Getting receipts in Iran is a laborious task. It has to be signed by an authorised person and then stamped with no less than two different stamps. I am almost in the van and turn outwards to shut the door when a middle-aged man clutching a bundle of flowers rushes towards me, hugs me and kisses me on the cheeks. I must have squirmed instinctively because he looks disappointed. His cheerful eyes turn sad as if telling me, 'Don't you recognise me?'

'Mahmoudi?' I shout.

Simpson shuffles at the back of the car. Mahmoudi was Simpson's driver during the revolution. The last time we were here with Simpson and Nick, we did a sort of profile of Mahmoudi in a big film for *Newsnight*. I have heard a story from Simpson many a time about how Mahmoudi saved his life or at least saved his eyes from being gouged out by some angry policeman during a demonstration in 1979.

The flowers are for Simpson. Thirty years on, Mahmoudi still works as a driver for foreigners in Tehran. He has heard on the grape vine that Simpson is here and has rushed to pay his respects. We all get out of the car and have a short polite conversation. Simpson casually asks him what he thinks of the anti-government demonstrations. He looks around cautiously and makes a gesture with his arms as if to say, 'Don't ask! It's serious.' I feel there is something he wants to tell us but he is afraid. My recollection of having conversations with him previously suggests that he belongs to the Rafsanjani wing of the political debate here – for a free market and better economic links with the West.

We tell him that we are moving to the Estaghlal and he is sad because he is a 'downtown man' and hangs around the Laleh most of the time.

The van leaves the forecourt of the Laleh and I have a sad feeling in my chest that I may never come back here again.

We turn right into Dr Fatemi Street and drive past the Interior Ministry on our left to join Vali Asr Street, one of the longest streets in the world. For the most part it is as straight as an arrow and is lined with sycamore trees on both sides. At times, it feels as if we're driving through a tunnel under the intertwined branches. We drive in silence through Vanak Square where we had our brush with the police and then past Mellat Park (formerly the Imperial Park) on the left, followed by the compound of the IRIB. Vali Asr Street is named after the 12th Shia Imam, who it is believed, together with Isa (Jesus Christ), will come to save mankind. He is known under many names, among which are The Mahdi, Imam al Zaman and Wali al Asr (The Prince of Time). The street was built by order of Reza Shah Pahlavi, the father of the last Shah, during the so-called 'modernisation' after he ascended to the throne in 1925. Reza Shah was an army sergeant who in the turbulent years of the First World War and the Russian Revolution that followed rose to General, overthrew the previous monarchy and set up a new dynasty. The grand street was initially known as Pahlavi Street. Briefly after the 1979 revolution it was named after the nationalist leader, Mohammed Mossadeq, who was deposed by the Anglo-American plot in 1953, but as the Islamic regime took hold it was renamed after the 12th Imam.

Approaching the hills of north Tehran, we leave the austerity of downtown Tehran behind and enter a new, very different world. The Islamic dogma no longer applies to people's clothes here. In a token gesture to Islamic tradition, women wear their scarves only lightly on the back of their heads. Heavy make-up and top Western fashion are the norm here. The houses are modern, most of them built to the latest anti-earthquake specification. Tehran lies on a fault line and has experienced devastation before. The air is cleaner and the Alborz Mountains seem closer.

We finally leave Vali Asr and pull up in the grand compound of the Esteghlal (which means independence). This must have been the place to be seen in Tehran in 1962 when it opened as the Royal Tehran Hilton. What strikes you first when you enter the hotel is not the spacious marble lobby with big windows overlooking a big garden, but the disproportionate number of men in black suits aimlessly milling around. I had been warned on a previous occasion that this was one of the most monitored places in Tehran. That's why I have always chosen to stay here and make my appointments in the hotel lobby. It tells these people that I've got nothing to hide. The hotel also boasts the only Thai restaurant in Tehran – generally considered to be the trendiest place in the city – the usual haunt for the rich young Tehranis.

We are given rooms in the new tower. The rooms are well appointed and clean. There's too much dark wood panelling for my liking but there is no comparison with the Laleh. I stayed at the original tower once, which is linked to the new one through the lobby, and thought it badly needed refurbishment. The hotel is now owned and managed by the Foundation for Veterans and Oppressed, a unique Iranian creation run by a cleric. The so-called revolutionary foundations control a sizeable proportion of the Iranian economy and were created after the revolution of 1979 to manage the assets confiscated from the Pahlavi dynasty and other important families close to the monarchy. In the early 1990s, in the aftermath of the Iran-Iraq war the government decided to sell state enterprises to war veterans and families of those who had lost their lives in the war. These people, however, lacked the money and the expertise to buy the state assets on offer, so the revolutionary foundations, which had already amassed great wealth, became their representatives. Today, the Foundation for the Veterans and the Oppressed is said to be the second biggest owner of industrial and agricultural assets in Iran after the state.

The translator tells us that there is going to be a victory rally for Ahmadinejad in Vali Asr Square. The final results have been announced. Ahmadinejad has got 63.6 per cent, Mir Hossein Mousavi – 33.8 per cent. At a news conference, Ahmadinejad said he'd been duly re-elected and those who didn't agree with the results had until the end of the day to appeal to the country's Guardian Council – the most influential body in Iran, controlled by hard-line conservatives.

We are getting a signal on our local mobiles, which suggests that the authorities feel more confident and are restoring the mobile network services. A victory rally is planned, so we must be there.

As we drive south along Vali Asr, we see the aftermath of the demonstration, this time pro-Ahmadinejad, which by definition in the current context means pro-Establishment, pro-Supreme Leader. It's always difficult to explain what 'the aftermath of a demonstration' means but we can see that thousands of people have passed down the street leaving behind the debris of human behaviour. Even if they have been very careful not to throw national flags or propaganda materials on the ground there is, of course, the usual legacy of plastic water bottles, paper napkins, ribbons, etc. The mobile metal barriers carefully arranged when the crowds were there now look scattered and abandoned. I get the feeling that we've missed the action but don't say anything because I know this will annoy Simpson. There's hardly any traffic. We soon find out why. Vali Asr is closed so there's no direct access to the eponymous square. We have to make a diversion and come down a parallel road, which cuts through the University of Tehran campus. There we see the aftermath of a more serious demonstration. There are broken windows, scattered chairs and smouldering dustbins, makeshift barricades. We find out later that police had stormed and dispersed a student demonstration at the campus. Some estimates suggest that about two thousand students had taken part.

At Vali Asr Square the pro-Ahmadinejad demonstration is still going on although we've missed him speaking on the podium. There are other speakers working the crowd. It's a different crowd, though – older, more conservative. Most women wear the hijab, the men wear dowdy old-fashioned cheap suits from the market and there's a more aggressive look in their eyes. Most of them have been brought here by coaches from the working-class suburbs or even from outside Tehran. Their support for Ahmadinejad is unswerving. He has played his cards as a man of the people very skilfully. He's ruined the economy but they still support him because he's good at handing out subsidies. There have been rumours of government handouts of rice, potatoes and cooking oil to the poorest parts of the country before the election. Ahmadinejad has also played the nationalist card very well. His pursuit of nuclear capability, although officially denied, has been received well by the poor and uneducated. The humiliating capture of British servicemen in the Persian Gulf featured prominently in his campaign videos. It's often underestimated in the West how sophisticated Ahmadinejad's media campaign in 2005 was. And now his main adviser is the film director Javad Shamaghdari, who created some of his campaign videos.

I once wrote a letter to Shamaghdari asking him to arrange an interview with Ahmadinejad after the first election victory in 2005. It caused a great commotion at the BBC because the top brass couldn't decide which presenter should do it. Would it be Simpson as World Affairs Editor, or Jeremy Bowen as Middle East Editor, or Jeremy Paxman as the rottweiler of British interviewing techniques? The management couldn't agree in time for my courier to take the letter personally to Shamaghdari, so I put Paxman's name on the letter. Shamaghdari is now Deputy Minister of the Ershad (Culture and Islamic Guidance), which formally approves the visas for foreign journalists. In fact, the approval comes from the Intelligence Ministry. In the ministry's literature the BBC is described as: 'The Psychological Operations Unit of the British government's spying agency.' Needless to say, the interview didn't happen but the whole episode created impotent panic among senior managers at BBC News, which highlighted the bloated and sclerotic nature of a structure designed to find work for self-serving managers with not very much to do.

Ahmadinejad still portrays himself as a man of the people. He is a demagogue but understands the importance of image in political life. He hasn't abandoned his trademark short rain jacket, which marks him out from the rest of the politicians here and around the world. The beige jacket is sold at the bazaar in Tehran as the 'Ahmadinejad jacket'. When Simpson and I went to his birthplace not far from Tehran earlier this year, the people there didn't think much of him. It was a relatively well-off small town, where people were preoccupied with the state of the economy instead of power struggles, uranium enrichment or relations with the West. He's also been on the receiving end of some pretty sarcastic jibes from the liberals and the religious establishment alike for his obsession with the 12th Imam and the supposed divine green light, which descended on him during his first speech at the UN General Assembly in New York in 2005. Love him or hate him, he's succeeded in building a recognisable image to go with his political aims. Although he's had some public clashes with the Supreme Leader, the latter has used his power and influence through the mosques and religious groups like the paramilitary basijis, responsible directly to him, to make sure that a large section of Iranian society voted for Ahmadinejad in the current election. Demographics in Iran are very complicated. Iran's young population is split along class lines – at the time of writing Iran's total population stands at 75 million, 64 per cent of which is under 30. Literacy rates have increased dramatically but unemployment has gone up sharply, too. Despite the growing urbanisation of Iranian society, or perhaps because of it, in 23 per cent of Iranian households all members of the family are unemployed.

I know that tonight's piece will not be very exciting but I also know that it will lead all BBC TV bulletins.

Monday, 15th June. I wake up tired after a restless night. We've only been here for four days but it seems like ages. I'm not sure if people in London understand how tiring it is to be permanently on your toes, making sure the team is in the right place at the right time. Driving in Tehran needs a lot of planning and I get easily irritated if things don't go smoothly. I'm getting calls from people in London just wanting a chat about 'what is likely to happen during the day'. It's very flattering but I'm not a clairvoyant. I am not in a position to predict that today will be the turning point in the disturbances.

The place to be today is Enghelab Square (Revolution Square) situated due east from the Azadi Tower, if you take Azadi Street. Enghelab Avenue continues along a straight line east of the eponymous square towards Ferdowsi Square, named after the 10th-century Persian poet, for many the national poet of Iran. Enghelab Square is close to Tehran Medical University. This is where Mousavi supporters are planning to gather for another protest. Although it's difficult to find out whether there is any organisation behind these protests, and we can't report that officially on the BBC, I have the feeling that there is 'an invisible hand'. To start with, there's the organisation behind Mr Mousavi's election campaign. The senior figures there, who stand to gain huge economic power should they come into government, have enough financial means to tap into the spontaneous anger of ordinary people who have had enough, and shape it into a popular revolt.

Today's demonstration has been declared illegal by the authorities but nonetheless huge crowds turn up. When we get there, Mousavi has been and gone. It's the first time he has appeared in public since the election. We shall see pictures of him among the crowds in his blue and white striped shirt, and gold-rimmed glasses, looking like a bank manager.

'People want respect, and they want their votes to be counted,' he tells his supporters, clutching a small black plastic microphone attached by a coiled rubber coated wire to an old-fashioned megaphone.

Iran hasn't seen anything like it in recent history – an opposition leader, who used to be part of the establishment, defies a government ban on demonstrations and addresses a huge crowd of supporters. This is a turning point.

The other event that makes today significant in the calendar of protests is that we are getting reports of the first fatality. A crowd of protesters apparently tried to storm a base of the feared paramilitary organisation, the basijis, near Azadi Square. Shots were fired from the windows and at least one protester is dead. The government accuses the demonstrators of trying to seize weapons from the base, thus justifying the killing.

Simpson does a piece-to-camera in Azadi Street among a crowd of protestors walking with him. They shout: 'Marg Bar Diktator!' ('Death to the Dictator!') The dictator has no name. Is it Ahmadinejad, or is it perhaps the unthinkable, the Supreme Leader? When we ask them what their demonstration is about, the slogan changes to a chant in English: 'We want freedom!'

We are now used to gathering only the minimum of essential material from the protests, then getting out. We film a well-dressed and well-fed man telling us in English that they have already said 'No!' to Ahmadinejad and 'Yes!' to Mir Hossein Mousavi in last Friday's election. The rest will be filled with agency pictures or amateur video posted on social networking sites. We shall get a still shot from a mobile phone of the listless bloodied body of the young man shot dead outside the basiji base in Azadi Square. The vast expertise of hard-working journalists at the coalface of the BBC in London has been channelled to verify the pictures and their provenance. The BBC Online service is very good at tapping into the experience of journalists at the World Service and Persian TV.

On the evening news in the office we witness one of the most astonishing U-turns in recent Iranian politics. The Supreme Leader, Ayatollah Khamenei, has ordered an investigation into allegations of vote rigging. Also, for the first time ever, the results of a presidential election will be announced in full detail.

After dark, the four of us go out again in the van towards Vanak Square. We play it safe. No getting out of the vehicle. Nick films as much as he can with the PD150 from behind the closed window. Riot police are everywhere. There is no sign of any mass crowds. The news of the first death of a demonstrator has obviously had an effect. Have the authorities finally prevailed?

Tuesday, 16th June. We wake up late. Breakfast at the Esteghlal is a much better experience than at the Laleh. To start with, there is more fresh fruit here, especially my favourite watermelon. I call my mother in Bulgaria and have one of our disconnected conversations that have become the norm recently. It's obvious that she is in the grip of advanced dementia. I feel guilty because both my brother and I live outside Bulgaria and she is in the flat in Sofia on her own. She has resisted any attempts to send her to a nursing home and I wonder how long this fuzzy arrangement will last.

'I'm in Iran,' I say when she finally picks up the phone.

'Oh, isn't it dangerous there?'

'No, Mum, the dangerous place is Iraq.'

'Oh, did you say Iran? The capital is Tehran, isn't it? Your mother still hasn't lost her marbles completely. Is the Shah still there? Mohammed Reza Pahlavi his name was…'

'No, Mum, he's long gone and he is dead now.'

'Oh, I am a bit confused. When are you going to come and see me? Who would've thought that I would be left on my own having raised two very clever boys?'

I know this is going to go around in circles and she will repeat what she always says in our telephone conversations, namely that she considers herself to be very lucky indeed because she is 80 and she's had a very nice life, while her brother died at the age of 55 of a heart attack, which was a great shame. I cut the conversation short under the pretext that I've got a lot of work to do.

When we get to the office, the surly producer in charge informs us that there is a ban on reporting the demonstrations by foreign journalists and that all our accreditations have been revoked. She has had a call from the Ershad, she says. Luckily, most British journalists will have to leave tomorrow because their visas expire. Simpson and I look at each other. She advises that we go and see the Ershad. Reluctantly, Simpson agrees. It's time to pay Ershad a visit.

I know the junior people there who deal with the foreign press because I have always taken a box of chocolates for them in the past. They are well-connected educated middle-class women. But I have never met the bosses. The structure there is a bit Byzantine, or should I say Persian, because the Persians invented Byzantine bureaucracy, as they were brought in to do the administration and tax collection.

Simpson is in a bad mood because he thinks we'll be chucked out. So far we haven't been able to produce anything close to our trademark cutting edge reports, insightful, engaging and flirting with danger. He is slouched on the beige velvet-covered sofa in the waiting room of the Ershad and sips his pale tea from a little ornamental glass. The autumnal colours of the waiting room are a throwback to the 1970s. The person who will see us is busy. Young women in light-coloured hijabs tiptoe around him. They have recognised him from their television screens. Watching BBC World News is illegal, as is all satellite TV, but they all watch nonetheless.

Finally, we are ushered in but there doesn't seem to be anybody in charge. The Head of Foreign Press is busy. Simpson is getting even more impatient. It looks like our trip to downtown Tehran has been a waste of time. Then a person who I have known since my first time in Iran four years ago walks in. The identity of this person will remain anonymous because of the tremendous importance of what was said in the room. The person says that the demonstrations are an exercise in democracy but all journalists should stay away from the protests for their own safety. I ask whether our accreditations have been revoked and the person answers, 'No.'

Other people come and go and the room is getting busy to the utter annoyance of Simpson. I persevere with the questions.

'What would you advise us to do?'

'You can stay in Tehran for the remainder of your visas. You can do your job. You can go shopping. All we are saying is that in the circumstances the government cannot guarantee your safety if you place yourselves in the crowds.'

'You can do your job' still rings clear in my head.

Then we are swiftly told that this person's son had been to many of the anti-Ahmadinejad demonstrations four years ago when the election went into a second round and his family did not stop him. Nothing was said about the son and the current protests.

On the way out I see the man who tried to set me up four years ago with the alleged phone call about an imminent explosion in Tehran. He now works for an American TV network. He is very unctuous and gives me his email address but quickly slips into the conversation that the visas for foreign journalists haven't been revoked as originally suggested. His American team are staying put. As a parting shot he says, 'We are told we can't work with foreign journalists any more. If we get caught helping any foreigners, we'll be in serious trouble.'

This is directed more at our translator. He doesn't look perturbed.

Back in the vehicle, I tell Simpson my interpretation of what we've heard. 'We've been encouraged to stay and carry on with our reporting. But we have to be more cautious. We must not get caught. This wasn't even coded. It's obvious that there is a strong pro-Mousavi camp at the Ershad.'

When I put together the jigsaw pieces in my mind it becomes obvious to me that Rafsanjani and his powerful family and allies are behind the support for the Green Movement. He was opposing Ahmadinejad in the last election four years ago and lost. And he doesn't see eye to eye with the Supreme Leader. Our person at the Ershad is a supporter of Rafsanjani.

Simpson admits that in the noise and kerfuffle inside the office he has missed that part of the conversation when we were told that we could do our job.

'We can stay in Tehran and go shopping,' I repeat.

He is now happy that we don't have to leave immediately. Both of us are even happier that the rest of the BBC team are leaving, and so are the competition. We've got another three days. Our translator looks on and nods. Then he drops a bombshell.

'I've been told that I'm no longer allowed to work with you. All contracts for translators working with foreign journalists have been terminated. I have been told to withdraw the car and the driver, too.'

'Let's discuss all this back in the office,' I suggest and the driver embarks on the arduous journey from downtown to northern Tehran. We travel in silence.

By the end of the day the anti-British and anti-BBC sentiment in government propaganda ratchets up. Everybody in the office seems stunned. All the staff, cleaners, office drivers, permanent translators and producers watch Iranian state TV in deep shock. We see pictures from a rally in support of Ahmadinejad where people carry placards denouncing the BBC and the British embassy for stirring up trouble. Working for the BBC doesn't seem like a good idea at this particular moment.

For once, London leaves me to deal with the situation on the ground without interfering. I have a private conversation with our translator. It would be inappropriate to disclose what is said but he decides to stay on and work with us in a private capacity. I will pay him directly instead of going through the intermediary. He undertakes to find a car and a driver who will also be paid directly by me. No one must know about our private arrangements. In fact, the situation is so fraught the intermediary, as it happens, doesn't want to know about anything. No one in their office wants to speak with me.

In tonight's piece Simpson goes out of his way to declare that there was no organisation behind the protests, that they were spontaneous. There were no leaders, which was 'both a strength and a weakness'. The mere suggestion that there might be a brain behind the protests would incur accusations that again it's 'the work of the British intelligence and its mouthpiece, the BBC'. The Americans are never blamed.

Our piece includes amateur video from inside Tehran University campus of students chanting 'Marg Bar Diktator!' and the first mobile phone footage of the events yesterday showing the shooting of demonstrators by basijis from their compound on the edges of Azadi Square. We drive after dark in search of a suitable place to do a piece-to-camera but caution prevails and we do it from the roof of the apartment building where the BBC office is situated. The unspoken agreement between Simpson and me is that we don't want to be arrested and expelled at a time when everybody else is leaving. We need to think about the next three days when we will be here on our own. As a consummate professional he turns his piece from the safety of the office block roof into a work of historical poetry, weaving into its content the eerie wailing from the rooftops after dark: 'Allah-o-Akbar' ('God is great'), a powerful form of protest for which no one can be arrested, interspersed with 'Marg Bar Diktator!' for which you could get into a lot of trouble.

But the authorities can't do anything about it. It's spooky when you hear it for the first time in the balmy night of northern Tehran under the shadow of the Alborz Mountains. Simpson says he remembers these chants from 30 years ago. This was how people protested against the Shah.

Wednesday, 17th June. I am looking forward to our lunch at the British embassy today. I first made contact with the embassy two days ago through the official channels, i.e. the press secretary. Things have moved on since then and I'm now in direct contact by email with the ambassador's wife. We'll have a private lunch. Unfortunately, I can't take our translator with us because that will get him into a lot of trouble. So, today it's just Simpson, Nick and me.

The Iranian authorities do not allow British security personnel even on the British sovereign territory of the embassy. The land in Ferdowsi Street in the heart of Tehran, north of the Grand Bazaar, was purchased in the mid 19th century and the grand Legation building was completed in 1876. The architect, James Wild, had a great vision that everything from the steel roof to the large glass panes should be manufactured in Britain. Transportation, however, was tricky. Therefore, it took more than 10 years to finish the project. But it was worth it.

Set on large grounds of mature gardens, it can only be described as a palace. It's situated just south of the much larger compound of the Russian embassy. The street, which divides the two great embassies of the 19th century's 'Great Game' is called Neauphle-le-Chateau, the name of the little village outside Paris where Ayatollah Khomeini spent his last months before returning to Tehran to take control of Iran in 1979. Churchill walked across that street in the late autumn of 1943 to attend the meetings, which were held at the Soviet embassy during the historic Tehran Conference, at which the shape of the post-war world was decided. The partition of Germany, the Polish borders and of course the opening of a Second Front against Germany in Europe were the main topics. The wheelchair-bound US President, Franklin Delano Roosevelt, stayed at the Soviet embassy for security reasons so that he didn't have to travel to the meetings every day. The conference was held in Tehran on Stalin's insistence because from here he could be in direct telephone contact with the General Staff in Moscow three times a day. Also, he didn't like long plane journeys. He travelled to Baku, the capital of Soviet Azerbaijan on the Caspian Sea by train, and then took a short plane journey to Tehran.

Iran had been occupied by Britain and the Soviet Union since August 1941 to counter the pro-Nazi leanings of the then Shah, although allied troops were all but invisible in the streets of Tehran. The main purpose of the occupation was to ensure a safe corridor, which became known in history as the Persian Corridor, for American supplies to the Soviet Union. Many Iranians today are quick to point out that Stalin and Roosevelt ganged up on Churchill during the conference by insisting that the priority of the Allies in 1944 should be a cross-Channel invasion of Europe rather than Churchill's idea of another front in the Mediterranean. There is a plaque on the wall by the main entrance of the embassy building commemorating the meeting of the 'Big Three' from 28th November to 1st December 1943.

This time we enter through the east-facing main gate in Ferdowsi Street. The street that runs at the back of the embassy used to be called Winston Churchill but it was renamed Bobby Sands, in honour of the IRA member who died on a hunger strike in the Maze prison in Northern Ireland in 1981.

The ambassador is a high-flyer at the Foreign Office. We sit under a thick shade on the veranda and drink gin and tonic. I'm not a great drinker but every time I go to a 'dry' country I feel like a drink. Is this my natural desire to defy the authorities? We briefly talk about the street protests but we all feel that this is not the right time, nor the right venue to talk hard politics. The ambassador's wife is concerned that ever since they arrived two-and-a-half months ago she has to take an Iranian security detail with her every time she goes out with her children. No British bodyguards are allowed even for the private use of the ambassador's family. 'It's quite disconcerting,' she concludes.

Mindful of our short time, lunch is served pretty quickly after the aperitif. A member of the household staff attends to us in his immaculately starched white livery. This is when the ambassador's wife mentions that while her husband was Deputy High Commissioner in South Africa she developed an interest in the South African author, JM Coetzee. Simpson can't hide his annoyance as the conversation goes deeper and deeper into the intricacies of Coetzee's plots and ideas. My favourite book is *Disgrace*. It's a short novel with a compelling plot, but also packed with ideas. The writing is incisive. It cuts through the flesh and touches the bone. It reads like a Greek tragedy.

Simpson visibly yawns when the ambassador's wife and I discuss the novel. I am conscious that once again I have hijacked the conversation but I love it and I won't let go. The Iranian secret service must have been totally baffled when they read the report about the conversations we had during our visit.

They probably thought there was something to read between the lines, coded messages or some such. It was, after all, a meeting between the BBC and the Foreign Office, the two entities which the government here publicly accuse of stirring up the protests.

We leave the embassy and head towards the nearby demonstration. Today, without any apparent organisation it takes the shape of a silent protest. Some of the protesters have got sticky tape across their mouths.

'Our voices have been silenced by the authorities,' they want to say.

We do a piece-to-camera from an elevated position, a pedestrian overpass, in the hope that we won't be spotted by any plainclothes policemen. After all, we are not supposed to be here. The small camera swiftly goes into a carrier bag and we hurry towards the car. Back at the office, everybody is fretting about the ban on reporting of unauthorised gatherings. They think we are mad to have been into a demonstration. The mobile phone network is down again. The landlines are unreliable and are supposed to be bugged. The only means of communication with London is the internet. They haven't pulled the plug on the broadband yet.

I am chatting by email to a fellow producer on the Ten O'Clock News desk. She mentions that she's seen some agency pictures of Rafsanjani's daughter addressing a protest rally in downtown Tehran today.

'Is this important?' she asks.

'Oh God, how have we missed it?' I admit. 'This is the most important development today. The rift in the Establishment – the power struggle within the ruling elite – has finally come out into the open. This is much bigger than a dispute about vote counting. We must definitely put it in the piece.'

This is how it works. Being in the eye of the storm doesn't necessarily give you the chance to have an overview of the various events happening around you. We, reporters and producers in the field, normally get round this impediment by reading news agency copy on the internet or by remotely accessing the BBC internal network. But here in Tehran, access is slow and sometimes impossible. Desk producers in the newsroom in London have a much better idea of what's happening because they have access to news feeds. They tell us what pictures they have in London and the reporter writes the script and records the voice track over blank tape. When we send the piece with 'black holes' in it, producers in London insert the missing footage into the 'holes', or 'paint pictures over the voice track', as the jargon goes. The most important job that we in the field have is to be on top of the interpretation of the story and to record the piece-to-camera, which demonstrates our presence in the right location. It's not always like that but in a restrictive and dangerous environment this is the only way to achieve value for money. As a crew of three, we can't be everywhere, at every press conference, at every demonstration. The BBC pays large sums of money to news agencies to gather material and we must utilise this investment.

As it happens, footage of Rafsanjani's daughter addressing a crowd of protesters has been broadcast on Iranian state television. The news agencies in London or Dubai simply record the output and then decide what is relevant to the story. All the relevant bits are compiled into a short agency feed for clients with a bit of written explanation, called the 'dope sheet', something like a written story board.

Rafsanjani's daughter told the crowd that they should stay in the streets 'until the final result is reached', i.e. until her father's arch enemy, President Ahmadinejad, has gone. Who made the decision to broadcast her appearance at the protests on state television? Around 500 political activists are reported to have been arrested already, some of them senior political figures. And not only was she allowed to speak to the demonstrators and urge them to keep up the pressure on the government, but news about this event and her words have been broadcast on the main TV channel from where most Iranians get their news. The rift in the system is now right out in the open.

Ali Akbar Hashemi Rafsanjani is a dominant figure in the Islamic Republic. As a theology student in the Holy City of Qom in the 1950s, he met, befriended and became a follower of one Ruhollah Khomeini who was a lecturer there. The rest, as they say, is history. Arrested and imprisoned for his activities against the regime of the Shah in the 1960s and 1970s he eventually became Ayatollah Khomeini's most trusted aide. It is often said that Khomeini listened to Rafsanjani's advice more than anybody else's. He was a key member of the Revolutionary Council after Khomeini took power in 1979. However, his greatest achievement is said to have been his role in the Iran-Iraq war of 1980-1988 during which he was de facto Commander-in-Chief. He was also credited with persuading Khomeini to show initial willingness for a ceasefire followed by a decision to end the war in 1998 on unfavourable terms for Iran. Ever the pragmatist, his argument was that to pursue the war any further would have meant detrimental loss of lives and bankruptcy of the state. In a way, that decision saved the Islamic regime because Khomeini, as well as most of the Establishment, and indeed the nation, wanted to continue with the war. They did not want to accept the humiliating terms first offered by Saddam Hussein in 1982. That meant that the last six years of the war had been in vain but the peace saved the regime.

Rafsanjani was rewarded with the presidency for two terms in 1989-1997. His predecessor was Ali Khamenei, the current Supreme Leader and the most powerful man in Iran. The rivalry between the two men must have begun in those early days of the Islamic Republic – Rafsanjani, the dashing, popular, Kalashnikov-wielding military commander who had the ear of Ayatollah Khomeini against the Tehran bureaucrat who dealt with budgets and administration and cultivated shady links with the all-powerful Revolutionary Guards. After Khomeini's death in 1989, Khamenei was elected Supreme Leader.

I heard a rumour some years ago that during the election campaign in 2005 in which Khamenei supported Ahmadinejad against Rafsanjani, an angry Rafsanjani said bluntly to Khamenei: 'Remember who put you in the post of Supreme Leader before you turn against me!' This highlights the nature of the power struggle between the two men, and the fact that Rafsanjani considers himself to be the power broker. Khamenei backed Ahmadinejad and effectively sent Rafsanjani into retirement. Now this rift has once again come out into the open.

But Rafsanjani and Khamenei are tied to each other like Siamese twins. The two of them allowed the Revolutionary Guard and the Intelligence Ministry to get involved in the economy, thus accumulating enormous wealth. The reason why this has happened is perhaps a realisation that unless you keep the people with the guns on your side they may turn their arms against you, like the Praetorian Guard in ancient Rome. This, according to some, has created a distorted market economy fuelled by corruption, intimidation, and even murder.

And here there are three men today – Khamenei, Rafsanjani and Mousavi. In the first years after the revolution and during the devastating Iran-Iraq war they were right at the top of the new regime. Thirty years later, they are involved in a bitter power struggle with constantly shifting alliances.

Rafsanjani is by no means universally liked. Similar to Mousavi, he comes with a lot of baggage. His detractors disparagingly call him the 'Kooseh', the beardless, because he can't grow a proper beard. His smooth face is graced with a wispy moustache and a thin goatee on his chin. But the word also means 'shark' in Farsi, an appropriate double entendre describing his political skills. Accusations of corruption and shady deals are rife. He is supposed to be the richest man in Iran and one of the wealthiest on the planet. Tales swirl around Tehran about how fabulously rich other members of the Rafsanjani family are. I once went to Dizin, a swanky skiing resort north-west of Tehran, and was immediately told by people working there that the place was the private playground of the Rafsanjani sons. They are estimated to be worth billions of dollars, a vast fortune which cannot be accumulated by hard work alone. His youngest son, Yasser, is rumoured to be controlling big chunks of real estate in Tehran's most exclusive suburbs. The eldest, Mohsen, a multi-millionaire, is running the construction of Tehran's super modern metro system. The third son, Mehdi Hashemi, is involved in oil deals.

But it's the daughter, Faezeh, a journalist, women's rights activist, and former member of parliament, who is in the news today. It's a bit unclear if she has addressed the crowd in a banned rally yesterday or today, but we've got the pictures today for the first time.

It is very difficult, almost impossible, to explain this complicated power struggle in 30 seconds. This is the length of the segment allocated to the power struggle in tonight's piece in the ever-dwindling duration of Ten O'Clock pieces. But we've identified it as a strong element and I'm happy that there's more than just reporting of the facts. It's my deep conviction that the viewer deserves more than just the bare facts of yet another protest and yet more arrests by a nasty regime. After a long conversation with Simpson, he boils it down beautifully into a paragraph without even naming the Supreme Leader.

There is one other element in our piece, a moving story from South Korea, where six members of the Iranian national team, including the captain, playing in a World Cup qualifier, appear on the pitch with the green armbands of the protest movement. These pictures have been shown live on Iranian television, with a placard raised by some supporters in English: 'Go to Hell Dictator.' In the second half, however, the armbands had been taken off. One can only speculate about how they'd been persuaded to remove them.

We drive around north Tehran looking for a suitable place to do a night piece-to-camera. This is how we've come to operate. After deciding on the structure of the piece, Simpson writes the script. We discuss with London what pictures should cover the voice track, which ones should be dropped into the piece in London and what original footage we have shot, and at the last possible moment we go out after dark to do another piece in addition to the one that we've recorded in the demonstrations during the day. This gives it a more up-to-date look but also allows us to incorporate the latest news, if any, which might come nearer the time we are due to go on air. The time difference is in our favour. It's GMT +3 hours and 30 minutes. This means that by the time the Ten O'Clock News goes on air in the UK, it's 1.30 am in Tehran on the following day. It gives us time to work till late. However, because the time difference is not a round figure it is confusing so I keep my watch on UK time and get the local time from my mobile phone.

Our van is stuck in traffic on Vali Asr facing north just opposite the compound of IRIB. There is a commotion outside, which looks like a demonstration but we don't get out of the car because the place is covered with secret police. We have a small camera hidden in a box of tissues on the dashboard. It records anything in front of the car but from time to time, Nick moves it sideways so that we can get a better shot. He decides to get the Sony PD150 out of the bag and film through the side window. He is pointing the lens away from the busy pavement across the incoming traffic towards the IRIB building. He hasn't pressed the record button yet when a man with a black beard runs in front of the vehicle making eye contact with the driver. He rushes towards the passenger door. We think he is just dodging the traffic but he bangs on the door and opens it straight away. There is a side arm clearly visible on his belt. He starts to remonstrate with the driver. The translator cuts into the conversation and all I can hear is the word 'BBC' mentioned several times. Mentally, I question the translator's judgement of divulging who we are but the man makes a gesture with his finger in front of the camera lens clearly meaning 'No filming!' and shuts the door. We all breathe a sigh of relief.

Time is running out and we decide to abandon the mission and drive back towards the office. On the way north, almost opposite the slip road which takes us to the Esteghlal Hotel, we pull up in a secluded lay-by off the motorway and record a piece-to-camera with busy night-time traffic behind Simpson. How disappointing for all of us!

Thursday, 18th June. For the sixth day running the centre of Tehran is paralysed. Hundreds of thousands of people are pouring out in the streets despite threats by the authorities that all illegal protests will be dealt with severely. Most of them wear black or have black ribbons on their clothes in memory of the people killed in the protests. It is now known that eight people died on Monday when shooting started around the basijis base in Azadi Square. Another seven have died in protests around the country. This is now not an isolated Tehran-based protest movement but is gripping the rest of the country. A vicious crackdown is expected.

We are in Imam Khomeini Square, which is the epicentre of the demonstrations today. It's all eerily quiet. No chanting, no shouting of slogans. The security services are keeping their distance. Most of them are situated on rooftops, carefully observing the stream of people with binoculars.

Suddenly, the mood changes. A vehicle carrying Mousavi drives slowly through the crowd heading towards Enghelab Square. 'Mousavi, Mousavi, get our votes back!' the crowd shouts. Mousavi himself is in the passenger seat. The vehicle is a Toyota pick-up truck tightly surrounded by a group of young men in casual clothes. They run around it like bodyguards and don't let anybody get close to it. The crowd is carefully ushered towards Enghelab Square. We don't have time to walk to the square because it's too far and go back to the car. Later, we see pictures of Mousavi's brief appearance there, where he urges the crowd to show restraint. So much for lack of organisation.

Ahmadinejad appears on television and sounds conciliatory. This does not bode well. I feel that a storm is brewing under the surface. The government needs another few days to get its act together and will come down on the protesters like a ton of bricks. For now it's only arresting selected people with political connections who have been identified as troublemakers. But that will soon change.

Tonight's piece is a little bland and I can feel that our friend and biggest supporter in the newsroom, the Editor of the Ten, sounds disappointed. It's been hinted that Bill Neally from ITN has been doing exceptional stuff. I saw him at the hotel yesterday and he said he was going back to London today because his visa had expired.

We are all tired. Doing a piece-to-camera while trying to avoid arrest and then being on tenterhooks about whether we'll make it on time to the office through the appalling Tehran traffic places an impossible burden on us. And when back in the office, we're faced with a grumpy and unfriendly attitude.

I had asked the producer in charge to pass a message on to the foreign desk in London that Simpson wouldn't be able to do a radio piece for them. For some reason this message wasn't passed on and the answer I got was, 'You should've told them yourself.' They are understandably angry. I waste a lot of time apologising.

There is an email from the ambassador's wife thanking me for sending her a 'lovely bunch of flowers'. I didn't send any flowers so either it's a mix up or a conspiracy. Simpson tells me to arrange flowers to be sent with a witty note. I spend more time arranging the flowers for the embassy than doing my job.

Friday 19th. This is supposed to be our last day here. Our visas clearly state that we have been allowed in for 10 days only. We entered the country on 11th June, therefore according to our calculations we should leave on 20th June, i.e. tomorrow. That's why before we left London we booked our return flight for tomorrow.

Last night before retiring to our rooms Simpson said that he needed a bit of rest. Should we take the morning off and meet for lunch rather than breakfast? We all agreed we needed more sleep.

I wake up early. My eyes are burning, I feel tired, but I can't sleep. My body is tense and my neck aches. There is less traffic noise coming from the motorway outside the hotel. It's Friday. The sky is blue and I get the familiar Sunday feel that I should be doing something interesting.

However, a blanket of dissatisfaction has descended on me. It's become perceptibly visceral: a hot wave rises in my stomach and travels up towards my head. It turns into anger. We haven't been daring enough so far. Have we wasted golden opportunities to shine? I think our pieces so far have been mundane, quite average, really. Why is that? Have we lost our golden touch?

The best way to deal with this anger is to get up. I am one of the very few people in the breakfast room. Most hotel guests are still in bed.

Mr M, the man from the facilities house which provided the translator and the car, has rung to say that he will come to the Esteghlal to collect his payment in the afternoon. I am not sure how much he knows about our informal arrangement with the translator after his services were officially withdrawn under government pressure. Mr M is a seasoned and well-connected former Revolutionary Guard of undetermined age – very fit, with strong arms and a big chest. Unfortunately, he dyes his hair. He looks as if he goes to the gym every day. I haven't seen him during this visit, but a few months earlier during the anniversary of the revolution we went to his office. It was a dingy building in a third-class shopping centre, one of these courtyards with cheap shops and cafés but in a good area of north Tehran, just off Africa Boulevard. It was again the three of us, Simpson, Nick and me. When he saw us he jumped up from behind his desk and, ignoring Simpson and Nick, gave me a friendly hug, which nearly crushed me. I couldn't understand the reasons for his friendliness. He said I was one of 'them': 'You look like an Iranian from Rasht, on the Caspian Sea.'

The girls in the office giggled. One of them, an educated woman in her forties said, 'People in Rasht don't have very good reputation…'

More giggles. This time I noticed a young man, who I had never seen before, laughing at his desk behind a glass partition.

'No, only the women in Rasht have this reputation,' Mr M tried to assuage my bewilderment. 'They have the reputation of being a bit loose.'

More giggles.

So, this is what passes for saucy jokes in present day Iran, I thought. 'Maybe some of my ancestors come from Iran,' I said. 'My grandfather was born in Istanbul, in the Ottoman Empire,' I embellished a little.

This wasn't the first time I met Mr M. I first came across him in 2008. Simpson and I got visas for just the two of us and worked with a local cameraman, a delightful Iranian man, who showed us the best bits of Tehran. The government had invited the foreign press to cover parliamentary elections and Mr M had set up shop at the Laleh with the intention of making money by providing satellite feeds to foreign crews. When an American network was caught using its own small private satellite dish to send pictures and do lives, the equipment was confiscated on the pretext that satellite dishes were banned in Iran. Mr M's business proposition didn't last very long because the government soon discovered that the foreign press corps was not grateful for the technical assistance and instead of friendly reports it disseminated what the authorities described as 'anti-Iranian propaganda'.

At that time I spent a lot of time talking with Mr M. He had rented a suite at the hotel and liked to have company for his afternoon tea. I found out that he had made numerous trips to Syria with young 'pilgrims', a euphemism for fighters, perhaps helping the Iranian-backed militant group Hezbollah. He even told me that two years earlier, he was operating in southern Lebanon when Hezbollah fought against the Israeli army during the minor war in the summer of 2006. He proudly boasted that he drank alcohol in defiance of the regime's official policy. And he gave me to understand that although he was already a grandfather, he was still partial to unmarried ladies. He almost arranged an interview with Rafsanjani which, although it didn't happen, gave

Me with my parents and younger brother during my father's internment by the communist regime, Red Riverbank, Bulgaria, 1959

As a conscript in the communist army, Karlovo, Bulgaria, 1975

My first school trip (front left), Shipka Mountain, Bulgaria, 1965

(Middle row far left) The 50th anniversary of the Bulgarian Section of the BBC World Service, Bush House, London, February 1990

Skiing with a friend in the Rila Mountains, Bulgaria, 1985, a few months before my escape to the West

With the President of Afghanistan, Hamid Karzai, and John Simpson, Kabul, 2007

Under a mulberry tree in Paktia province, Afghanistan, November 2002, with the ruthless warlord, Pacha Khan Zadran

L-R: Sir Robin Knox-Johnston, me, Simpson and Sir Ranulph Fiennes in Kabul during the filming of *The Three Dogs* documentary, September 2008

Recording a radio documentary, Nadir Shah Mausoleum, Kabul, August 2009

With Taliban supporters at a tea house in Maidan Shahr, Wardak province, Afghanistan, January 2010

Tora Bora Mountains, eastern Afghanistan, not far from the Osama bin Laden caves, September 2008

Kabul book market, August 2009

Outside Kabul, June 2006

With friends in Chongqing, the biggest city in the world, China, April 2010. Joe Phua (far left) is a cameraman with whom we frequently worked around the world

With Simpson and his son, Rafe, on a break after an assignment in Hong Kong, June 2009

Tiananmen Square, on the eve of the 60th anniversary of the revolution, September 2009

Departing from Kashgar airport after a controversial one-day trip to the enigmatic city, October 2009

Under the statue of Mao Zedong, Kashgar, October 2009

Outside Ahmadinejad's hometown, Aradan, south-east of Tehran, February 2009

Tea at the bazaar in Tehran, February 2008

In the holy city of Qom, Iran, February 2008

On a rare solo trip in the Alborz north of Tehran, June 2005

One of the last remaining Jews in Iran, Moshe Baba (between Simpson and I), runs an antiques shop opposite the British embassy. His assistant is on the far right. Our Iranian minder refused to go into the shop – Tehran, February 2008

With the crew of Iranian state television at a polling station, June 2009, on the eve of the violent demonstrations which became known as the Green Revolution

The Old City, Peshawar, Pakistan, June 2010

Visiting a madrasah, Peshawar, June 2010

The road to the Khyber Pass, Peshawar, June 2010

With the Pakistani journalist, Rahimullah Yusufzai, and his son – Peshawar, June 2010

In the Al-Qaida stronghold of Al-Joulan, Fallujah, Iraq, March 2010

Walkabout in Sadr City, Baghdad, a no-go area for Westerners, November 2006

Travelling in a van with closed curtains to avoid detection, Baghdad, November 2006

Recording *Simpson's World* in Saddam's hometown of Tikrit on the day after the collapse of the regime, April 2003

With an American soldier in Tikrit, April 2003

Interview with the Iraqi Prime Minister, Nouri al-Maliki, 2006

With the 101st Airborne Division,
Mosul, Iraq, November 2003

Green Square, Tripoli, March 2011. We were promised mass
demonstrations in support of Gaddafi

Recording a piece-to-camera in Misratah with Gaddafi supporters, March 2011

Gaddafi forces firing at rebels in Misratah, March 2011

After the interview with HM King Abdullah in Jeddah, October 2007.
BBC cameramen Duncan Stone (far left) and Tony Day (second from the right)

Jeddah, October 2007

The Arab Spring, Tahrir Square, Cairo, February 2011

Victoria Falls, Zimbabwe, after an undercover assignment
with cameraman Nigel Bateson, April 2009

On Ceausescu's balcony, Bucharest, December 2009, during the filming of a
TV series for the 20th anniversary of the collapse of communism in Europe

us a picture about who the right people were in Rafsanjani's entourage. It also identified that Mr M and his business outfit was firmly in the Rafsanjani camp.

So Mr M is due come to the lobby of the Esteghlal at 5 pm to get his money. I go back to my room and try to read. *Scoop* by Evelyn Waugh had been in my bag since my previous trip earlier this month. We were in Hong Kong for the 20th anniversary of the Tiananmen Square massacre in 1989. Simpson and I were not given visas for China, so we went to Hong Kong instead. It was basically a one-day story but it was worth it. I thought we did an excellent film with lots of archive footage and a good historical explanation. The candle-lit vigil in Victoria Park was visually stunning and we managed to get bird's eye footage of it from the roof of our hotel.

I try to read but my thoughts go chaotically from memories of previous trips to plans for future ones. Then I fall asleep and wake up in time for lunch. The sleep has done me a lot of good. I am less angry. Downstairs in the lobby, I bump into Nick who also looks well rested. The translator is also there. But there's no sign of Simpson. I decide against ringing his room and the three of us have lunch at the restaurant. There is still no sign of Simpson. We move to the café. Nick and I order Turkish coffee. The translator asks for tea. There is no English cake at the Esteghlal so I get some baklava.

At about 3 pm Simpson rushes out of the lift, spots us in the café and comes to our table. He looks puffed up and not very healthy. The translator says that the Supreme Leader is supposed to lead Friday prayers at Tehran University. Huge crowds in support of Ahmadinejad have been bussed in from the provinces. The opposition has called for a big demonstration around the University, too. Clashes are possible.

Simpson looks at me with sad puffy eyes and says, 'Oggy, have I got time for a cup of tea?'

I say, 'Yes,' but my heart sinks.

By the time we reach the vicinity of Tehran University, we realise that if there has been a story, we have missed it. The area outside the prayer hall is empty. Forlorn barriers lay scattered on the ground. Cleaners are sweeping the debris from the crowd of government supporters. There is no sign of any opposition rally. We drive around in the empty streets in the hope that something will turn up but there is a cast iron inevitability that it's all over for the day.

In silence, we drive back to the office. The resident correspondent has already done a piece on the day's events and we sit down to watch it on BBC World. He understands that we've missed the story but doesn't gloat. We have a pleasant chat about what's happened.

The sermon by the Supreme Leader was very tough. The message was: 'You can't change the election result through street protests! You have to accept the result because this is how democracy works!' Ahmadinejad was sitting obediently in the first row in his signature beige jacket. The Supreme Leader has confirmed him as the election winner and there is no going back. Mir Hossein Mousavi was invited to attend Friday prayer but wasn't there. The battle lines have been drawn. It's now up to the opposition to decide how to respond.

There haven't been any clashes between opposition and government demonstrators. At least, we haven't missed that. Simpson is silent. His face is like a thunderous cloud. This is our last day and we've got nothing to show for. Not even a piece-to-camera outside Friday prayer. What a disaster.

I stand on the little office balcony on my own and sip pale sweet tea from a small glass. The sugar goes straight into my blood and I feel better. I rack my brain to find a solution. What can we do? We can go out later tonight and try to find an opposition gathering to film but judging by today's events it's very unlikely there will be any. Then like many radical solutions, a simple idea appears in a flash.

I walk into the small room allocated to us. There are three desks there. Nick is occupying one with his laptop for film editing and is fiddling with some camera batteries. Simpson sits at the other one writing something on his laptop. I've never used my desk. I normally use the office PC in the main room which has a cable connection to the broadband. I shut the door behind me. They both look up.

'We can't go back on such a flat note,' I say looking directly into Simpson's eyes. 'We've missed the story today but there wasn't much of a story, anyway.'

Silence.

'I have a simple solution. We don't go back tomorrow. We stay another day. Tomorrow is Saturday. The opposition is bound to respond with a big demo and we'll try to get right in the middle of it.'

'But how…' Simpson's trying to intervene.

I take my passport out of my pocket and open it on the page with the Iranian visa.

'Look, it says the visa is valid from the 11th to 21st June. True, it also says "duration of stay 10 days," but does it mean we have to leave on the 20th if it also says our visas are valid until the 21st? If you look at the Islamic dates on the visa, we can argue that we can legitimately leave on the 21st.'

Simpson looks at me with incredulity.

'But let's not worry about this now. We'll worry about it if the immigration people at the airport spot anything wrong. However, I doubt that they will.'

Nick opens his passport and surveys his visa. 'Yes,' he says, 'valid until the 21st.'

Simpson's face lights up. 'Shall we do that then?'

'I think we should. It's a risk but it's a small one. The benefits outweigh the cost. And we have to make sure we do a cracking piece tomorrow.'

Nick lifts his eyes from the passport and murmurs with his typically Yorkshire dry sense of humour, 'You've got your uses sometimes.'

'Are you happy to stay with us and change your return flight?' I say officiously.

This is what's required by the BBC health and safety rules. I have to have everybody's explicit agreement.

Nick smiles and says, 'Yes.'

Simpson smirks. I don't bother asking him.

The mood in the room has changed. Simpson is perky again and starts writing an email to his wife about the change of plans. I call the BBC travel desk to change our flight. Once all that has been done I open the door of our room and announce it to the producer in charge. On hearing it, she has a fit. The resident correspondent who has been really friendly and helpful thinks there is a huge risk, but then he adds, 'Knowing how the Iranians operate, they may not notice. But if they do, you are in big trouble.'

The bosses in London have been notified about our idea of staying one more day and are uneasy about it. I explain that tomorrow is a crucial day and we can't afford to miss it. I hope it fulfils its potential.

Saturday, 20th June. It's a glorious, clear, hot day. There's determination in all of us to do our best. We have breakfast on time and decamp to the office for a while. When we get the first reports on social media sites that there's an opposition gathering, we jump into the car and head downtown. We've been told the main demo is around Azadi Square and along Azadi thoroughfare eastwards towards Enghelab Square. We are very lucky with our current driver. I'm not sure where and how our translator found him but he's been a real gem. He had suggested that driving in a van was very suspicious because most media crews hire vans for their filming expeditions, so vans have become a target for the police. It's easy to carry our equipment in a van – tri-pod, rucksacks with batteries and cables, big camera, spare lenses. But we are now in an old green Volvo sedan. Very inconspicuous!

The driver watches out for hidden dangers and warns us in advance. We only have a very small digital camera, which is hidden in a plastic shopping bag. We arrive in the area around Azadi Square by mid afternoon when the opposition protest is in full swing.

The crowd is perceptibly more aggressive. We don't get out of the car but I can feel the dry, crisp tension in the air, like a dry powder keg waiting for a single spark. The security presence is more visible. It's evident that the authorities are determined to put an end to the street protests. We can spot riot police in their protective gear, ordinary police in their blue uniforms and lots of basijis. The basijis are a volunteer paramilitary force attached to the mosques and personally loyal to Ayatollah Khamenei. The only way to describe them is 'thugs in civilian clothes', mostly T-shirts and jeans. There is a lot of hatred in their eyes. You can spot them easily because they normally carry truncheons or thick wooden sticks, with which they beat up any suspects. They don't ask for permits. If they spot you with a camera, Iranian or foreigner, you are toast.

The volunteer force is called 'Basij'. An individual member is a 'Basiji'. The organisation was formed by Ayatollah Khomeini in the first months after the revolution as 'people's militia'. During the Iran-Iraq war the basijis became cannon fodder. Tens of thousands were killed, some of them as young as 12, in the so-called human waves, which cleared mine fields and drew enemy fire on themselves away from planned offensives. They were indoctrinated in schools and mosques, and through effective media campaigns. I have heard that each was given a 'key to paradise' made of plastic to wear around his neck so that when he dies he can unlock the gates of heaven with it. But I haven't seen any of these keys myself. In peacetime, the basijis became, in effect, a grass roots intelligence organisation, snooping on anybody in the neighbourhood suspected of un-Islamic behaviour. They have been notorious in implementing the ban on alcohol. I've been told they often rummage through people's rubbish to check for any empty bottles.

Today, we can see them on their motorbikes or on foot, often with pistols tucked into their belts, waving their trademark sticks. We drive around Azadi Square and back along Azadi Street but cannot find a suitable place to stop. On occasions, a snooping face will peer into the windows of our car to check who's inside. Simpson is sitting in the front passenger seat dressed in a cream, freshly ironed cotton shirt. The basijis and the police are looking for young people or anybody wearing the colours of the protest movement, like green bandanas or green armbands. We, apparently, look safe and are waved through. The demonstration is illegal because all public gatherings were banned a few days ago but there are thousands of people around us, blocking the traffic. The police can't cope with this influx of people. The riot policemen sit in the back of their pick-up trucks, their commanders seemingly unsure about what orders to give them.

We make another loop around Azadi Square but are unable to stop. Back into Azadi Street in the direction of Enqelab Square, we see the same plain-clothes policemen monitoring the traffic. Making these loops is getting more and more dangerous because we could come under suspicion if they remember us. Simpson is someone who can easily be recognised. We drive eastwards towards Enqelab Square until we find a turning to go back. That stretch of the road is now getting very busy. The protestors chant angry slogans. The police are getting more and more nervous.

When we reach Azadi Square we realise that it's too dangerous to make the same loop again. The only decision we can reach is that we must find a side street suitable for parking the car and try to get out on foot. The translator explains to the driver what we want to do.

The green Volvo drives slowly back along Azadi Street. Before we reach the group of police who have already seen us driving in the same direction several times, the driver turns right into Dr Houshyar Street, which takes us diagonally south of the main boulevard. It is eerily quiet. Behind a block of houses, the thunderous noise of the demonstration becomes muffled. A few yards down the road, we reach a turning to the left, called Ebrahimi, which unfortunately is a cul-de-sac. I don't like parking the car in a dead end street and the driver agrees. He makes a U-turn facing Dr Houshyar Street and parks on the corner.

'This is a good place,' he says.

We sit in the car trying to hatch a plan.

After thinking in silence for a few seconds, Simpson says, 'Oggy, you look Iranian. Why don't you and I get out with our translator and leave Nick in the car.' Nick is a tall fair-skinned Yorkshire man who will stick out like a sore thumb. 'Well, I don't look Iranian either,' he continues, 'but I've got to be there. Can you do the filming on your mobile phone? That won't attract attention because everybody does it.'

I look at the translator. He nods in agreement. I ask him to explain to the driver to stay here no matter what. 'If he has to move under the threat of death, we must arrange another rendezvous nearby. Where do you suggest?'

The driver and the translator begin a long conversation, which annoys Simpson. 'Can you just arrange another meeting point? What is there to discuss...'

An emergency rendezvous is arranged but only the translator knows where it is. If we get separated, Simpson and I will be lost. Or we can get a taxi. Ha-ha.

If you face south-east on Dr Houshyar Street and Ebrahimi, there is a small park on the left. Further down there's a little crossroads where five streets congregate. I need to remember all these details because we have to be able to find our way back in a hurry. There are people coming out of the side streets and rushing north to join the main demo. We can't see any police here. One of the streets at the crossroads, Geranmayeh, leads north directly to Azadi Street. This is where we mingle with the crowd. We advance north and I film Simpson walking among the demonstrators. Suddenly, the crowd turns back and runs in panic towards us at the bottom of the street. Riot police must have charged into them at the other end. Then the panic abates as suddenly as it has started and we proceed cautiously north.

Bang, bang!

Two single shots rip the air right next to us. A man drops down. More panic and shouts from the crowd. I crouch on the ground and crawl towards the injured man filming with my mobile phone. The man is covered in blood. I get closer and realise he's wounded in the arm. He lies on the ground surrounded by fellow demonstrators. One of them administers first aid.

Who fired those shots? This is when I realise that the crowd around us is infiltrated by secret police but events unfold far too quickly to dwell on such a realisation.

I get up and look around for Simpson. He is standing nearby looking towards the main street. I film him standing in the crowd. Then again we hear 'Bang, bang!' More shots are fired, this time in the distance. The crowd turns back in a panic and we are swept back towards the crossroads.

The shots, apparently with live ammunition, have galvanised the demonstrators. They start beating the traffic barriers with stones. The noise is deafening.

Nearby, I see a young man propping himself on a whitewashed wall. His arm is covered in blood. We ask him what happened. He explains that his arm has been slashed with razor blades, one of the favourite weapons of the basijis. He is a skinny urban youth with a trendy haircut, exactly the type the basijis hate. I take a few medium and close-up shots of his arm without showing his face.

The wind brings down tear gas which has been fired at the demonstrators at the top of the street. I dab my eyes with my shirtsleeve. The eye contact I establish with Simpson says: 'Time to go back.' I am not sure what I've got recorded on my mobile phone but, as a cloud of tear gas starts to envelop us, now is not the moment to start checking. The translator has been inconspicuous but every time I've located Simpson in the crowd, he's been next to him.

The car is waiting where we left it, Nick and the driver eagerly awaiting us. After we've pulled out of the danger zone, I check the footage on my mobile. It exceeds my expectations. The sound is superb. This is when I first notice that the crowd had been chanting: 'Marg Bar Diktator!'

The excitement, the exhilaration of the experience has made me forget that tomorrow we are going to be faced with the uncertainty of leaving Iran with an expired visa.

Today is the day that the history of the Green Movement is written. Close to where we were, only minutes after we left, a young woman, Neda Agha Soltan, is murdered. Her story galvanises the world. Late, we see footage shown on Iranian television of basijis being attacked by protestors and their motorcycles burnt. We see pictures of demonstrators throwing stones at the riot police, a critical departure from the relatively timid protests so far. The Supreme Leader threatened the protestors yesterday, vowing to stop the demonstrations with a show of force. He failed to do so today.

We are sitting in the garden of White City, one of the BBC buildings in west London. There's a microphone on the table. Two other producers are directing a complicated conversation between the three of us about our experience in Iran. BBC Radio 4 is doing a special programme about what has happened in Iran over the last 10 days and our participation in the coverage of the momentous events.

We recall how on the following morning we approached passport control at Imam Khomeini airport with great trepidation. It's not a busy airport, Iran being under sanctions, so immigration officials were a bit puzzled when we stopped at the yellow line, reluctant to step forward.

'Oggy, you first!' Simpson said with a broad but uneasy smile, an in-joke between the two of us. It referred to a story attributed to the legendary Hollywood director Fred Zinnemann of *The Day of the Jackal* and *A Man for All Seasons* fame. In the 1980s during a meeting with a young Hollywood executive the elderly Zinnemman was asked by the hapless producer to list some of his best achievements. Not wanting to boast of his Oscars for films like *High Noon*, *From Here to Eternity* and *Oklahoma!* Zinnemann casually said, 'Sure. You first.'

I turned around and before I crossed the yellow line I said quietly, 'If I get arrested, go back and call the embassy for assistance. Don't try your luck with another passport official.'

The immigration officer nonchalantly stamped my passport and I was through. Simpson and Nick followed me into the departure lounge. They thought it was all over, but I was nervous. There was an episode from my first trip to Iran back in 2005, which made me subdued with doubt. I met someone, who was widely credited with starting the blogging revolution in Iran, Hossein 'Hoder' Derakhshan. We interviewed him for one of our election previews. He was bold enough to say that young people in Iran aspire to do what any young person in the world wants to do: go to parties, drink and have sex. A few days later, after the inconclusive first round of the elections, he called me and requested a meeting in the evening in one of the trendy cafés in Fereshteh, just off Vali Asr. When I arrived there, he was with his father, an affluent-looking gentleman who, I found out later, was in the carpet trade. Both of them looked nervous. He said he wanted to tell me something confidential. I took out the battery of my local mobile phone. Silently, they did the same. Hossein told me that he had tried to leave Tehran for Canada the day before. He had dual citizenship. The immigration official stamped his passport and just when he thought he was through, the secret police arrested him in the departure lounge. What they said to him was very ominous. 'You have now officially left Iran. We can do anything we like with you and no one will know…' After some interrogation about his blogging activities, especially his blog posts about internet censorship in Iran, he was allowed to return to his father's house in Tehran but his passport was confiscated. He was now afraid that something might happen to him. Would it be possible for his father to call me if he suddenly disappeared so that the BBC could alert the world about his fate? I said this would be a legitimate story for the BBC to do. The relief on his father's face was visible. I didn't hear from 'Hoder' until later in the year when he suddenly turned up in London. Our meeting in London was our last. After a bizarre but well-publicised trip to Israel the following year, 2006, he returned to Iran only to be arrested and sent to jail. The charges were unclear and speculation ranged from 'spying for Israel' to 'insulting religion'.

Simpson, Nick and I drank pale Iranian tea, ate nuts and laughed in the departure lounge. In order to get the Derakhshan episode out of my mind, I started explaining the background and the acquired meaning of the 'You first' joke to Nick. I knew that Simpson was a great admirer of Fred Zinnemann as well as another of his European contemporaries, Billy Wilder, who made it big in Hollywood. I wanted to talk about Zinnemann's realism and desire for authenticity, at times grittiness, but Simpson directed the conversation towards Italian neo-realism. One of his favourite films is Vittorio de Sica's *The Bicycle Thieves*. His eyes became tearful when he talked about it. Although the film is nominally about the hardships of a working-class family in post-war Italy where a young father is frantically looking for his stolen bicycle without which he can't hope to find a job, it is much more than that. When I saw it again recently, it struck me how romantic it was in portraying the relationship between a bumbling inept father and his streetwise nine-year-old son. The son stood by his dad in the face of all adversities. Here, at Tehran airport's departure lounge, I felt the film had touched a string in Simpson's heart because of his own young son, the precocious Rafe.

The sun is trying to peek through the June clouds over White City. The conversation between the three of us is a bit erratic despite the efforts of the Radio 4 producers to moderate it. They steer us towards concrete memories, which can define and help explain the momentous events in Tehran.

I recount how Mr M came to the Esteghlal at the agreed time to collect his money. He was prompt. I looked at the invoice to check that it ended on the day the government banned foreign journalists from covering the demonstrations. This was the day when Mr M withdrew his services. He diplomatically refrained from asking about what we did after the ban was imposed. I offered him a cup of tea, he accepted and the waiter took the order. Simpson never liked Mr M and was very cold towards him so Mr M turned towards me.

'I have worked with many foreign journalists in Iran. As you know, I helped you with your visas. So, remember me! Remember that I helped the BBC.'

This came like a bolt from clear sky. It took me a few seconds to realise the significance of his words. They meant that the game was up for the regime. Mr M knew it instinctively and was thinking about the future. He thought that helping the BBC would get him off the hook. I looked at Simpson. 'I don't like this creep' was written all over Simpson's face.

It was very symptomatic that Mr M tried to associate himself with the BBC in such a manner. By the time the Radio 4 programme went on air, Iran had already blamed the BBC for fuelling the protests. There were even more ludicrous allegations. One website reported that the BBC had hired hit men to kill Neda Agha Soltan, the 27-year-old woman who was killed by a gunshot to the chest in the protest not very far from where Simpson and I were filming on that Saturday afternoon. A newspaper accused the BBC resident correspondent, Jon Leyne, of hiring Neda's killer personally. Jon was expelled from Iran.

There was controversy about Neda's identity. Neda's death was recorded on video by a bystander and posted on the internet. It went viral. The protest movement, but much more importantly, the media around the world, needed a martyr, a hero, and Neda fulfilled that role. But every hero needs a face. Frustrated journalists trawled the social media networks for a photograph of Neda Agha Soltan and found one. Unfortunately, that was a picture of a completely different young woman, Neda Soltani, a 32-year-old university lecturer. She unsuccessfully tried to remove her picture from the internet but it was too late. In the crackdown that followed the protests, Neda Soltani's life became intolerable. She was accused of 'endangering the security of Iran'. She had to flee her country and is now in Germany where she was granted political asylum. The real Neda didn't find peace in her death. Her grave was desecrated several times by pro-government thugs.

Over the following months, the crackdown was brutal. The opposition claimed that more than 80 people had been killed during and after the protests, a figure never confirmed by the government. Detained opposition supporters, women and men, were raped in prison. An opposition politician, Mehdi Karroubi, documented a number of these cases and posted his findings on the internet. The government acknowledged some incidents but dismissed them as 'negligence' on part of prison guards.

Ahmadinejad served another four years as president, a term that was marred by controversy, accusations of economic incompetence, and efforts to impeach him. He was mocked in Iran for his obsession with the 12th Imam. A mobile phone video of him describing how the green light of the 12th Imam descended on him during his first speech at the United Nations was derided even by senior clerics. He was deplored abroad for his outlandish pronouncements on the holocaust, homosexuality and his hatred of America. His detractors continued to claim that he was one of the captors who held American citizens hostage at the US embassy in Tehran in 1979. And pictures were circulated in an attempt to prove that.

But Ahmadinejad relentlessly pursued Iran's nuclear programme, skilfully avoiding any drastic measures by the West. The threat of Israeli attack on Iran diminished, especially as a new crisis unfolded in Iran's client state, Syria.

For me the most defining memory of the events that took place in those fateful days in June 2009 was the absence of fear. The authorities might have succeeded in putting down a peaceful rebellion but the new post-revolution generation have demanded more and more freedoms. The Islamic revolution of 1979 means nothing to them. Most of them don't even remember the devastating Iran-Iraq war because they were born after it ended. But above all, the authorities have found it more and more difficult to deploy their most powerful weapon: fear. People, young and old, defied repression in those heady days of June 2009. They found their voice and that voice can only become louder and louder.

Simpson and I haven't been back to Iran. I shall miss walking around Tajrish Square in north Tehran, sitting in the trendy cafés and drinking pomegranate juice with my Iranian friends. I shall miss my trips to Darband, just north of Tarjish, with its amazing concentration of different style restaurants. And I shall miss buying pickled walnuts from the street vendors there or ordering 'Bulgarian kebab', a long sword with lamb chops skewered through their flat side. I'm not sure why they call it Bulgarian when I've never seen it in Bulgaria. And I hope that one day I shall see Hossein Derakhshan, who is still in prison in Tehran.

KASHGAR, CHINA, OCTOBER 2009

Here we are at last, closer to Baghdad than to Beijing, and yet in China, on the ancient silk route. We decided to test the government's goodwill, and on the day after the 60th anniversary of the republic, we flew to the capital of Xinjiang, Urumqi. Only three months before, the city was the scene of the most grotesque ethnic violence between local Uighur youths and ethnic Han Chinese, the majority group in China. More than 200 people died, some of them bludgeoned to death in mindless anger.

Urumqi is famous for being the furthest city inland from any of the world's oceans. The nearest coastline is over 1,600 miles away, which places Urumqi in the so-called Eurasian Pole of Inaccessibility, a geographic construct which denotes the centre of the huge combined landmass of the continents of Europe and Asia. It is also the capital of Xinjiang Uighur Autonomous Region of China. Urumqi means 'beautiful pasture' in the local tribal language. The city is anything but.

Skyscrapers, new buildings and big roads appear beneath us as our plane descends towards Urumqi airport. It all looks gleaming and modern from the sky. The four-hour flight from Beijing is surprisingly pleasant. The aircraft is new, the stewardesses beautifully turned out, the food bearable. Gone are the days when an internal flight in China was like a death sentence. In the 1990s Chinese aircraft were dropping out of the skies like stones because of poor maintenance.

Our arrival coincides with the Chinese Moon Festival. It's celebrated on the 15th day of the eighth month of the Chinese calendar during full moon. This year, 2009, it falls on 3rd October. Last year, the communist government declared the Moon Festival a public holiday across the country.

However, for all its bright lanterns, burning of incense and moon cakes, not many in Urumqi celebrate the Moon Festival. The indigenous Uighur people are Muslim. The traditional moon cakes – pastry filled with bean paste or lotus seed paste – are for the Han Chinese people, who have been coming to Urumqi in large numbers in recent years. The locals see them as economic invaders. The

Uighur people are now only 50 per cent of the population in the region and feel they have been displaced in a deliberate effort by the central government in Beijing, which is trying to secure a permanent foothold in Central Asia. Some Uighur activists even claim the government is trying to crush their culture and subjugate the region. The reality is, as ever, much more complicated.

The original Uighur people were a Turkic-speaking tribe from the region of the Altai Mountains in Central Asia. They enjoyed their golden age in the 8th and the 9th centuries AD when they had a vast empire called the Uighur Khaganate. After the collapse of the Khagane in 840 AD, the Uighur tribes migrated south and west, and dispersed. Some of them converted to Islam in the 10th century, others not until the 15th century. The term Uighur was all but forgotten. Western travellers in the 19th century called the Muslim people in Xinjiang Turki, the Russians – Sart. The locals identified themselves by the name of the oasis they came from.

Uighur nationalism started in the 1920s when the Bolshevik Revolution took hold in Central Asia. The Soviets met Turkic Muslim nationalists from Xinjiang in Tashkent in 1921 and created the so-called 'Revolutionary Uighur Union', a nationalist Bolshevik organisation designed to spread Soviet influence in Xinjiang and wrest the province from Beijing's control. However, the Turkic inhabitants of Xinjiang were not officially called Uighur until 1934 when a local ruler, Sheng Shicai, started to promulgate Uighur national identity on Stalin's orders. Xinjiang at the time was under virtual Soviet control and Sheng Shicai was a puppet governor. Stalin even made him a member of the Communist Party of the Soviet Union. By 1944 Sheng had gone but Uighur nationalism in Xinjiang had taken root.

We arrive at Urumqi airport, a well-maintained modern structure, without any hitches. On this trip to China, Simpson and I are travelling with a delightful Chinese man from Singapore who is our cameraman. Joe has worked with us in Afghanistan and Iraq. He is calm and well composed in adversity.

Two other people travel on the plane as part of our team but they pretend they are not with us. One of them is a human rights activist, D, who I've employed as a translator and fixer, and a local Uighur girl from Urumqi, who now lives in Beijing. She is involved in charity work but will be our conduit to eyewitness accounts of the riots in her city.

We are under no illusion that the authorities are tracking us down. At Beijing airport, our fixer surreptitiously managed to point out to us a man in a casual black leather jacket who had quite openly been giving an account of our movements through the airport to somebody on his mobile phone – from check-in to the departure lounge. The man, masquerading as a passenger, sat on a bench just opposite the three of us in the lounge but never got on the plane.

A car with two men inside follows us from Urumqi airport to the Ramada Tunhe Business Hotel in the centre of Urumqi. It's a run-down four-star hotel with a tired façade. The surveillance car unashamedly pulls up in front of our taxi outside the hotel and the two men walk in and sit down in the lobby while we are checking in. The big marble lobby adorned with red propaganda slogans is deserted. We can't see many hotel guests around. The staff – all in black suits – look Han Chinese and are very friendly. I'm sure that they know who we are. They've got the demeanour of people who have been expecting us. Unfortunately, the pretence that our fixer D and the Uighur girl are not travelling with us unravels very quickly because I have to guarantee payments for their rooms on my credit card.

We have been allowed into China for the 60th anniversary of the People's Republic. Simpson travelled briefly to Beijing last year ahead of the 2008 Olympics but my visa application was conveniently delayed and the visa was only offered after the Games were over. I am not sure how much this delay was due to usual Chinese suspicion about the role of the producer in a news crew.

As I have already mentioned, every time Simpson and I decide to go to a particular part of the world, the main struggle begins with the local BBC office. Before we even start the battle with officialdom in the target country, we have to fight BBC bureaucracy. BBC Bureau Chiefs don't like Simpson stomping on their patch but dislike even more the idea that his producer will be managing the story and they won't be able to have control over it.

Soon after the Beijing Olympics, which were an undeniable success, I suggested to Simpson that I should approach the Chinese embassy on his behalf requesting a meeting with the ambassador, Madam Fu Ying. Simpson had a better idea. 'Why don't we invite her for lunch at the Garrick?'

Simpson is a member of the Garrick Club and justifiably proud of it.

Women are only allowed to visit the all-male club in the company of men. The Garrick, in the heart of London's 'Theatre Land', is one of these quintessentially British institutions which are both hated and admired. We were pleased when Madam Fu accepted the invitation.

A black diplomatic limousine pulled up in front of the club at exactly 1 pm on the agreed day and Madam Fu got out of it together with a female assistant. Simpson and I were waiting at the top of the stairs. Madam Fu was impressed by the grand staircase and the old paintings on the walls, and showed some interest in the history of the club. Simpson briefly explained who the actor David Garrick was and mentioned some of the club's most famous members: Charles Dickens, H. G. Wells, Somerset Maugham, A. A. Milne, T. S. Eliot, and Jeremy Paxman. Madam Fu actually knew who Jeremy Paxman was.

Over lunch, she mentioned in passing that she had seen Simpson's report from China, which was broadcast on the BBC's Ten O'Clock News ahead of the Olympics. In it, he tracked down a Chinese Christian activist detained by the authorities. She also mentioned that we would not be allowed to visit China around the beginning of June 2009 to coincide with the 20th anniversary of the Tiananmen massacre or, as it's known in China, 'The June the Fourth Incident'. And although she didn't promise, she gave us to understand that we would be issued with visas for the 60th anniversary of the revolution.

Madam Fu, a career diplomat, was a tough cookie. She was the epitome of a Communist Party apparatchik of modern times, fluent in English and suave. Immaculately turned out in black, with a conservative hairstyle graciously emphasising the grey, she'd obviously taken advice about the rules of the Garrick. Behind the smiley façade, however, there was firm determination that she would take no nonsense.

When you have a meeting about visas you don't bring up the subject of human rights in China, but she brought it up herself by denouncing what she called 'the demonisation of China by the Western media ahead of the Olympics'. I changed the subject by pushing my luck with a request that our visas should allow us to arrive not just on the day before the National Day Parade on 1st October 2009 but perhaps a week in advance, so that we could do a bigger and more thoughtful piece about how China is changing. Her assistant was taking notes frantically and I felt sorry for her because she couldn't enjoy the nice lunch.

Madam Fu Ying went on to become Deputy Foreign Minster, or as they prefer to call it in official jargon 'Vice Foreign Minister of the People's Republic of China'. I didn't see her again but Simpson and I were introduced to her successor as ambassador in London, Liu Xiaoming.

National Day Parade, the reason why we are in China, was yesterday. It was a great success. The man in charge of the weather should get a promotion because there wasn't a single cloud in the October sky over Beijing. And this is not a joke. The People's Liberation Army has a special Weather Modification Programme. It employs more than 30,000 people and costs hundreds of millions of dollars. The cloud busting troops fire substances like silver iodide and solid carbon dioxide (dry ice) in the form of chemical pellets into the clouds to induce precipitation. The process is called cloud seeding. Cloud movements are being monitored by satellite and if they head towards Beijing, they get busted before they arrive. More than 20 cloud seeding aircraft and 50 fog dispersing vehicles had been at work in Beijing to ensure clear skies for the grand parade.

It was a hot October's day. Nature had almost conspired with the regime to bring an Indian summer to the Chinese capital. We chose to stay away from the parade in Tiananmen Square.

This is the secret of successful reporting of set-piece events: you don't stand all day with other journalists and photographers penned in a small area designated for you by the authorities. It's a recipe for disaster.

In this instance, to start with, journalists were required to clear security in Tiananmen Square at the ungodly hour of 5 am. The parade started at 8 am and finished at midday. With an event like this, your movements and view are normally restricted so you can't see very much from where you are, you get thirsty and hungry, and it's too complicated, sometimes impossible, to go to the toilet for many hours. On top of that, if anything happens, like a terrorist attack, for example, or other disruption of the parade, you are the last to know about it (unless by a miracle it happens in front of you) because journalists are 'kettled in' to prevent coverage of the disruptive event. So it's much better to get up at leisure, have breakfast and watch the event on television. You get the benefit of an overall picture, as well as the ability to browse various websites for coverage and commentary of the event. When the event is finished, you have the advantage of being fresh and composed. You can go out and do a well-judged piece-to-camera rather than a frantic one while being pushed and shoved during the parade without the ability to analyse what's going on.

Therefore, we relinquished our places to whoever wanted to take them. People at the BBC Beijing office were shocked when we announced that we didn't want to be at Tiananmen Square. The three of us watched the parade, and after that the evening fireworks and laser show on television.

The parade was staged down Chang'an Avenue (The Way of Heavenly Peace) from east to west and culminated in Tiananmen Square. The Communist Party leaders – past and present – viewed it from the balcony of Tiananmen (The Gate of Heavenly Peace) above Mao's portrait. Tiananmen is located in the northern part of the vast square and was built by the Ming Dynasty at the beginning of the 15th century. The building was the actual gate to the Imperial City, within which is situated the Forbidden City, the residence of the Chinese emperors and their households. For centuries, the Forbidden City was the heart of Chinese power. Now it's only a symbol of that.

The parade reminded me of similar events I had watched on television from Red Square in Moscow, and far less grandiose parades in Bulgaria when I was a child. They followed the same pattern. I must admit that as a five-year-old boy I was smitten by the powerful military display in front of Lenin's mausoleum in Moscow, especially the huge intercontinental rockets. And this is what the parades were designed to do in those days, to instil a sense of power and superiority in ordinary people.

It's often forgotten where it all started. In the 1920s, the Soviet commissars were the first to create a powerful propaganda display, the most powerful in the history of mankind. They also recognised the power of cinema in perpetuating the propaganda. Most of the filming techniques and camera positioning for a grand parade were the creation of early Soviet cinema and they have endured until the present day. Hitler, Mussolini, Mao Zedong, Kim Il-sung and his descendants, all owe a tremendous debt to early Soviet cinema.

But what was the purpose of yesterday's military parade? It's hard to believe that the intercontinental rockets on display were meant to threaten Washington or London. We are now more threatened by China's new economic power. This is what we discussed with Simpson while watching the event on television.

The parade went off without a single hitch; everything was perfect. Residents of Chang'an Avenue had not been allowed to open their windows for days before the event, the sale of knives had been banned, and most dissidents had been silenced by either being under house arrest or banished from Beijing.

In the evening, Tiananmen Square was host to a spectacular show for an audience of 60,000 carefully selected members of society. Ordinary folk were not allowed anywhere near the Square. The leadership had entrusted Zhang Yimou, famous for his 1987 debut film *Red Sorghum*, to direct the show. Mr Zhang was a trusted pair of hands. He had also directed the opening and closing ceremonies of the Beijing Olympics in 2008. The film that propelled him to fame, *Red Sorghum*, although sometimes described as a work of magical realism for its romantic portrayal of peasant life, was ultimately an example of government-approved communist propaganda – patriotism and the teachings of the party eventually prevail.

The laser show in the evening was spectacular albeit somewhat sterile. The fireworks were great but you could watch only so much of them. After a dazzling few minutes at the beginning, they started to look just the same.

I thought the piece we did for that evening's Ten O'Clock News was one of the best pieces Simpson had scripted in the years we had worked together. It was funny, incisive, analytical and, above all, watchable. There were ironic references to the style of the parade: 'Distinctly retro', 'Mao Zedong jacket', 'The North Korean Look'. It was clear to us that the leadership was afraid to emphasise how capitalist China had become and in times of rising unemployment and anger about corruption, it deliberately chose to go back to basics, i.e. it's communist roots, for the duration of the parade at least.

The killer sequence in the military parade from our point of view was an absurd regiment of women volunteers, The Iron Roses, dressed in pink jackets and matching miniskirts. They marched in immaculately straight lines clutching their assault rifles. The absurdity of it all was in their white berets, white handgun holsters and knee-high white boots, to go with their pink uniforms. 'Not quite Maoist,' Simpson scripted, 'but definitely 60s.'

The piece made a great impression on the BBC audience in the UK. The Chinese, though, murmured that the tone was a bit flippant and didn't match the solemnity of the occasion.

Simpson adores China, Chinese culture and especially Chinese tea. He's been here many times before. For me, it's the first time. In the last 15 years I have travelled the world but somehow China has eluded me so my knowledge of the country has been theoretical. In the last year, since the financial crisis, the so-called credit crunch, has engulfed the Western world, I have debated the Chinese economic model with my friends in north London. Some of them, although liberal and individualistic, have begun to suggest that China's centrally managed economy might provide a much more durable model than the paralysing Western namby-pamby decision making through endless parliamentary debates and impotent checks and balances. I have always believed that freedoms for the individual stimulate intellectual creativity. Centralised dictatorships are doomed to unravel sooner or later because they are not flexible enough to let steam out when the pressure for the individual becomes unbearable.

It's been said that the Chinese authorities have conducted in-depth studies of the collapse of the Soviet Union so that they can manage the transition to market economy without the big cataclysmic events that led to the break up of the Russian communist empire. The Soviet Union was confined, to use a well worn out cliché, to the dustbin of history because it essentially became bankrupt. Its economic model was unsustainable. Bankruptcy is China's biggest fear. That's why it hoards money and tries to look at least 20 years into the future when it makes its plans for economic development. It's very easy to push through plans, albeit with the best possible intentions, if you are not accountable to an electorate and you don't have to worry about a huge social security bill. But this top down heavy-handed decision making will become more and more difficult to implement with the rise of the middle classes and organised labour. Modernising the economy will lead to demands for modernisation of China's social model, too. And that is what scares the ruling elite.

There's another problem, too. To all intents and purposes, China is the last colonial empire, which holds together countless nationalities and ethnic groups, ruled by the centre and kept obedient by the biggest army in the world. If you look at the biographies of the top Chinese leaders, everybody's ethnicity is clearly stated. But statistically the Han Chinese group dominates not only the ruling Politburo but also the army and the police. Communist ideology dictated that national identity should be encouraged, and language and culture should be preserved but only within the confines of communist dogma. What this means in practice is that if, for example, you are a Uighur and communist you can freely express your ethnic identity. If, on the other hand, you are a Uighur and Muslim and separatist, you become an enemy of the state. As economic prosperity spreads to the far-flung parts of the empire, demands for self-determination will become louder and louder.

On Simpson's suggestion, we stayed at a typical Chinese hotel, the Jianguo, in the Chaoyang district of Beijing where most of the foreign embassies are based. It's on Jianguomen Street, not within walking distance of Tiananmen Square but a short drive away. From the hotel entrance, if you turn right and take the street due west it will cross Dongdan Street and will morph into East Chang'an Avenue. The Jianguo is not a high rise. It's set in a Chinese garden, with faux waterfalls and a small imitation river going through the compound and is an example of communist folklore architecture. Although I didn't like this style in Bulgaria and Russia during communist rule, I loved it here. I guess I was a bit nostalgic.

On the morning after our arrival, I met D, who would be instrumental in organising our trip to Xinjiang. Simpson and I were drinking a pot of strong Pu'er tea in the hotel garden by a small waterfall when D arrived. Simpson had worked with him before on a couple of occasions and spoke very highly of him. I knew he was an economic commentator in his own right and a human rights activist so I had a preconceived idea about what he might look like, which couldn't have been further from reality. D is a youthful-looking man of undetermined age, quite tall, with a broad open smile and very bad teeth. To say that he was dressed casually would be an understatement. The nearest description I could find for him would be that he looked like an environmental activist, an eco-warrior, who'd been living in a tree in protest against the building of a new road. A Chinese Swampy of a kind. He is fiercely intelligent. And we clicked.

Our visas allowed us to spend almost a week in Beijing in advance of National Day Parade and we were intent on doing a solid investigative piece. D was the right man to help us. We also had a Chinese translator, a girl with superb command of English and even better knowledge of the best Chinese restaurants in Beijing.

The first thing I wanted to see was an old-fashioned hutong, a warren of alleyways so typical of old Beijing. Hutong is a Mongolian word meaning 'water well'. The water wells were the focal point for settlements when Beijing expanded in the 13th century. And the quintessential courtyards, linked with countless alleyways, were born. Although most of the hutongs have disappeared in the last 60 years to make way for wide boulevards and skyscrapers, some areas like Xicheng and Gulou have preserved them. Some of the alleys are so narrow that if two people meet they have to turn sideways in order to pass. The Gulou area around the Bell and Drum Towers, north of the Forbidden City, is now gentrified and most of the courtyards in the hutongs there have been turned into trendy cafés and restaurants, a Beijing version of Hoxton, if you like.

Just like in trendy east London, Gulou is the place to be seen if you are a good-looking young person with lots of spare cash to spend. One evening Simpson, Joe, our Chinese helpers and myself were having a meal there. Simpson had gone to the loo and was returning to our table when a well-dressed young Chinese man made a beeline for him. A group of young people were looking on. Simpson's big frame and white hair had marked him out in the crowd and obviously drew their attention. I watched how in the course of the conversation Simpson's cold and slightly annoyed look changed first into a polite demeanour and eventually into animated friendliness. It turned out that the man was a graduate of Simpson's Alma Mater, Magdalene College, Cambridge. They had apparently met a few years previously when Simpson went to speak to students there about careers in journalism. The man, James, now reads the news on the English channel of CCTV, China Central Television, the state-owned broadcaster.

On a different night, we ate Peking duck in a run-down hutong in the Xicheng district, west of the Forbidden City, but appearances there could be quite deceptive. The restaurant was like a shed in someone's garden – dirty, smelly and unkempt, but the food was delicious. There was no menu, only loud discussions in Chinese between D and the owner. When the bill arrived I thought it was extortionately expensive. Needless to say they didn't take credit cards. That night I tried Chinese Maotai for the first time in my life. Maotai is a traditional Chinese alcoholic drink, distilled from fermented sorghum, which in its purest form can be very expensive. On another visit to China the following year, Simpson and I had further Maotai experiences, that time with detrimental consequences.

In Beihai Park, the former Imperial Garden to the north-west of the Forbidden City, we had one of the most elaborate Chinese meals I've ever had. And sure enough we visited the Liulichang hutong, south-west of Tiananmen Square, the home of some delightful antique shops. Just for the record, it's common knowledge that everything that's sold in Liulichang does not fall under the definition of 'protected antiques', the sale of which is proscribed by the Chinese authorities. The things that we bought there were replicas manufactured by government-sponsored factories. But they were very charming nonetheless.

We aimed to have a very ambitious piece for the evening before National Day Parade but in the end it came out a bit flat. We filmed at an internet café in the centre of Beijing where youngsters were all too willing to show us that the BBC website in Chinese had been blocked. There was no fear in any of them but they didn't want their faces shown, just in case. The manager had allowed us to film freely in his establishment so long as individuals were happy to be filmed. We tried to track down a leading dissident residing in one of the run-down hutongs but by the time we reached his house, he had been taken away by the authorities. We interviewed his wife in the little two-room house but the interview was disappointing because she wasn't very articulate and the political message was somehow lost. The sequence that made the biggest impression on editors in London was from the little suburban village of Xi Bai Xin, north of Beijing, where we filmed in a street market overflowing with fresh fruit, vegetables and meat. Everybody who we asked in the market said how good life was compared with 15-20 years ago. BBC World News asked me to send them an edited version of just that sequence which they ran over and over again for 24 hours. Adjacent to the village, which was in Beijing's commuter belt, we filmed a new housing development. Shocking as it may sound the asking prices were almost as high as in the south of England.

The idea of going to Xinjiang crystallised the day before the military parade during one of our brainstorming sessions over copious amounts of Pu'er tea. Simpson and I must have exceeded the recommended dose per day because both of us complained of insomnia. The potent fermented black tea from the southern province of Yunan is strong enough to wake up a dead horse. It was in one of these hyper moods that both of us dared each other to do reckless things.

'You wouldn't consider going to Kashgar?' I said, thinking more about the opportunity to see the ancient monuments rather than anything else. I also relished the idea of the frenzy with which this announcement would be met by the Beijing Bureau Chief and the BBC managers in London. Urumqi was thought to be a dangerous unpredictable place. A month after the July riots, a spate of bizarre syringe attacks unsettled the fragile atmosphere in the city and the whole province. Reportedly, 250 people became victims of these attacks but no toxic or radioactive substances, nor HIV infections were found. Some of the attacks resulted in robberies. Three Uighur people were sentenced to up to 15 years in prison for the attacks. The previous year, just before the Olympics, 16 Chinese soldiers from the border force were killed in Kashgar by attackers armed with knives and explosives. They drove a truck into a group of about 70 soldiers jogging in the street and started stabbing them randomly, and threw hand grenades.

'Of course, I would,' Simpson replied. 'I think we actually have to use the remainder of our stay here more productively. And going to Xinjiang will be one such opportunity.'

The female translator looked at us in disbelief. D on the other hand was intrigued.

'Can we actually book tickets to Urumqi and Kashgar without any problem? Do we need any special permits to fly to Xinjiang?' I said.

'No, you don't need any permits. Anybody can buy tickets and arrive in Urumqi or Kashgar. Whether you will be able to do any filming there is another matter,' our female fixer said.

I hesitated. It was too good to be true. It was too good an opportunity to be missed. But both Simpson and I knew that before we tested the goodwill of the Chinese authorities in such a sensitive place as Xinjiang, we needed to have our battle with the BBC for permission to go.

Once again this battle unfolded along familiar lines. I informed London about our decision. I didn't ask for permission. My email to the Foreign Editor simply stated that we had a possibility of flying to Urumqi and then to Kashgar on the day after the parade. He replied that it was a good idea but added that I should speak to the Beijing Bureau Chief to iron out any safety and security implications. This was what I dreaded most. Bureau Chiefs don't like their lives disturbed by outsiders who fly in onto their patch, stir up trouble and then leave them to pick up the pieces. I must admit that if I were a Bureau Chief I would feel the same. That's why I adopted the tried and tested policy of avoiding any direct contact with the Bureau Chief. I only emailed him to say that we had bought tickets for Urumqi and Kashgar and then refused to respond to his numerous orders to call him. He ominously suggested that travelling with D, who in his words was a 'known political activist', would expose our team to danger and we would be prevented from doing any filming there. He was only partially right.

The story was so much up our street, fraught with uncertainty and danger, the possibility of arrest, but above all, the chance to find out why ethnic grievances erupted with such violence between Uighur and Han Chinese youths.

All we needed now was D's opinion and whether Joe, our cameraman, would be willing to come with us. Simpson and I had made a pact that if no one else wanted to go, the two of us would travel to Urumqi anyway. I would do the filming on my mobile phone.

D was very receptive to the idea. He suggested that we take a Uighur friend of his with us who would be able to help us get interviews with eyewitnesses of the violence three months ago.

After checking in at our hotel in Urumqi we convene downstairs for a chat and a plan of action. We all agree that there is no point in hiding what we are doing because this will make matters even worse. Let's carry on openly and see if the police decide to stop us. In that vein, we decide that our interviewee, a girl who has witnessed the violence, should come here and we shall film the interview in the hotel café. That will save the secret police the effort of following us outside, something they have already done quite openly.

The girl arrives and we offer her a cup of tea. She is not nervous at all and that makes me nervous. 'Have we got a genuine eyewitness or is she a plant?' goes through my mind. I share this thought with D. He says that the girl will be telling us that she saw Uighur youths attacking Han Chinese shops and beating two Chinese men to death. Nearly 200 Chinese people died in the violence. This is the official Chinese propaganda line, therefore there's nothing for her to worry about. This answer restores my confidence in the project. No one interrupts our interview.

Encouraged by the success of the interview, we venture out into the streets. We walk to the nearest mosque. People are gathering for afternoon prayer and while Joe is filming outside, I go in with D to find out if anybody in authority is willing to speak to us. We openly say we are from the BBC, which produces a mixture of bewilderment and fear. Some of the people we speak to inside the mosque like the attention, others are openly hostile. The imam, a youngish soft spoken Uighur man with bright eyes and white turban, is intrigued but refuses to speak to us and does not allow us to film inside the mosque. However, he agrees to have his picture taken with me and even manages to produce a faint smile under his well-groomed pencil moustache.

There's riot police at every corner in the centre of Urumqi. Joe takes a few discreet shots from a distance but when they notice the camera they get angry. We move away and they don't follow us. I look at my watch. We've been on the ground for about four hours and haven't got very much material. I take D aside and ask him to find out from our Uighur girl if she can take us to a typical Uighur area of the city. She comes up with the idea of Gulistan, a solidly Uighur slum area where people live in poverty. We set off in our hotel car, followed by our friends from the secret police. They, however, keep a very polite distance.

Gulistan is on a hill on the outskirts of Urumqi. When we approach, the place reminds all three of us of Afghanistan. The low-rise rickety houses are built on a slope almost on top of each other. The dominant colour is ochre, the colour of the surrounding hills. Dusty cables run erratically over the streets and the alleyways create a wire mesh, which envelops the whole settlement. By the main road, before you enter the village, there's a market from which emanates the unmistakable smell of rotten vegetables and freshly slaughtered meat. Old men with Central Asian features wearing the tubeteika (Uzbek skull cap) sit passively on their doorsteps. Small children are playing in the dirt. The air is dusty.

We drive deeper into the slum. The unpaved streets are narrow and very difficult to navigate. We look around to find someone to talk to but the place is deserted. People are hiding inside, fearful of any contacts with foreigners. According to human rights organisations 43 men and teenage boys were taken during police raids on Uighur districts like this one in Urumqi after the riots and have since disappeared without trace.

Suddenly, when we turn a sharp corner, we see three cars, one of which has come to grief. Two men are pushing it to dislodge it from a hole in the ground. It becomes very obvious to us who these people are. These are the undercover cops who've been following us. Joe carries the camera on his shoulder and openly films their effort to push the car. Simpson mocks them. 'Can we help you? We can push with you…'

One of the men in a mauve short-sleeved shirt waves at him dismissively. The other two cars have disappeared round the next corner. Eventually, the men manage to push their car out of the hole and it speedily drives away. We've recorded this whole sequence on our camera.

Now Simpson, Joe, D and myself, walk down the unpaved street. Our car follows behind. The street leads us to an open space like a little square. Two kids are playing with some plastic bottles at the far end of it. A woman with an empty shopping bag, oblivious to the fact that there are foreigners around, is walking down the street towards us. D approaches her and starts to negotiate the possibility of a short interview. She violently shakes her head in refusal. Eventually, she agrees to be asked questions but not to be filmed. As we gather around her, she spots something in the distance and rushes away. Then we see someone waving at us. He is a well-fed, tallish man in a white shirt with some sort of ID card hanging on a string around his neck.

Our group moves down towards him. Joe still carries the camera on his shoulder and I give him a nudge to film. He says the camera is already rolling. When we approach the man in the white shirt we see two other men with him, all wearing the same type of badge around their necks. The man in the white shirt makes a sign spreading the fingers of his hand in front of the camera lens. The meaning is all too familiar to us. 'No filming!' D tells Joe to move away but to continue filming and then inspects the man's ID.

We understand that these three people are quite different from the ones who have been following us. They ask for our accreditations. All of us have the Tiananmen Square media passes around our necks. They have obviously expired because they were only issued for the big parade yesterday but despite that they make a big impression on the men. D hijacks the conversation. He hates all manifestations of gratuitously applied authority and is trying to tell these men that in today's China you can film anywhere in public spaces without explicit permits. The men are not aggressive. They are really polite. They want to know the purpose of our visit to Urumqi and, more specifically, Gulistan. We tell them the truth. Simpson says that the world is really interested in what happened in Urumqi three months ago and we want to find out the source of the anger, which resulted in so many deaths. I tell them that Urumqi is an open city. Anybody can buy a ticket and arrive here.

Then it's our turn to ask questions. We find out that these people are members of a special task force created after the disturbances to smooth things out between the two communities. They are half policemen, half social workers, if you like. Their main task is to look out for any signs of emerging violence, but also to listen to the grievances of the Uighur people and recommend action to the government. Perhaps not surprisingly, all three of them are Uighur.

At this point my mind drifts away. I remember in the 1980s just before the fall of communism there was a nasty campaign by the Bulgarian authorities to assimilate the Turkish minority. It involved the forcible change of their Islamic names into Bulgarian-sounding Christian names. The campaign backfired. Almost a million Bulgarian Turks left for neighbouring Turkey. But some of them stayed in Bulgaria. The ones who stayed were members of the Communist Party. They put ideology above ethnic identity. This is what's happening here. There are ethnic Uighur who put their party allegiances above their ethnic identity. Not all may do it out of ideological adherence. Some may do it for career progression, material benefits, or power over their peers. But nonetheless there are Uighur who work for the government here.

We shake hands with the three men and wander down the road to the market to do some more filming. We think we have got some material but not enough to make a decent piece out of it. I ask our Uighur helper to take us to the spot where the main rampage took place three months ago. I know from memory that the riots started in one particular street. Also, there is a spot where most of the violence against Chinese shopkeepers occurred. The girl is a bit confused because she lives in Beijing and wasn't in Urumqi when the riots happened. Then D casually throws a bombshell at me: 'You know, her father is a high-ranking police chief in Xinjiang.'

Now I am confused. Have we been manipulated subtly by the Chinese secret service?

'Don't worry,' D continues. 'She is genuine.'

We eventually drive down a street with lots of boarded-up shops. It's deserted and we can see the aftermath of fire. But our girl is not sure whether this is the correct street. It's getting late, so we decide to abort the mission and go back to the centre of town. We've spotted a bazaar by the central mosque earlier and Simpson wants to go back there.

The bazaar is called The Desert Jade. We are not interested in the spices, the foods, the pelts and the silk but head towards the antiques stalls. Many of the sellers are Han Chinese and they are tough to haggle with. Simpson sets his eyes on a white porcelain statue of Mao Zedong in a winter coat in front of a tall microphone. The statue, probably a foot tall, looks quite fragile because of the thin stem of the microphone, rising from the ground and reaching Mao's face. The seller, seeing a foreigner as a prospective customer, ups the price immediately and asks for $250. We move away and start looking at other Mao Zedong memorabilia. But Simpson is obsessed with the microphone statuette and we go back. After a lot of haggling and threats to walk away, the price comes down to $150, at which point the statuette is wrapped carefully in bubble wrap, then in paper, and eventually put in a Tesco plastic bag. It's astonishing to see a British supermarket bag in Urumqi and we ask if there's a Tesco's nearby. The seller smiles and says that the bags are manufactured here.

I'm very excited to be here. The atmosphere is completely different from that of Beijing. Right next to the hotel we can see shop signs in Russian. They invite you to go upstairs to the second floor to purchase mink, sable and other rare furs on sale at 'very reasonable' prices. We, however, want to sample the food of Central Asia and ask the hotel to recommend a restaurant. D takes the details.

The restaurant is a short walk away, but we don't like the look of the building when we arrive. It's a concrete shopping mall, very cold and unappealing. We have to take a lift to the second floor. The whole experience is bizarre and we are about to give up but curiosity prevails and we walk into the establishment.

Simpson and I gasp in unison when we lift the black curtains covering the entrance door. It's not a restaurant, it looks more like a nightclub but that's not the point. It is furnished and decorated in impeccable 1970s style. We both know this isn't deliberate. Whoever designed the interior of this place probably doesn't remember the 70s under the austere Maoist dictatorship, a far cry from today's China. This is definitely thought to be the latest fashion. The nearest to this prime example of 1970s interior design that I have seen before was about 10 years ago in Cape Town. I can't even remember the name but it was in Green Point and had an inimitable James Bond 1970s feel – all furnished in autumnal colours, including the dark beige leather sofas, with a sprinkling of chrome.

This Urumqi restaurant-cum-nightclub is one step further. Dark walls, lighter semi-circular leather seating around chrome tables, an enormous bar with hundreds of bottles of alcohol on display, and a black round dance floor in one corner. You sort of expect waiters in starched white uniforms to usher you through but the barman, a Han Chinese, is in a T-shirt and trainers as if deliberately trying to shake off the spell this place has cast upon us.

D and the girl look on matter-of-factly, evidently not impressed but not disgusted either. Joe is more concerned about whether we can get any decent food here. D asks and we are given menus straight away. The menu is in English but I don't understand any of it. The names of the dishes in the food section don't mean anything to me. Joe nods and says, 'I can get some rice. Don't worry about me.'

This isn't very encouraging but Simpson and I are determined to have dinner at this surreal place. There are no other customers. We are either early or it's extortionately expensive by local standards. And, of course, it is the Moon Festival and most people celebrate it at home. I suspect the club is designed for visiting Central Asian millionaires. I ask D but he says that the prices are relatively cheap compared with Beijing.

I am not a great drinker but I'm in the mood for celebration tonight. We made it to Urumqi. I can also feel that Simpson is in a mood for a drink. D discusses with the waiter, another Han Chinese, the prices of Maotai and we order a bottle of the most expensive. After some explanation by the waitress, D translates to us that the food here is predominantly Central Asian with Russian influence. Joe is not impressed. Simpson and I love it. For us it's a throwback to the Cold War.

Xinjiang has a very small border with Russia in the north but you can feel the Russian influence through the other neighbouring countries: Mongolia to the north-east, Kazakhstan to the north-west, Kyrgyzstan and Tajikistan to the west, all former Soviet Republics, except Mongolia, which was nominally independent but under heavy Soviet influence: even the Mongolian alphabet is Cyrillic, borrowed from the Soviets. To the south-west, Xinjiang has borders with Afghanistan, Pakistan and India, and to the south is Tibet.

We order some of the main Xinjiang dishes. Laghman noodles – staple food for the Uighur – when covered in fried peppers, tomatoes, onions, garlic, green beans and spices, with bits of mutton in it, it's called Suoman. Nokot – boiled chickpea salad with shredded carrot, vinegar and fresh herbs, fried mutton dumplings, steamed mutton dumplings. Uighur bagels arrive unprompted. Polo or Plov is a variation of Pilau rice with added chickpeas, carrots and raisins, and of course the inevitable mutton chunks. Joe is not happy with the Plov and asks for plain steamed rice, which raises eyebrows, but the waitress eventually brings it.

The Maotai flows, as does the conversation. I ask for the most typical dish in Urumqi and after some to-ing and fro-ing, D says that it must be horsemeat. By that time the Maotai has gone to my head and I order horsemeat. Simpson squirms but says that he will try it. The locals only have horsemeat as a starter but we order it anyway. Before too long a medium-sized plate arrives with slices of boiled meat. I don't understand why some of it is dark, and some of it is white. I'm told that younger horses have whiter meat when boiled and older horses – dark. I'm not sure whether to believe that or not and try a piece of the lighter. Even the influence of the Maotai doesn't mitigate the weird taste. I have had smoked horsemeat in Europe but the taste of this is very different. The smell makes me gag, it's tough and I have to swallow the whole slice because I can't chew it.

In terms of culinary experience, this has been a disaster but the Maotai has put everybody at a very friendly disposition. The conversation inevitably veers in the direction of how well China has done in the last 20 years and how rich it has become. I want to know if D is happy with the levels of personal freedom he has at the moment.

'So long as you don't criticise the government and the Communist Party, you can do virtually anything,' he says.

'So, what happens if you do?' I challenge him.

'Well, it still depends on whether you criticise individuals or you challenge the right of the party to govern. If you expose corrupt individuals, you can get away with it, but if you call for a change in the system, you're in trouble.'

'I don't understand what you mean by change in the system. China is no longer a communist country. It may still be governed by the Communist Party, but the system is capitalist. It already has been changed.'

D is confused. I can feel he wants to tell me something but there is a barrier. Even now, under the influence of the Maotai and away from the ears of any spies, he exercises self-censorship. This is why the system is still so powerful.

I try to spell it out for him. 'You mean that you can't challenge the right of the ruling elite to govern. What you have here is the return of the imperial system in China: the sons and grandsons of Mao Zedong's closest associates govern the empire now and they are not going to give up the reigns of power. It's the new red aristocracy that rules China now.'

There's an awkward silence around the table. I understand that I've entered forbidden territory and decide to change the subject. Still in a belligerent mood, I begin to criticise the intellectual vacuum in the West, which I blame for failing to produce any radical ideas about how to deal with the financial crisis.

Simpson intervenes. 'Until the Second World War every generation in the Western world had produced its own culture. However, in the last 70 years, that's almost three generations, there's been no radical change in the way we think, in the way we dress, in the music we listen to. My father's generation listened to a completely different type of music. Since the late 1950s we've been listening to variations of the same music. Mick Jagger is only one year older than me. People like him and me listen to the same music as our sons and daughters and our grandsons and granddaughters...'

'That's because we in the West have lived in peace for an unprecedented length of time.' I try to offer an explanation. 'Apart from some local wars, not on our territories, there haven't been any big cataclysmic events to shake up the world. The Cold War was a period of stagnation not only for the Soviet Union, but for the West, too.'

'No, I don't agree. I think it's because the world hasn't been able to produce great thinkers and visionaries in the last 70 years,' Simpson concludes.

'Oh, I think that when the world needs giants, it produces them. The political and economic circumstances have not been conducive to producing great thinkers. We have lived in a consensus society for far too long and this stifles free thinking.'

'Oggy, that's so Marxist. You are going back to your roots.'

It's already midnight. Joe is bored. We need to rest because tomorrow is a big day. We are flying to Kashgar, the heartland of Uighur nationalism and until recently a forbidden city for foreign journalists. And we still need to do some filming in Urumqi in the morning before our flight.

Joe hasn't drunk at all but Simpson and I are pretty drunk. D is remarkably sober for the amount he's imbibed. We walk back to the hotel talking loudly in the street. Surprisingly, Urumqi has come to life after dark. Shops, restaurants and cafés are open. We walk past a giant hairdressing emporium on two or three floors. It's open and there's a pretty girl outside inviting people to come in. Simpson and I look at each other. We collect haircuts, as we often joke. We've had our hair cut in Baghdad, Kabul, Beirut, Tehran, Amman, Jerusalem, Johannesburg, and in numerous other places. To Joe's consternation, we decide to go in. He tells us he will walk back to the hotel on his own. Our Uighur female fixer had already bailed out while we were at the restaurant. D decides to stay with us but doesn't want his hair cut.

The young girls are faffing around, looking at me and giggling. I ask D to translate what they are chatting about.

'They say you look like a Hollywood actor and are wondering if you really are,' he says.

'Here we go again,' I say. 'Which actor do they want me to be?'

'Dustin Hoffman,' he says.

When he mentions the name 'Dustin Hoffman' there's a burst of giggles all around. I sit in the chair waiting for them to decide who is going to cut my hair.

Simpson feels a bit left out because they don't recognise him.

'Oh, well,' I say, 'Dustin Hoffman is 20 years older than me and about three inches shorter but never mind, tell them that I am Dustin Hoffman. I've come to Urumqi to shoot my new movie.'

The girls giggle again but I don't think they believe me. After more faffing around, washing, cutting, drying we eventually get our hair done. When I look at my watch it's almost 1 am. I am in an excellent mood but I know I'll pay for it somehow. We walk back to the hotel and I slump on my bed, falling asleep almost immediately.

The symptoms of the migraine are unmistakable. I wake up at about 4 am with a throbbing headache. It hurts behind the eyes, on the sides, and on top of my head. The vein on the left-hand side of my neck is pulsating. This is going to be bad. I'm tired but I drag myself out of bed and swallow two Nurofens with some water. I lie down and force myself to sleep but the headache gets worse. I try to breathe deeply and put my fist behind my neck to press on the pulsating vein. This raises my head from the pillow, which makes it impossible to sleep. The pain abates for a few seconds only to come back with a vengeance. It's one of those moments when I think I'm better off dead than alive.

I gradually realise that the room stinks of cigarette smoke, something that hadn't bothered me before. The carpets, the curtains, the bed have absorbed the smell over many years and turned it into a mature disgusting odour. My throat convulses and I rush to the toilet to throw up. The retching is violent. The contents of my stomach come out in three gushes. The stench is unbearable. I can see bits of horsemeat, chickpeas and carrot in my sick. That makes me retch again and more semi-processed food comes out. I flush the toilet and sit down on its lid. The retching has increased the supply of blood to my brain and I feel marginally better but I know it's not over yet. I take two more Nurofens and lie down but my stomach won't process the medication. I jump up and retch again over the toilet. More mushy substance comes out.

The throbbing ache in my temples is unbearable. There's nothing I can do but wait. I lie down on my back and try to think of anything to keep my brain occupied. I begin to sketch in my mind the structure of a television piece of about three minutes. I go through the material that we've already filmed: a skyline of Urumqi shot from a park on a little hill halfway between the airport and the city; street shots; military presence; shots of people going into the mosque for prayer – we must use as many close-ups as possible of the Central Asian faces outside the mosque; an Uighur slum area; the guys who followed us; the guys who questioned us. It all looks a bit flimsy, insubstantial. Oh, yes, we have the interview with the eyewitness of the violence. It's not great but it's essential to the story. So, what do we have to do tomorrow? I turn on my side and drift into a slumber, something between proper sleep and being awake. I shall be impossibly tired tomorrow.

I wake up and look at my watch. It's almost 5 am. I've been asleep for barely half an hour. The headache is abating but it hasn't gone yet. I take two more Nurofens, hoping that they will work this time. So, what do we need to film in the morning to make a complete piece? I go through the structure again but apart from the interview it all seems like wallpaper to me. Ok, we need to go to the street where the riots started and film a piece-to-camera. This should be easy enough to do. Then… then… I fall into slumber again.

When I wake up 30 minutes later the main headache has stopped but my head feels like a balloon – light and swollen. I start thinking about the structure of the piece again. Sometimes, in this state of heightened tension when all my senses are strained, very useful ideas come to mind. I suddenly remember that when we walked to the restaurant last night we passed by a wall in the street covered with posters of wanted Uighur youths in connection with the violence three months ago. The posters have been battered by the weather but you can still see the faces. We must go there and take a few shots. These shots will be the bridge between our Urumqi sequence and the Kashgar footage, which we hope to get later today. I can even suggest to Simpson what to say over the poster shots.

'Most of the people wanted for starting the riots did not come from Urumqi, they came from Kashgar, a thousand miles away, the bedrock of Uighur nationalism. And this is where we are heading next.'

It will work like a story told in chronological order. I fall asleep again.

The telephone by my bed must have been ringing for some time because when I pick it up I hear Simpson's firm voice. 'Oggy, where are you?'

I look at my watch. It's 8 am, an hour after our agreed time for breakfast. I don't say very much by way of excuse. It takes me five minutes to get dressed and splash some water on my face. I look terrible – sunken red eyes with dark rings and an ashen face.

The vast breakfast room is almost empty. It's just our group and some middle-aged Chinese women. I walk past the buffet table and the smell of food makes me retch again. I sit down with a cup of black tea.

'I am sorry for being late. I had a terrible night. If I said that I had a migraine, you'd laugh because you might think it was a hangover.'

'Oggy, what are we going to do today? We haven't got much material,' Simpson says.

I outline the structure the way I saw it in my migrainous slumber this morning.

'And I have a suggestion for this morning: we go out to the street where the riots started and do a piece-to-camera to say: this is where it all began, etc. Then we walk down the road and film the wall with the posters of the wanted men. Fifteen hundred people were arrested after the violence. Most of them came from Kashgar. This is our bridge to the Kashgar sequence. Let's hope we get something more interesting there.'

Joe looks happy. All cameramen are happy when there is a plan of action. It will take us an hour to accomplish all that and then we'll head for the airport. It's going to be a busy day but it will be fun.

'I hope you get better,' Simpson says almost gently. He can see that we've got a piece.

We arrive in Kashgar on the day of the autumnal equinox when the Chinese Moon festival is celebrated. The airhostesses, impeccably dressed in blue uniforms for the festival, give us little boxes with moon cakes. The distance from Urumqi to Kashgar is a thousand miles but for me this is the shortest flight ever because I sleep deeply all the way, missing the spectacular views of the snow-capped Tien Shan Mountains below. But it's just as well that I got some sleep because no one could have anticipated the events that unfolded in Kashgar during the following day and night.

As we leave the plane, we see a uniformed policeman checking the passports of all passengers at the point at which they leave the jet bridge and enter the airport building. We look at each other. Joe, John and I stay together. D and the Uighur girl are ahead of us, travelling as a couple. The policeman checks their passports and lets them through.

A few seconds later he opens mine and shouts something to his colleague further down the corridor. The policeman doesn't look at me but quickly grabs John's passport and scans the crowd behind him. Joe hands over his Singaporean passport.

'I found them!' Joe whispers in my ear. 'This is what he said to the other policeman. Obviously, they are expecting us.'

The policeman who's taken our passports has two stripes and two big silver stars on his epaulettes, which makes him a lieutenant colonel, identical to the Russian insignia, although the uniform is blue, not green like in Russia. He still avoids my eyes every time I fix my gaze on him. He is a small man, probably in his early fifties, with a haggard face. We've been told with sign language not to move. Eventually, after all passengers have filed out of the plane, three more uniformed policemen arrive and we are duly escorted through the building, down two flights of stairs to what looks like the basement, and into a small room.

The room is bare, with a desk in one corner and a few chairs lined up against the walls. We are told to sit down on the chairs along the wall and everyone disappears. The door is left open. We look at each other but don't say anything. It's common practice to leave suspects on their own and then monitor their behaviour and conversations. I notice that the red recording light of Joe's camera has come on and I smile in silence. I cover the camera with my jacket. After a while, the uniformed lieutenant colonel returns with a young Chinese man with a very intense face. He is dressed in casual clothes, almost too casual: white trainers, T-shirt, and a faded mauve sweat top with a big print on the back. He speaks excellent English.

'You are journalists, right?' he says. 'I must tell you that you are not allowed to do any interviews in Kashgar.'

Not a great start.

John explains that we are accredited journalists and Kashgar is not a closed city, so we are not breaking any law by being here.

'I know who you are,' he says calmly, 'but you are not allowed to film in Kashgar; this is the latest order from Beijing.'

The lieutenant colonel sits calmly behind his desk in the corner and observes. The young spook is sitting in a chair just opposite us. His body language is very intense, leaning forward when he speaks. An angry exchange follows between him and John.

'Are we under arrest?' asks John.

'No, not at all. You are free. Welcome to China, but you can't film in Kashgar.'

'So, can we go to the city then? We've got a hotel booked there. The Macartney House.'

'No, you can't go to Kashgar.'

'So, we are under arrest then. If you don't let us go to Kashgar you have to keep us in prison.'

'No, you are not under arrest. But journalists are not allowed in Kashgar.'

'Why?' I intervene. 'We checked with the Ministry of Foreign Affairs in Beijing and they said we could travel to Kashgar. That's why we bought our tickets. Our return flight is tomorrow.'

I have lied about the ministry, hoping that he can't check it with Beijing.

He says something to the lieutenant colonel and walks out of the room.

We wait in silence. The lieutenant colonel pretends he's busy by leafing through some files. I get the feeling he's a bit embarrassed by the whole situation.

After a long awkward silence, maybe 10-15 minutes, the young man, who I think is a well-trained undercover agent, comes back. He attempts something like a smile and says, 'Ok, you are allowed to go into Kashgar, but NO-O-O filming. You are not allowed to use the camera.'

'So what will happen if we do?' I push my luck.

'You are not getting it,' he says. 'I'll put so many of my people around you that you won't be able to do anything.'

'Ok, let's try,' I say and get up. 'Either arrest us or let us go. We would like to go to our hotel now.'

The lieutenant colonel, who's been silently looking on, picks up our passports from his desk and stands up. He points with his head towards the exit.

We only have hand luggage, so we quickly make our way towards the exit, flanked by the uniformed lieutenant colonel and the young spook. Outside, we see D and our Uighur translator loitering by the taxi rank. The police ignore them, which makes me very suspicious but there's no time to discuss that with John.

John, Joe and I get into a taxi. D and the Uighur girl get into a different one. As we pull out of the airport compound, we notice that we are being escorted by two unmarked police vehicles: one in front, the other one behind us. There is a hidden benefit in that because the road to Kashgar is chock-a-block. With the police car leading the way, we jump the queue. The taxi driver is enjoying it. It doesn't happen very often that you go through the main checkpoint into the city without being searched. In fact, the checkpoint is the reason for the traffic jam.

In the taxi, we are trying to decide on a plan of action.

John says, 'I don't think it's worth trying to film surreptitiously because we won't achieve anything. They will prevent us anyway and we may get banged up. This is what the BBC Beijing Bureau said would happen and I would like to prove them wrong. The benefit of cooperating is that we'll get to see Kashgar with our own eyes and that, although not perfect, is better than not seeing Kashgar at all.'

'Did we get any shots from the police station at the airport?' I turn to Joe.

He nods affirmatively. But then adds, 'I would like to be able to work in China again.'

'So would I,' says Simpson.

We decide to cooperate.

The hotel, Qini Bagh (Chini Bagh or 'The Chinese Garden') is an unremarkable concrete structure, an example of communist architecture. Behind the disappointing concrete block, however, across a small car park, one can find nestled awkwardly in the corner of the compound the old house of Sir George Macartney, the first British Consul General in Kashgar. Macartney, an officer in the British Indian Army, was a fascinating character. His mother was Chinese from southern China, a descendant of one of the leaders of the Taiping rebellion against the Qing dynasty in the mid 19th century. On his father's side, he counts the First Earl Macartney, the 18th-century British diplomat and colonial administrator, as his relative. The old Macartney, who in his long career had been a special envoy to the court of Catherine the Great in Russia, governor of Madras, and the first British ambassador to China, is credited with coining the famous quote after the Paris Treaty of 1763.

'Britain now controls a vast empire, on which the sun never sets.'

We give our passports to the hotel receptionist and impatiently wait to be checked in. I try to make small talk with the young spook who is standing next to me and ask him what his name is.

'You can call me Tommy,' he says. 'Chinese people have a Chinese name and an English name. My English name is Tommy.'

'Nice to meet you, Tommy,' I say and stretch out my hand. He takes it warmly and we shake hands. 'My name is Oggy.'

'Oggy? This is not an English name.'

Here we go again. 'No, it isn't. It's Bulgarian. Oggy is short for Ognian, which means fire.'

'Oh, Agnian? It's just the same in Russian,' he says, pronouncing my name with a Russian accent. When the 'O' is not under stress, it's pronounced as 'A' in the Russian language.

'Do you speak Russian?' I say.

'Yes, I do,' he says in English and continues in Russian, 'when did you leave Bulgaria?'

'A long time ago,' I say in Russian, deliberately avoiding any details.

The lieutenant colonel's ears prick up. It's so easy to forget that we are actually in Central Asia where Russian is the lingua franca.

Before we head for the rooms to leave our bags and freshen up, Tommy warns us that we must not carry any cameras or recording equipment when we come down.

'And please, don't wear any jackets or overcoats. When we go out in the town you must wear only shirts or T-shirts.'

We look at each other. It dawns on me that they want to make sure we don't carry any hidden recording equipment in our clothes. We are grateful that the weather is pleasantly warm despite the altitude of nearly 4,000 feet.

A few minutes later we meet in the paved courtyard, which separates the concrete hotel from the old house. We admire the magnificent ancient elm tree still standing in the middle of the courtyard. A cheap metal table with a top covered in white and green gingham oilcloth sits forlorn under the tree. There are no chairs.

The house itself is an unassuming two-storey whitewashed building with a terracotta tiled roof and red ochre trim around the windows and along the edge of the walls. Dark green wooden pillars support a large first floor balcony, thus creating a spacious porch. It is no longer a hotel but a Uighur restaurant. Simpson and I rush in to take a good look because we don't know when the goodwill of our escorts will be exhausted. The interior shows signs of disrepair. The wooden staircase leading to the second floor is creaking but the atmosphere of past grandeur still lingers in the air. Intricate plaster mouldings cover the walls of the dining room, which is the main space of the current restaurant. One would expect to see pictures of Sir George Macartney or his wife, Catherine, on the staircase but there aren't any. The green carpet throughout gives the house the unmistakable feel of a government-run establishment. Eventually, we find a black and white photograph on the wall of a small room on the first floor, which shows a man in a British army uniform with slight Chinese features among a large group of men and women dressed in European clothes. So, this is the famous Sir George Macartney.

We walk out onto the first floor balcony from where distinguished Edwardian visitors like Sir Aurel Stein, the British-Hungarian archaeologist, would've admired the famous English garden created by Lady Catherine, once dubbed the most famous garden this side of the Karakorum Mountains. There's nothing left of the gardens now, except an elm tree.

I am elated. I can't believe my luck that I am in the land once called Kashgaria and ruled as an independent kingdom by one Yakub Beg, a Tajik adventurer turned king, at the height of the Great Game. The term, the 'Great Game', was coined by another fascinating Brit, Arthur Conolly, an intelligence officer who travelled undercover in Central Asia as a British spy. At the age of 34, he was beheaded in Bukhara by the local ruler in 1842. The Great Game, introduced to the general public much later, in 1901, by Rudyard Kipling in his novel *Kim*, is a term describing the struggle between the Russian and the British empires for domination of Central Asia and spans almost the whole of the 19th century.

After the death of Yakub Beg in 1877, the Qing dynasty re-conquered Kashgaria. Legend has it that Yakub Beg's surviving son and grandsons were castrated and turned into eunuchs to work at the Imperial Palace in Beijing. Over the following years, the Chinese established the province of Xinjiang ('New frontier') and brought it firmly under Chinese political and cultural rule, dropping the old name Huijiang ('Muslim frontier'). This is what the Communist Republic inherited in 1949.

Over a cup of tea in the courtyard under the ancient elm tree, Simpson indulges our hosts in a brief history lecture about the Great Game, the upshot of which is that the game, at least in Xinjiang, has ultimately been won by the Chinese. The lieutenant colonel, who we now understand is called Mr Zhu, and the young plainclothes spook, Tommy, love the story ending.

Tea is followed by fresh fruit, sweet grapes and Chinese dates. The latter causes a great deal of discussion because we can't find an English word for it. It has the shape of a date but tastes like apple. Its scientific name, we found out afterwards, was Jujube.

Half an hour later after numerous phone calls between our minders and their bosses, Tommy announces that because we've been very cooperative we can bring our photo cameras to take 'holiday' snaps of the Macartney House, and later on of the old town and the streets of Kashgar. We've been offered a guided tour of the city and we can't believe our luck.

By now it's already 6 pm but still light because Kashgar is forced to live on Beijing time. In fact it's only 4 pm astronomical time. On the steps of the ground floor entrance of the house we invite the lieutenant colonel and our young spook to have their pictures taken with us. They refuse. I discreetly take a couple of distant still shots of them from across the courtyard.

Walking out of the hotel is quite a sight. Tommy and I lead the way, followed by John and Joe, followed by our fixers. But if you looked around, you would spot at least four men in black uniforms and several plainclothes policemen, some of them ethnic Uighur, keeping their distance but watching our every move. They are all armed.

Tommy ushers us into the main commercial street, lined with numerous little shops – butchers, bakers, and blacksmiths. Kashgar is famous for its handmade knives. The smell of burning charcoal and grilled mutton mixed with spices takes me back to Afghanistan. For a moment I think I'm in Kabul. No wonder the Hollywood director Marc Forster used Kashgar as a backdrop for his 2007 film, *The Kite Runner*. It was too dangerous to film in Kabul, and Kashgar was the nearest he could find for the 1970s Kabul sequences in the film.

Local Uighur youths look resentfully at our party. There is an air of sadness and resignation in their eyes. What a pity we are not allowed to speak to them.

'Don't take pictures of the soldiers,' Tommy warns me when I get my camera out.

A squad of soldiers, all of them Han Chinese in brand new green uniforms, marches past.

We are carefully guided into the square in front of the main mosque, the Id Kah Mosque ('the place for praying and festivities'). Its distinct yellow front gate is flanked by two minarets and leads into a four-acre compound. Behind the gate we can see the tops of lush poplar trees. It's tempting to go in but we need to see as much as possible of the real life in the streets, so we decline the invitation. We know we are being monitored so we don't try to evade our minders. However, we separate and browse in the shops on the edges of Id Kah square, making it difficult for them to follow each one of us. I engage in haggling over the price of a Chinese lynx skin. It gives me enormous pleasure to bargain with people who think of me as an easy prey, ready for fleecing. The price comes down immediately. However, Tommy cuts me short. He doesn't want me to drive the price further down. The shopkeeper, a Uighur boy of about 20, is very curious. He doesn't know what to make of me but I'm sure he's sussed out who Tommy is.

The main square, under the towering statue of Mao Zedong, is packed with green army trucks. Our first impression is that Kashgar looks like a city under military occupation. We linger around the monument under the pretext of taking pictures of Mao Zedong's granite statue, a prime example of communist propaganda. Mao is in a buttoned up overcoat and a worker's flat cap, his gaze fixed in the void over Kashgar and his right arm raised in the air greeting imaginary masses. Our minders have their eyes fixed on our cameras so that they don't point at the soldiers positioned all over the square.

We then head for the old city which, according to Tommy, is being restored to preserve Uighur ethnic culture and folklore. I try to separate Tommy from the rest of the party and walk faster, ahead of the main group.

'Tommy, where did you learn to speak such good English?' I ask.

'In Pakistan,' he says.

'And what were you doing in Pakistan?'

'Just a visit to study English,' he replies and changes the subject. He is too young to have been involved in the Chinese effort to help the mujahideens against the Russians in Afghanistan. But his father might have been. The fractured relations between China and the Soviet Union during the so-called Sino-Soviet split (1960-1989) meant that China trained mujahideens in camps in both Pakistan and in China itself. Another result of this geopolitical game was that China beefed up its military presence in Xinjiang.

As we move away from the centre of Kashgar and walk across a bit of wasteland towards the old city, Tommy in turn asks me how many countries I have visited. I say I haven't counted.

'I'd love to travel,' he says, 'but I have no money and I'm very busy with my job.'

He tells me that he is 27, born in Kashgar, a local boy, as he describes himself. He desperately wants to get married but there aren't enough Chinese girls in Kashgar. The city is 90 per cent Uighur. He will have to find a bride elsewhere.

I look back and see that Simpson and the rest are trailing far behind us. Tommy and I are alone and no one can hear our conversation. Then out of the blue I hear the following: 'I'm so sorry for being rude to you and your colleagues at the airport.' His stern façade melts away. 'But we are only doing our job.' He looks vulnerable. 'Why did you leave Bulgaria?' he ventures a personal question.

'Because I didn't like the communist regime,' I reply quickly.

'Oh, so it was a long time ago,' he says pensively. 'I would like to come to London one day.'

I don't say anything. There's an awkward pause.

'I'm sure you will. If you do come to London, please get in touch,' I say.

His face lights up but he remains silent. I feel I have to reassure him that everything will be fine, that he'll get married and maybe one day he'll travel to Britain. He smiles sadly and says he wants to see Big Ben and Buckingham Palace.

We are now approaching the part of the old city, which is like a theme park. We even have to buy tickets to get in. Inside, along the quaint narrow alleyways we are invited into restored little mud-brick houses where Uighur families have been made to wear folk costumes and parade for the cameras of foreign tourists. The authorities want to show that Uighur culture is being preserved.

Tommy allows me to take some pictures from the rooftop of a mud-brick house, which is being refurbished. I take a panoramic shot of the neighbouring area, the stronghold of Uighur nationalism, where many of the so-called 'terrorists' come from. It consists of the same mud houses but un-restored, and with a thick net of power cables drooping over it. Many of the wanted men might still be there, just a stone's throw away from us. The area is earmarked for demolition. When you look around you can see that big swathes of the old mud houses on stilts outside the theme village have already disappeared under the encroaching avalanche of nondescript high-rise concrete blocks.

I breathe in deeply, savouring the dry desert air, trying to memorise its smell. I always do when I know that I'll probably never come to a particular place again. Marco Polo, if you believe the legend, passed through Kashgar around 1273. Genghis Khan had conquered it a generation earlier; Tamerlane the Great, the Tartar despot, ransacked it a hundred years later in pursuit of his dream of building the biggest empire in the world. Imperial China had vied for control of this oasis city and the arid land around for many centuries. And here I am today, at the start of the 21st century, looking at the remnants of this ancient city condemned to destruction to make way for a new, more powerful China.

Earlier in the year the central government in Beijing announced something called 'Kashgar Dangerous House Reform'. The plan involved knocking down most of the Old City on the pretext that the houses were unsafe for human habitation. They would be replaced with gleaming office blocks, symbols of modern day China, and a small portion would be restored, fortified against earthquakes and kept as a museum. Uighur nationalists saw this as a sinister move to deal a deathblow to Uighur culture. Others thought that demolishing the slums would smoke out the 'terrorists' who were thought to be hiding there. There was also a very pragmatic view, which said that demolishing the houses of people with no property rights would open the gates to enormous riches for developers who would pay huge bribes to officials.

In the evening Tommy takes us to the best Uighur restaurant in town, the Altun Orda ('Golden Palace' in Uighur). Again, I have the feeling that I'm in Kabul. The garishly decorated restaurant smells nicely of freshly baked bread and grilled mutton, mixed with the sweet smell of smouldering charcoal. Despite our protestation, we are afforded a private room. Our minders think it's best not to mix with local people too much. Mr Zhu, the uniformed lieutenant colonel, makes his excuses and disappears to celebrate the Chinese Moon festival with his family. Tommy stays with us and makes suggestions about what to order. Simpson orders a bottle of Maotai. I think the hair-of-the-dog will do me good, so I have a glass. Tommy has a glass, too. Before the food arrives, Tommy surprises us and says that he will have to leave in order to celebrate the Moon Festival with his family. Just as we think that we'll be left alone at last, two plainclothes policemen, both of them ethnic Uighur, enter the room. They will be our new minders for the evening. I recognise one of them – he was in uniform earlier and was part of our escort around the city.

A sumptuous meal of Central Asian cuisine follows. However, my taste buds are dead and I don't enjoy any of the dishes. I am intrigued by an offering of local red wine from the Gobi desert, which proves to be a revelation. We expect with trepidation that horsemeat will be served at some point but it never arrives. I don't have the energy to chew the tough mutton chunks on skewers, something I've never refused in the past. There is, however, Ququ, delicate mutton-filled dumplings, an Uighur specialty, which is my favourite.

After the main meal, the Maotai flows freely around the table and loosens the tongues of our Uighur minders. We are treated to untranslatable local jokes, with D and our Uighur translator struggling to convey the meaning.

Towards the end of the meal, our lieutenant colonel turns up. He's very keen on the Maotai and after a few drinks he says he is very sorry that things have turned out the way they did; we should come another time as tourists to enjoy Kashgar hospitality. When he gets his pension, he says, his ambition is to visit London.

We have a toast to good friendship. And another one to China! And another one to Britain… Simpson keeps repeating that we are not here to make trouble for them because they are only doing their job and could we, please, take pictures of ourselves with them – we wouldn't publish them. But despite the drink, they refuse.

When the bottle is empty, the lieutenant colonel offers to pay for the meal but I refuse. We can't accept hospitality from the Chinese police while investigating a sensitive story. I pay the bill.

Mr Zhu, by that time visibly drunk, decides to take us on a midnight walk in the deserted streets of Kashgar to demonstrate how safe his city is. It's now revealed that he is the local police chief. That's a big honour for us. We also find out from him that he knows the father of our Uighur translator from Urumqi who, as we already know, is also a high-ranking commander. I feel that there's something wrong with all these connections. That makes me uneasy but that's a discussion for tomorrow when we start editing our television piece in Beijing.

We stop at a Pakistani-owned restaurant and the owner greets us warmly. He knows who Simpson is and is very proud that we stop in front of his restaurant. Next door there is an off-licence, which is still open. Mr Zhu is very keen to point out that this means that there is no hard-line Muslim influence in Kashgar.

There is, however, something absurd about our midnight walk in this ancient city, escorted by one of the most feared police forces in the world, talking about friendship. Only a few years ago we would have been booted unceremoniously out of Kashgar. The leadership today has showed a degree of flexibility. It adapted the rules by letting us in. The Chinese leaders know very well that in the modern world of global communications you cannot stem the tide of information. After all, what sparked the July riots was a relatively minor incident a month earlier some 2,000 miles away, in the southern province of Guangdong. A brawl in a toy factory between ethnic Uighur and Han Chinese workers ended up with two Uighur workers dead. The Uighur community, which sees itself as an aggrieved Muslim minority, demanded justice. Details of the incident spread as wild fire through instant messages. And the pent up anger boiled over into extreme violence.

Despite our friendly banter with the Chinese police, in the balmy midnight air of the Central Asian desert, I sense that something ominous is unfolding around us. Down the road among the run-down mud-brick houses of the old city destined for destruction, young blood is boiling into an explosive mixture of anger and dissatisfaction. It is only waiting for another spark.

On the following morning Tommy and Mr Zhu meet us in the hotel lobby. They are both wearing dark suits and ties, rather funereal, I think. Tommy looks smaller in his big jacket, and rather awkward. They say they'll escort us to the airport. I understand from Joe that our rooms had been under observation all night. He couldn't sleep and got up early for a walk around the block but the policeman stationed on our floor didn't let him go out.

At the airport, Tommy hugs me as an old friend. I've known him for less than 24 hours but I've become very fond of him. Mr Zhu shakes my hand. I make a point by shaking hands with the two Uighur plainclothes policemen who also accompany us. Mr Zhu has accomplished his job admirably. He can report to his superiors in Beijing that he has successfully prevented Simpson and his team from filming in Kashgar. He may even get a promotion as a result of that.

We, on the other hand, gathered enough material to do an interesting piece for the Ten O'Clock News. The piece included our undercover filming at the police station at Kashgar airport. Mr Zhu's face was not shown. Tommy was not even mentioned in the film.

After our return to London, news reached us that a Chinese court had sentenced 12 Uighur youths to death for their part in the July violence. I never heard from Tommy again.

FALLUJAH, IRAQ, MARCH 2010

We've just passed the notorious Abu Ghraib prison, driving westbound on the motorway, which eventually takes you to the Jordanian border. A huge green sign 'Fallujah' looms above us. My heart sinks with apprehension. Even now, seven years after the war, driving in Iraq is an unpredictable experience. A few months of negotiating, fixing and cajoling has finally paid off and our battered inconspicuous Toyota Landcruiser sails smoothly towards one of the most dangerous places on earth, the hard-line Sunni stronghold of Fallujah. Al-Qaida had its base here after the US invasion and the feared Abu Musab al-Zarqawi was rumoured to have had a safe house here. Zarqawi was the mastermind behind the murder of hundreds of people, including the bombing of the UN headquarters at the Canal Hotel in Baghdad in the summer of 2003, in which the UN special envoy Sergio Vieira de Mello was killed. The CIA accused him of personally beheading two US hostages, Nick Berg and Eugene Armstrong, whose executions were recorded on video and posted on the internet.

But that's not what's bothering me. Zarqawi has been dead for nearly four years and Al-Qaida in Iraq today, 2nd March 2010, seems emasculated. However, suicide bombers still strike in the morning traffic. Statistically, the suicide attacks happen between dawn and 11 am but we have to be in Fallujah by 11 if we want to have at least half a day of productive filming. Simpson and I are returning to Fallujah after two years. The last time we were 'embedded' for a couple of days with the US troops based here. Now we are 'freewheeling', i.e. we do not have any military escort or protection. Our only security personnel are two lightly armed civilian British ex-special forces men employed by the BBC. But I have put my trust in our fixer, a former engineer, who has worked tirelessly in the last few months to get us here with the permission of the governor of Fallujah. For understandable reasons I'll refer to our fixer as S. He has had death threats and had to move house after his neighbours found out that he works for the BBC. He comes from an old illustrious Baghdadi family. Needless to say, he is a Sunni.

What bothers me is the thought that any foreigner is a potential target, even those like us, who are now doing a story about the cruel legacy of the war for the Sunni part of the population. I am about to make an admission on this page, which I haven't shared with anyone before, even with those closest to me. Ever since the death of an acquaintance in April 2005 on the infamous Baghdad airport road, I have butterflies in my stomach every time I set off on a road journey in Iraq. Marla Ruzicka was a young American woman who I first came across in Kabul in 2002, and subsequently saw a few times in Baghdad after the invasion of 2003. We weren't friends but I was smitten by her young age, vivacious character, inexhaustible energy and her great sense of adventure. She was an aid worker and an activist. In Iraq, she created a charity, CIVIC (Campaign for Innocent Victims in Conflict) and was often a guest at the BBC house. One afternoon, in the middle of April 2005, she and her driver were travelling towards Baghdad airport when a suicide bomber struck. Her vehicle wasn't the target. The aim was a passing convoy of security contractors. Marla's car was caught up in the blast and burst into flames. She was conscious while she was burning to death. Eyewitnesses said they heard her voice, 'I am alive. Please help me…'

It's not the fear of death that makes me nervous. I have often thought of that during my assignments in places like Iraq and Afghanistan. I know that getting killed has been a possibility. But the words: 'I am alive. Please help me…' relayed to the inquest by an American army paramedic at the scene had a very disturbing effect on me. I still haven't been able to dislodge them from my brain. I don't want to die like that.

I keep these morbid thoughts to myself. Once we are out of the Baghdad traffic, the drive to Fallujah doesn't take very long. The distance is only 45 miles from the centre of Baghdad. I'll deliberately avoid explaining here how we get on the Abu Ghraib Expressway to Fallujah because the BBC still has an office in Baghdad and it's not appropriate to divulge the routes to and from the BBC house. We vary the routes several times a day just in case the exit points are being monitored.

Before the entrance of the city, there is a big roundabout fortified with concrete blast walls. The traffic grinds to a halt because all vehicles are being checked. S gets out of the vehicle and shows the commanding officer at the checkpoint a piece of paper. This is our invitation to visit Fallujah to investigate a story about genetic damage in the city's children born after the suppression of the insurgency here at the end of 2004, the so-called Second Battle of Fallujah. The commander reads it carefully. This takes a long time. Then he hands it back to S, smiles broadly at us and waves the vehicle through. 'Welcome to Fallujah,' he says as the Toyota drives past him.

Fallujah straddles the Euphrates in one of the most fertile valleys of Mesopotamia. There's been a conurbation here since the time of Babylon. During the Ottoman Empire, the town was a minor stop on the main road from Baghdad to Damascus and the Mediterranean. One of the most enigmatic British spies of the early 20th century, Lieutenant Colonel Gerard Leachman, was murdered here in 1920, after the British took control of this part of the Ottoman Empire under the British Mandate of Mesopotamia. Working for military intelligence, Gerard Leachman travelled extensively in Arabia and Mesopotamia under the pretence that he was a naturalist from the Royal Geographical Society. His language skills and dark looks often helped him disguise himself as a Bedouin. Most of the time he travelled alone. In the summer of 1920, he went to Fallujah to mediate with the sheikh of a rebellious local tribe but was shot in the back by the sheikh's son in a minor dispute over a robbery. Leachman was played by Oliver Reed in a little-known film financed by Saddam Hussein in 1983, *Clash of Loyalties* (Al-Mas'ala Al-Kubra).

The Iraqi Hashemite dynasty created by the British after the First World War drew fervent support from the unruly Sunni tribes around Fallujah. Saddam Hussein, after assuming supreme power in 1979, gave lucrative employment to many loyal Sunni from Fallujah. Some of the leading members of the Ba'ath Party came from Fallujah. That privileged position was shattered after the US invasion in 2003, which led to the establishment of a majority Shi'a government. Fallujah became part of the so-called Sunni triangle, a densely populated area north-west of Baghdad defined by three points: Baghdad, Ramadi (the capital of Anbar province) and Tikrit (Saddam's birth place). The area became the stronghold of resistance to the US occupation and to the Shi'a led government in Baghdad.

I first went to Fallujah in the autumn of 2003, a few months after the invasion. The residents were still shell-shocked by their loss of power. The organised insurgency, an amalgam of former Saddam military forces, Ba'ath Party activists and Al-Qaida operatives, was just beginning to gather pace. No sooner had we come out of the car in the main shopping street than a hostile crowd gathered around us. We were wearing body armour, which obviously annoyed them. I still remember the angry faces, the dirty robes (dishdasha) and the pungent smell of sweat. A young man in a cream dishdasha and eyes seething with anger looked at us and unashamedly made a gesture with his hand as if cutting his throat. This was what he was going to do to us.

I was there as producer for Caroline H, a competent BBC reporter and fluent Arabic speaker, to do a story on a new confidence-building approach by the Americans in this part of the Sunni heartland. The Americans had come to realise that even Saddam Hussein could not subdue the local tribes – he had to buy them off. I had been told that in some instances he even handed over cash to the heads of the big clans. The US Central Command had brought in an Arabic-speaking anthropologist as a liaison officer with the tribes. The strategy was simple – get the tribal leaders on your side and you in effect would control Fallujah. I had arranged an interview with the commanding officer. He had promised to let us film during his meeting with the tribal leaders. The fact that they had agreed to see him for a second week running was a success in itself. I also hoped that I might persuade him to let us go out on patrol with one of his Sci Ops guys, a psychologist, whose job was to talk to the local population and try to combat the so-called 'cultural misunderstandings'. And there was a lot of that right across Iraq – from hand gestures and tone of voice to the ludicrous idea that American binoculars or even sunshades could see though their clothes.

Still euphoric with the success of the invasion, the Americans were ridiculously underprepared for the aftermath. Here in Fallujah, in the autumn of 2003, I listened to a young bespectacled lieutenant who was telling us how he dealt with local grievances. He ushered us into a room where a Tajik looking man was given a licence for a gun repair shop.

'You see,' the lieutenant said, 'we don't want to damage the local economy. We even license gun shops providing they keep only four guns on the premises and no ammunition.'

I couldn't believe my ears. This was out of touch with reality. The Americans at that stage still hadn't realised that the civil war had already started. But I wanted to meet the Arabic-speaking anthropologist. And there he was, standing at the other end of the corridor. Captain Smith, I wasn't sure if that was his real name, was tall, blond, with fair, almost transparent, skin. There was something very intense about his face. He looked as if he was in pain. The uniform did not suit him – his pale complexion, slightly stooped posture and intelligent blue eyes made him stand out. He looked unhealthily skinny among his soldier colleagues. I quickly introduced myself to him. He had studied Arabic in Alexandria, Egypt, he said. I wanted to ask him a lot of personal questions. Why did he choose Arabic? Where did he come from? What did he want to achieve here? But there was no time. We were ushered into a room where a big table was laid out with fantastic Arabic food. The local dignitaries dressed in pristine dishdashas and golden embroidered jalabiyas, started eating quickly with steely determination. No one spoke during that stand up ten-minute feast during which they ate with their hands. The total lack of warmth and friendliness in the demeanour of the local sheiks didn't escape the attention of our American hosts.

I knew then that the battle for the hearts and minds was lost. Six months later, on 31st March, 2004, a unique event occurred in Fallujah, which changed the political landscape here. Insurgents ambushed a convoy of US private military contractors from a company called Blackwater, setting two of their vehicles on fire. What followed next was a defining moment in the American involvement in Iraq. Local residents, overwhelmed with joyous revenge, removed the bodies of the four contractors from the burning vehicles and in scenes reminiscent of the ill-fated US involvement in Mogadishu in 1993, dragged the charred corpses through the streets, shouting: 'This is our city. What are you doing here?' Two of the bodies were then hanged upside down from the overhead girders of the old bridge on the Euphrates. Pictures taken from this gruesome event were released to news agencies and within hours were shown on billions of TV screens around the world.

But something even more disconcerting emerged later in a US Congressional investigation. Soldiers from the Iraqi Civil Defence Corps, created by the Coalition Provisional Authority in September 2003, led the Blackwater convoy into the ambush, blocked their escape routes and then disappeared. The Corps, made up of local recruits who lived in their communities, was described by the Americans upon its creation as the force that 'can do things we can't'. Its existence was short-lived.

We have an appointment at the new hospital in Fallujah. It's situated on the right when you take the main road after entering the city through its eastern checkpoint, not very far from the fortified roundabout. It's known locally as the Private Hospital. It has been built with American money. It's brand new and smells clean. We have all the necessary paperwork allowing us to film here but a policeman stops us in the lobby and says, 'No filming! Filming not allowed here!'

It's a familiar story. S takes the document issued by the governor and a long drawn out process of reading starts. At the end of it, he folds it and hands it back to S. But we are still not allowed to film. He gets his mobile phone out and calls his boss. It's puzzling why in Iraq something that you can say in one sentence always takes a long-winded explanation, which sometimes goes on forever.

The policeman delivers a two-minute monologue on the phone. Then he listens for another two minutes. I am getting impatient and look anxiously at S. He gives me a reassuring sign that all will be fine. A few more minutes of pleasantries on the phone and we are allowed to climb the stairs to the children's ward. A male orderly is attached to us to show us around.

The children's ward is impressive – the rooms are spacious and well lit. The incubators – brand new. The floor is spotless and shiny. Mothers in black hijabs sit on chairs calmly watching their babies in the incubators. There's no fuss, no cries. Some of the babies are connected to respirators. We are allowed to film freely the sickly infants with their mothers' consent. Simpson and I watch with interest through the door but stay in the corridor so that we don't seem too prurient.

'What are we looking for?' I say.

Simpson shakes his head. I ask the orderly to find a doctor so that we can speak to somebody in authority. He disappears. I then send S to look for him. Both Simpson and I know that it will be difficult to find someone to challenge the official version of the Shi'a government in Baghdad that there is nothing unusual in Fallujah: congenital defects are only slightly above the national average.

Eventually, S comes back with the orderly. The news is not good. The doctor doesn't want to speak to a TV crew. This is more than just disappointing. It's disastrous. Without an interview at the hospital our piece will be worthless. It's unthinkable. 'Let's just hang around here,' I tell the cameraman, 'and keep close to Simpson. We must try to doorstep the doctor when we see her.'

I have already mentioned Simpson's doorstep with Fidel Castro, but here's the time to relay another of his memorable anecdotes, this one from his days as a young political reporter in London. Apparently, Harold Wilson once punched him in the stomach for asking an impromptu question he was not supposed to ask.

S uses his initiative and having asked the orderly some questions tells us that the doctor is due to visit the ward shortly. She is supposed to come from the other end of the corridor. We rush there and position ourselves strategically by the door. The camera is running and the microphone is switched on. A few minutes later she appears from the lift and rushes purposefully towards the door. She knows who we are but doesn't look as if she wants to talk to us. We follow her. She wears a white headscarf and has a big mole on her right cheek, on the same level as the tip of the nose. A white stethoscope clings around her neck. She is already in the doorframe when she turns back towards Simpson. He smiles and asks if she speaks English. She smiles and says she does 'a little bit'. In fact her English is fluent. Her body language says that she wants to talk to us.

'How many cases of birth defects do you see on the ward?' Simpson asks.

She is nervous and looks around.

'One or two per week?' Simpson perseveres.

'No, no, no, two or three cases per day,' she says and lowers her eyes towards the floor. 'Mainly cardiac defects.'

'What is it that happened in Fallujah that means that these defects exist in such numbers?' he fires the killer question.

She smiles almost imperceptibly, closes her eyes and takes a deep breath. That gives her time to think. 'I am a doctor,' she says, 'I have to be scientific in my talk. I have no proof and nothing documented… but I can tell you that year by year, the number is increasing.'

She doesn't want to talk any more but gives us her name, Dr Samira al-Ani. Her name eventually became very well known among scientists and journalists who continued to research the story. She also became more and more outspoken, giving details about not only congenital heart defects but also about babies with one eye, two heads, skeletal disorders, and so on.

Our next stop is a clinic for disabled children. When we leave the hospital I am tempted to walk. For the first time since the invasion we are not required to wear body armour in Fallujah. But I get a nasty look from our bodyguards so I get in the car.

Before leaving Baghdad I spoke with an official from the Health Ministry who told me that the high rate of birth defects among Fallujah's children was due to 'inbreeding' among residents. Such is the blind hatred between the two sides in the sectarian divide in Iraq – the majority Shi'a who had been suppressed but are now in government, and the minority Sunni who had been the dominant sect since the creation of Iraq in the 1920s but now have lost their privileges. In a nutshell, the Shi'a think the Sunni get everything they deserve.

The clinic is a single-storey building. We are ushered into a room, which is furnished like an average Iraqi living room: cheap sofa and two armchairs upholstered in large patterned prints and covered with fitted transparent plastic sheets. There is a small desk by the window. From there I can see our bodyguard standing by the metal gate, separating the street from the paved garden in front of the clinic. He is looking nervously at the small crowd gathering outside. Suddenly, as if by some invisible prompt, a stream of parents with disabled children starts to file through the gate and fill the small reception room of the clinic. No one is talking to us. We feel like extras on a carefully arranged film set. Our fixer S is trying to find someone who can introduce some order in all that. Then a small man in a yellow-brown suit and checked shirt appears. He's got distinguished white hair and a short grey beard. He is the director of the clinic. In fact this is not a clinic in the strict sense of the word, it's more like a charity distributing funds to parents with disabled children. He has no doubt in his mind about the cause for the rising number of congenital defects in children born in Fallujah after 2004.

'The Americans used some kind of weapons in the battle with insurgents in the city at the end of 2004, which are causing this suffering now,' he says.

This, of course, is unproven. Some will say it's highly improbable. But we are shown pictures documenting severe birth defects. Some of the children on the pictures are no longer alive. There is one particularly disturbing photograph of a baby born with three heads. The director tells us that the official advice to women in Fallujah is not to have children.

I ask Simpson to hold the photographs in his hand so that our cameraman can film close-ups of the photos but I know that most of them will be too disturbing to show on the BBC, especially before the 9 pm watershed.

The children who have been brought in here look the right age. The oldest is not more than four. Most of them are mentally handicapped. Some have congenital spinal defects. I have the feeling that this is carefully orchestrated and that these people are not doing this exercise for the first time. In fact, the medical story of Fallujah and its battle for media space started almost immediately after the end of the military Battle of Fallujah, the most severe urban warfare the Americans had fought since the Vietnam War.

During one of my stints as a BBC Baghdad Bureau Chief in April/May 2005 the BBC was accused by pressure groups of failing to investigate claims that the US had used banned weapons during the so-called Second Battle of Fallujah from 7th November to 23rd December 2004. These reports appeared on the internet, citing allegations from volunteer medical staff who went to Fallujah in the aftermath to treat injured civilians. We at the BBC Bureau, as well as other big media organisations, treated the reports with utmost care. There was no hard evidence although the emotional stakes were stacked against the Americans. The BBC felt obliged to answer its accusers publicly. Reporters who had been embedded with the US Marines during the battle said that the US troops did not use NBC (Nuclear Biological Chemical) protective kit during the assault on Fallujah, which they did during the invasion of 2003 when the predominant opinion was that Saddam Hussein had weapons of mass destruction. I was asked about whether I could send a team to Fallujah in May 2005 to investigate. My reply was that it was too dangerous to travel to the city. Moreover, researching the story during the aftermath of such an event needed forensic investigation and statistical surveys, involving medical staff. That only became possible after the insurgency abated in 2009 and journalists were able to travel to Fallujah independently of the US military. Today we are here in Fallujah because empirical evidence started to emerge about the number of birth defects, which shows it's above average. There's no proof yet about the causes.

There have been accusations of the use of 'unusual' weapons in the assault on Fallujah, which virtually flattened the city, right from the beginning. The argument was reignited a year later when an Italian documentary *Fallujah: The Hidden Massacre* by the state broadcaster RAI accused the US Marines of using white phosphorous as a burning agent. The use of such incendiary weapons against civilian targets is banned by international treaties. The US initially said that white phosphorus was only used for illumination purposes. However, evidence from soldiers who took part in the operation confirmed the use of white phosphorus shells. One account said: 'We fired "shake and bake" missions at the insurgents using white phosphorus to flush them out and high explosive shells to take them out.' The nature of the ferocious urban battle meant that the US soldiers didn't always know who they were hitting with these shells.

Eventually, the US officially admitted that it had used white phosphorus as an incendiary weapon against enemy combatants, a humiliating retraction of its initial denial. After that, more and more anti-American websites started to mention controversially that 'depleted uranium' might have been used, although this has never been proven.

We are going to have an impossible task to do this story, which we knew right from the start would annoy both sides of the argument. The director of the clinic tells us that the worst cases are to be found in Al-Joulan, an area of the city close to the river. My heart leaps. Al-Joulan was the scene of the heaviest fighting six years ago. It was a no-go area even for most Iraqis. Highly trained Islamic fighters from Chechnya, Bosnia, Saudi Arabia and Syria were rumoured to have been based there. I look at Simpson, then at our security adviser and get the nod from both of them. The director is happy to facilitate a visit there immediately. He gives us one of his assistants to accompany us.

We drive slowly along narrow unpaved streets deeper and deeper into the neighbourhood of Al-Joulan. Most of the houses are newly built or re-built with grey breezeblocks, unrendered and unpainted. Al-Joulan was all but demolished in the Second Battle of Fallujah. Most of the rubble was then bulldozed into the river. Residents of Al-Joulan still get their drinking water from there. Sanitation is a problem: dirty water runs freely along the unpaved streets.

The car stops outside a small house. We get out apprehensively. The street is deserted. However, in the following few minutes at first children, then adults start to come out and hang around the gates of their houses. Ostensibly, they are not looking at us. I take a few pictures and they don't object. It's an interesting crowd, mostly men. The older are dressed in light green traditional Arab dress, the dishdasha. Most of the young are in tracksuits or Western trousers and shirts. They look remarkably fit. It reminds me of the time in 2003 when, after the fall of Saddam, Simpson and I drove from northern Iraq to Baghdad. As we approached Baghdad from the north, the main road was closed by a military operation so we detoured through some date plantations. In the small villages we passed on the way, we saw young well-fed men with short hair dressed in tracksuits standing by the gates of their houses giving us an angry look. At the time we were convinced those young men were members of Saddam's armed forces, which melted away with the fall of Baghdad. But who are these people here in Al-Joulan today? I ask S if I can talk to them. He says it's not a good idea.

Through a small courtyard, we are ushered into a house built of grey breezeblocks. We take off our shoes and enter a large room, which is only reserved for guests. There is a green rug in the middle placed over a larger patterned carpet. Three armchairs are lined up against the wall. Next to them there is a small sideboard containing teacups and saucers. Cushions are lined up against the opposite wall so that visitors can sit on the floor. The gauze curtains are drawn to keep the sun out. Three kids are crawling on the floor – two partially paralysed boys and a girl with brain damage. This is what the mother tells us. The girl is dressed in a smart pink skirt and matching pink jumper. Two cute pink hair ribbons are attached to her nicely combed jet-black hair. The boys are in smart black woollen jumpers. It's obvious that they have been expecting us. I wonder if this is another part of our pre-arranged guided tour of Fallujah. The grandmother is here, too, but she stays in the background and doesn't intervene. Both women are well dressed, with painted eyebrows and their hair is covered by patterned hijabs. The grandmother wears a black abaya, the traditional Arabic dress for women, and her light-coloured hijab is covered by a black headscarf. The mother speaks on camera and blames the Americans.

Our cameraman films the kids who are intrigued by the camera but I have the feeling that it's not the first time the family has seen a camera crew in their house. Outside, we are virtually ambushed by a man in Western clothes who's brought his disabled daughter. The girl, four, nicely dressed in a red knitted jumper, has six fingers on each hand and six toes on each foot. Her nails are painted red. She has a pearl bracelet on each wrist and golden earrings. The father shows us some paperwork in a plastic folder documenting his child's condition. Again, he blames the Americans and tells us that he wants compensation.

I have a quick conversation with Simpson about the material that we've got so far. We both agree that the material so far is good but our interview at the hospital is what will make the piece. Without that doorstep we wouldn't have a piece. The last stop of our journey is the old bridge, or the 'Blackwater' bridge, as it's known here. The idea is to get a few shots of the river, from where most residents still get their drinking water, which could be a possible cause of the birth defects.

The old bridge is on the far western side of Fallujah. When you cross the bridge, the road takes you to Ramadi, the regional capital of the Anbar province, another nasty place of Sunni fundamentalism. The city sprawls on the eastern banks of the river. I do remember the entrance of the bridge from two years ago when Simpson and I made our first trip to Fallujah together. Then we were escorted through the city by a group of heavily armed American soldiers, led by a Captain who had survived an IED (Improvised Explosive Device) attack a year earlier. He nearly lost his eyesight but recovered so well that he volunteered for a second tour of duty. We wore body armour and our wrists were marked with indelible ink so that we could be identified if we got injured or killed in an attack. The number written on our wrists contained information about our names and blood group.

No such thing today. We roam freely at the entrance of the bridge and take photographs. I remember the building opposite the bridge. Its concrete roof collapsed as a result of heavy bombardment. It had taken a direct hit in 2004 and rubble still hasn't been cleared. The atmosphere is less hostile but I'm not sure how much of this is due to the fact that we are doing a story about how badly the residents have fared. Word travels very fast in this city and most people already know why we are here. However, S advises us not to stray too far down the main road towards the mosque by the market. We take pictures of ourselves in front of the bridge. There is a photographic poster attached at the entrance showing King Faisal I, the first king of Iraq installed by the British, inaugurating the single lane bridge in 1928.

After about forty minutes gathering material around the bridge, we are ready to head back to Baghdad. We get into our vehicle, all in one piece and in a very good mood. As we leave the outskirts of the city, I turn back for one last look, in an effort to memorise a mental snapshot of this unruly place because I don't know if I shall ever come back here again. I suddenly feel tired.

However, a more exhausting and tortuous battle started only after our piece had been broadcast on the BBC the following day.

It's often said in our industry that on any assignment the cameraman gets the money, the reporter gets the fame and the producer gets the blame. Our piece is a success. It leads all the news bulletins on both radio and television. We congratulate ourselves on a successful high-impact story. However, for me this is short-lived. The following day I receive an email from an assistant of the BBC's Head of News who forwards the following email and asks me to comment on it so that the BBC can reply officially. Although the email is unclassified, I have censored the names:

Sent: 05 March 2010 16:33
Subject: Fallujah
Hi H
I was surprised to see this story, with the link below, leading on all BBC platforms yesterday. The way the story was promoted, it gave the strongest possible impression that the US was the reason for an increase in birth defects in Fallujah. But the story was thinly sourced and seemed to be driven more by images than facts or research. My office facilitates hundreds of interviews, embeds, visas and meetings for BBC journalists every year, because you are a quality operation. This story, however, was nowhere near BBC standards.
Regards,
Z
Public Affairs Officer
American Embassy London

I look back at what was written in the last 24 hours. The BBC website headlined the story as follows:

A BBC investigation in Iraq has confirmed a disturbingly high number of birth defects among children in the town of Fallujah. Six years ago, in 2004, there were fierce battles as US forces subdued two uprisings in the town.

I spend all day drafting my response. For the sake of clarity, I have cut it down:

DRAFT LETTER TO THE US EMBASSY, London

Dear Z,

Thanks for your email and I am sorry that you felt that our story from Fallujah fell short of our high standards.

The BBC has been aware of this story since 2005 when the first allegations surfaced through a Dubai-based human rights organisation. During 2005/2006 some Western pressure groups criticised the BBC for ignoring the story. At the time we explained that it was too dangerous for any Western team to reach the area. We had to rely on second-hand reports and then try to verify them from afar, which was not at all satisfactory.

It is common knowledge in Iraq that Fallujah has a high number of birth defects, although the Iraqi government says that this is due to inbreeding and taking medication during pregnancies.

We sought an official US response to the allegations of a link between the birth defects in Fallujah and the weapons of war used there, and received this statement:

We are not aware of any official reports indicating an increase in birth defects in Fallujah. We always take very seriously public health concerns about any population now living in a combat theater. No studies to date have indicated environmental issues resulting in specific health issues. Unexploded ordinance, including improvised explosive devises, are a recognised hazard.

Indeed, this is precisely the point that our World Affairs Editor, John Simpson, made throughout the material, which we produced for radio, TV and online. Here is an extract from his script:

Their mother blames the Americans. Until there's a proper independent investigation we won't know if she's right. But what's certain is that thousands of children in this place have been terribly cruelly damaged.

Our material was based on an interview with a specialist at the children's ward who said she saw two-three cases a day. Our team visited a charity where we saw for ourselves disabled children born since the fighting in 2004. On the basis of what we saw we thought it was fully justified to raise awareness of the problem. Throughout the reportage John Simpson made it absolutely clear what the sources of our information were. In addition to that, BBC programmes in London interviewed separately Professor Alastair Hay, environmental toxicologist from Leeds University, who took great care to explain that the cause of the birth defects in Fallujah was still unknown…

In summary, I believe this was a legitimate story to cover. The way it was scripted and presented, and the additional expert observations from Professor Hay enabled our audiences to make up their own minds.

Professor Hay made it clear in his interviews for BBC outlets that the most effective way to clarify the issues raised in our film would be an independent scientific investigation. If that happens, please be assured that BBC News will report the findings.

I hope that I have addressed your concern.

By the time I finish, the sun has gone down and a dark blanket of dry warm air is covering Baghdad. We sit on the veranda of the house overlooking a small garden. The generator is humming at the far end. This means there is no mains power. Seven years after the invasion, the infrastructure is still inadequate.

Simpson is smoking a cigar, leaning back on the plastic chair. He looks at me inquisitively.

I say, 'If we have managed to piss off both sides, we must have done a good job. First, we stand accused by some of ignoring the story, now we've been hammered for overcooking it.'

He smiles but doesn't want to talk about work. What is it going to be tonight? Ah, the Coen Brothers. He's been watching their films on a hard drive he carries with him on our journeys. I don't want to take part in the conversation. I like *No Country for Old Men* but Simpson has reservations about it. He loves *Fargo*.

I sit silently and look at the new banisters of the veranda. On advice from the BBC health and safety people, the old ones have been replaced. I wonder where they've gone. They had hexagram patterns, the Star of David, because the house was originally built as a Jewish school. I look with admiration at the original floor tiles on the veranda. This house has seen a lot of upheavals since it was built. At the end of the First World War, 40 per cent of the population of Baghdad was Jewish. It was a prosperous community, which built nice houses, especially in what was then the lush suburb of Karada and along the banks of the Tigris. By the beginning of the 1970s, most Jews had already gone and their houses handed over to friends of the Ba'ath Party regime without any deeds. The Jews of Baghdad survived the pogrom of June 1941 when violent mobs went on the rampage with knives and guns. This happened in the power vacuum after the collapse of the short-lived pro-Nazi government of Rashid Ali. Controversially, British cavalry was only eight miles from Baghdad but failed to intervene to stop the violence. Nearly 200 Jews were killed and there was widespread looting of Jewish property. It spelt the end of a Jewish community, which dated back to Babylon. In 1969, when Saddam Hussein was deputy prime minister 14 people were hanged, 11 of whom were Jews, on charges of spying for Israel. Crowds were forced to parade and dance past the scaffolds. In response to international pressure, in the early 70s, Saddam, by then the Iraqi leader, quietly allowed the remaining Jews to emigrate, leaving their property behind without any compensation.

I wonder if any of the children who attended this Jewish school once upon a time are still alive. The palm tree in the garden gently moves in the warm breeze from the Tigris. I stay on the veranda until very late into the night discussing quantum physics and the theory of probability with a colleague.

Five months later. I am standing in the courtyard of Television Centre in London. It's known as the 'horse-shoe' because of its shape. We've set up the camera to interview a man called Chris Busby, who's one of the authors of a report based on a study carried out in Fallujah at the beginning of the year. In fact it was carried out just a month before we visited the city in March. The report's press release is headline grabbing: 'Genetic damage and health in Fallujah worse than Hiroshima.' The project was organised by Malak Hamdan, an Iraqi woman with a degree in chemical engineering who now lives in London. She has been campaigning on behalf of the citizens of Fallujah and has kept Simpson informed about the progress of the study.

I had trouble selling the story to the Ten O'Clock News. There's general mistrust of stories based on such studies. We checked the credentials of Chris Busby and he seemed fine. But I must admit I didn't know how to interpret the methodology of the survey and couldn't make a judgement on the reliability of the findings. There's also the added problem of how to deal with the Americans after we broadcast the story. I'd sent the report to the Pentagon with a request for comment but there'd been no response despite my numerous naggings on the phone. Luckily, yesterday I received a detailed critique of the report from Alastair Hay, the environmental toxicologist and a regular commentator on the BBC. He pointed out that the survey involved a great degree of risk, which did not diminish its value – quite the reverse. His main concern was the methodology. Residents of Fallujah were asked to fill in questionnaires. In some areas, the authors abandoned questioning because of hostility to the team. Iraqi state television had warned people not to take part in the survey because 'it was carried out by terrorists'.

He also said that not even a sample of medical data from the questionnaires was checked against medical records. It was hardly an overwhelming endorsement but not an outright dismissal either.

But we knew that the survey had been done in good faith and as honestly as possible despite its limitations. We were satisfied with the credentials of the people who organised it. Given the difficulties of carrying out such a study in Fallujah and based on what we saw with our own eyes, Simpson and I decided to go ahead with the story. We simply couldn't ignore it.

Today, in the 'horse-shoe' both of us are a bit subdued. We've just come back from Peshawar where we had a wretched time. He had a terrible bout of diarrhoea. I had a suspected case of flesh-eating disease, leishmaniasis, caused by some rare parasites. Dr Chris Busby is on time. He calls from main reception and we go to sign him in. We walk down a long corridor to reach the 'horse-shoe'. His appearance is a bit unusual. I knew that he was based in France but was a bit surprised to see him wearing a black French beret. Anyway, this is a good look for television.

The interview is short. We know what we want. He makes the comparison with the aftermath of Hiroshima. 'Far fewer boys were born in Fallujah after 2005 than girls,' he says. 'This is a well-known expression of genetic damage, which was found after Hiroshima. And the interesting thing also is that the spectrum of illnesses was very similar to the Hiroshima, but much, much worse.'

Our new piece contains a lot of footage from our visit to Fallujah. The only new things are the interview with Chris Busby and a computer-generated graphic outlining the main findings of the report:

Child mortality in Fallujah – 80 per 1000
By contrast, in neighbouring Jordan – 17 per 1000, in Egypt – 20 per 1000
12-fold increase in childhood cancers since 2004
Ratio boys to girls has changed dramatically, from an average of 1000 boys to 1000 girls, to only 860 boys per 1000 girls

I suggest Simpson does the piece-to-camera in an edit suite where we show pictures from our trip to the hospital in Fallujah on the screens behind him. This is the segment in which he has to explain the shortcomings of the survey due to the inherent dangers of working in Fallujah plus a bit of context about why the predominantly Shi'a government in Baghdad is not interested in the welfare of the Sunni population of Fallujah.

I understand the sensitivity of our piece. But I wasn't prepared for the first reaction I got from the Ten O'Clock News. There's new editorial management there and the new editor doesn't trust us implicitly like the previous one. They say that the piece will not run tonight unless we get a response from the Pentagon. This is an impossibly high bar. I tell them that the Americans have no incentive to respond quickly. And when they do, it will be the usual denial on the basis that there hasn't been any reliable study.

After a lot of discussions about the reliability of the report, reading and re-reading of Professor Hay's response, and general arguments about why we should be doing the story, I am told that that we have to wait for the American response for another 24 hours. At this point I realise I have to widen the circle of people involved in this story. I call the BBC Washington Bureau with a request to chase the Pentagon. I talk to my own department, Newsgathering, to explain the reluctance to run the story. The campaigning eventually pays off. More and more people are now saying that because the BBC has already been to Fallujah and we have first-hand evidence of birth defects it will look very bad if we don't run the new story. No one questions the credentials of the people who organised and carried out the research.

The following afternoon I approach the Ten O'Clock News desk armed with the paperwork on the story. The people editing the programme have already seen our piece. I think that it's a done deal. I am prepared for minor arguments about the script but I am shocked by what I hear.

'If your story is so good, if this survey is so important, why has no one else picked it up in the last 48 hours?'

I look at the person who's made this statement with disbelief.

'Do you think that Simpson and I would have wasted our time and effort if we didn't think the story was worth doing? The underlying story has been in the public domain for a long time. It has been done by most of the British broadsheets and some of our television competitors. The current survey is just a further development…'

I am not allowed to finish.

'If you say it's an important development, why hasn't anyone done it again? They've seen the study, haven't they?' she says.

I raise my voice in desperation. 'If you don't trust us and you think that the BBC should wait for the *Independent* or the *Guardian*, or Sky News to do the story before we do it, what's the point of employing Simpson and me to work here? It doesn't make sense. I repeat, we stand by our story.'

Everybody on the desk is looking at me. I apologise for raising my voice, put my papers into the folder and walk away without waiting for a decision.

When I call Simpson a few minutes later to tell him about the conversation, he says not to pursue it any further.

'They will run it eventually,' he says.

The story went out on the Ten O'Clock News that same evening without any response from the Americans and without any cuts or edits. I avoided the Ten desk for the following two days. On the third, the *Independent* published an article with the headline: 'Toxic legacy of US assault on Fallujah "worse than Hiroshima".' I note that 'worse than Hiroshima' is in inverted comas. It was a quote from the report.

By the end of the year, the same team, this time including Dr Samira al-Ani, produced another report, which was picked up by the *Guardian*. Later studies started to link the birth defects in Fallujah to the military action there. Scientists studied hair samples of the population in Fallujah and found that levels of lead were five times higher in the hair of children with birth defects than in other children and they linked this to increased exposure to metals released by bombs and bullets.

Eventually, the World Health Organisation (WHO) commissioned an inquiry into the occurrence of birth defects in Fallujah. It may never be possible to prove with scientific certainty that weapons used in the assault on Fallujah were responsible for the increased number of birth defects. It may never be possible for the people of Fallujah to get any redress.

I made one more trip to Iraq for the BBC. During that assignment Simpson made a factual error in one of his reports and I failed to spot it. The piece was broadcast with the error. Editors and producers in London only found out about it on the following day after a viewer called to point it out. That caused a lot of embarrassment for us. There were sniggers behind our backs. It put pressure on our partnership. But during that trip I was able to visit an area of Baghdad I had never been able to visit before, Mustansiriya, in north-east Baghdad, close to the Ministry of Finance. It was the site of Mustansiriya University, one of the oldest universities in the world dating back to the early 13th century. It bears the name of the 36th Abbasid Caliph, al-Mustansir, who established it. The university was spared when the grandson of Genghis Khan sacked Baghdad in 1258. In the civil war after 2003, it became the focus of grotesque sectarian violence. It was even closed temporarily in 2009 following a spate of murders, torture and rape by a shadowy student group. However, in the summer of 2010 we walked in the courtyard of the restored building of the original Mustansirya Madrasah. And this is my last memory of Baghdad.

PESHAWAR, PAKISTAN,
JUNE 2010

The heat is unbearable. It's the end of June and Peshawar struggles to breathe under a giant lid of dry hot air. There's hardly anyone in the streets in the midday sun. The door of the van slides open and a smiley face peers inside. The man is dressed in a police uniform. An automatic rifle hangs on his shoulder. This is the first checkpoint in our approach to the provincial police headquarters. The police chief is expecting us for an interview. Sending a message about our arrival to the heavily fortified police compound takes time, so I get out of the van. I am still confused about the geography of the city because the minibus that we've been given has curtains in the back and they are always closed for security reasons when we are on the move. Peshawar is a dangerous place for Westerners.

Simpson is not with us this time. I'll be doing the interview because he is back at the hotel with a terrible bout of food poisoning. We've eaten the same food and drunk the same drinks since our arrival here. But yesterday at Jalozai refugee camp for Afghans displaced by the fighting in their country since the Soviet invasion, he couldn't refuse a glass of tap water offered at a meeting with the military commander. It's customary here to welcome visitors with a glass of cold water. I declined despite the feeling that it would be considered impolite. Anyway, this is my suspicion for Simpson's stomach trouble.

Our cameraman, Nasir, a Pakistani man from Islamabad, is talking to me from inside the van. I am half listening to him when I hear a soft whistling noise followed instantly by a dull thud at the base of the concrete block by my left foot. From the brick wall to my right comes the sound of a gentle peck. I look down at the chip off the roadblock then to the brick wall and gradually realise the gravity of what's happened – a bullet fired from the guards' hut on the road behind us has ricocheted from the reinforced concrete slab and has come to rest in the brick wall opposite. I see a few uniformed guys scuttling around the hut.

'Get into the car straight away,' Nasir says.

My feet feel heavy, as if my boots are filled with lead. I am a bit disoriented but get into the van. The barrier in front of us lifts and we are being hurriedly waved through. The driver zigzags carefully between the concrete blocks towards the next checkpoint. There's deadly silence in the car.

Eventually, we enter the compound through big metal gates. We are ushered into a waiting room. Pale tea in small glasses miraculously appears carried in a tray by a small man in tribal dress.

'It was an accidental discharge,' our translator Arshad finally says.

He is a young man with receding hair. A long jet-black beard surrounds his friendly face. He has studied in Portsmouth and his English is perfect.

I'm trying to block the thought from my mind and concentrate instead on the questions I'm planning to ask the police chief.

'Don't worry. Let's not talk about it now,' I say.

'But you must tell the police chief,' Arshad insists.

'As you said, it's an accident. Why bother?' I shrug my shoulders.

A tall thin man dressed in a white shalwar kameez, the traditional Pakistani dress, enters the room. Arshad stands up and greets him warmly, from which I infer that this is someone important. He introduces himself to me as the head of media relations for the provincial police chief.

The province used to be called the North-West Frontier Province but a constitutional amendment pushed through parliament in Islamabad just a couple of months ago changed its name to Pukhtunkhwa (The Land of the Pukhtun or the Pashtun). The old name was considered a British colonial anachronism, dating back to the British Raj. Pashtuns are the largest ethnic group in the province, although almost all speak Urdu as a second language. Peshawar is the provincial capital. The geographic proximity to Afghanistan with its dominant Pashtun population, from which the Taliban draws its traditional support, has made the province a battleground in the so-called War on Terror since 2001. Strictly speaking, the province does not share a border with Afghanistan. There is a thin slither of territory called FATA (Federally Administered Tribal Areas), a series of semi-autonomous territories called 'agencies', almost homogenously Pashtun, directly administered by Islamabad, which lie between the Pukhtunkhwa province, also known as the Khyber Pukhtunkhwa, and the Afghan border. These 'agencies' are ruled by a system of village elders and tribal chiefs, although at the top of each one there is a Political Agent, directly responsible to the president and the appointed governor of the Khyber Pukhtunkhwa province. The Khyber Agency holds the most strategic geopolitical entity in the region, the Khyber Pass, part of the ancient Silk Road. I have been on the Afghan side of the Khyber Pass at the border crossing of Torkham but my hopes of approaching it from this end have already been dashed. On this trip, neither Simpson nor I will be allowed beyond the western gates of Peshawar. The official line is that it's for our own safety. We might be able to get permission to send our Pakistani cameraman to get some pictures.

Last year was a turbulent year for Pakistan. On 3rd February 2009, the Taliban blew up a bridge on the Khyber Pass cutting off the main supply route for NATO troops in landlocked Afghanistan. The Taliban were in the ascendance in the tribal area of South Waziristan and in the Swat Valley. The Swat Valley was once famous for its ski resort and breathtaking mountain views. However, for obvious reasons the vibrant tourist industry had fallen on hard times. In the last few years, the Taliban have taken virtual control of the valley. The central government in Islamabad had even allowed Sharia law to be imposed in the area in an effort to pacify the bitter Islamic insurgency. Violent attacks shook major Pakistani cities, most notable of which was the strike on the Police Academy in Lahore, where militants stormed the compound, took police cadets hostage and barricaded themselves in. In the ensuing battle, 18 people died. The leader of the Pakistani Taliban, Baitullah Mehsud, vowed to launch two suicide attacks a week until the Pakistani army withdrew from the border areas and the US stopped its unmanned drone attacks on Taliban bases.

The army didn't withdraw. On the contrary, at the end of April it started an offensive for the recapture of the Swat Valley from the Taliban. The offensive began with relentless airstrikes on Taliban positions, followed by ground assaults. Faced with overwhelming military power, the Taliban retaliated with high-profile suicide attacks. Peshawar bore the brunt of it. The hotel that we are now staying in, the Pearl Continental, was the target of one of the most spectacular terrorist attacks. On the night of 9th June 2009, the heavily fortified compound of the hotel was breached in a daring raid. CCTV footage released later shows a white car approaching the outer perimeter of the hotel from the main road. It stops in front of the barrier. You can see one guard slowly returning to the guards' hut after having checked a visitor on a bicycle. Another one casually lifts the barrier, consistent with a cursory inspection of the vehicle and finding nothing suspicious. As the car enters the hotel grounds, it slows down, shots are fired, then it speeds towards the hotel entrance. The guard who has opened the barrier runs after the car, thus abandoning the checkpoint. While everybody's attention is on the white car, a lorry containing the explosives speeds across the barrier and enters the compound. A few seconds later, you see a white flash.

Fifteen people were killed in the explosion, some of them foreign nationals working for the UN and NGOs. The explosion was so powerful that part of the hotel was destroyed. The façade was literally peeled off revealing the interior of the rooms. A Taliban spokesman, Maulvi Omar, admitted responsibility for the attack. For the rest of the year, the central government having established control over the Swat Valley started an offensive in Waziristan, part of the tribal areas. Peshawar, however, experienced several more attacks. Despite the killing of the leader of the Pakistani Taliban, Baitullah Mehsud, in a drone attack, and the capture of their spokesman, Maulvi Omar, in the summer of last year, the attacks continued. The deadliest of them was on the Meena Bazaar (the market for women and children), in which 118 people were killed, although the Taliban denied responsibility. There was an attack on the headquarters of Pakistan's intelligence service, the ISI (Inter-Services Intelligence), and a man blew himself up as he attempted to enter the Press Club.

Unexpectedly, in the last few months Peshawar has been remarkably quiet. The PC, as the Pearl Continental is affectionately known, reopened for business on 1st January this year. This window of relative calm has allowed us to travel to Peshawar despite resistance from our bosses at the BBC. And this is what I am going to ask the police chief. What has happened in the last six months? What has led to the dramatic reduction in attacks in the city?

The police chief sits comfortably in front of the camera. He's pleased to be interviewed by the BBC. Among the general propaganda lines that he skilfully dishes out, there's something valuable, a gem of newsworthiness, and in his opinion it is unclassified. A new strategy implemented a few months ago is paying off. He explains that the police together with the army have identified key roads leading into Peshawar from the tribal areas, and have blocked them. The nature of the terrain means that you only have to block just a few mountain-passes and secondary roads, and the flow of explosives into Peshawar has dried up. Hence, there have been no attacks in the last six months.

While he speaks I am thinking about my next question. *Why wasn't this implemented earlier?* It's hardly rocket science. When he stops, I ask the question.

'Well,' he says, 'now we have the manpower to do it, whereas we didn't have enough people to implement this plan before.'

I admire his well-rehearsed answer.

I find Pakistan fascinating. Ever since I started coming here in 2001, I've been transfixed by the complexity, the vibrancy and the violence in Pakistan's society. There's something very schizophrenic about life here. For example, it's a dry country, which means that the sale of alcohol is prohibited, but you can take your own in a brown bag to certain hotel restaurants and there is plenty of bootleg liquor at private parties. The Islamic Republic bans homosexuality but I have met openly gay people who are not afraid to talk about their same sex partners despite the severity of the law about same sex sexual acts. Pakistan's legal system is a bizarre combination of British colonial law and Sharia, so for the same offence one can face either secular or Sharia punishment, or in some cases both. For homosexual acts the law theoretically stipulates a punishment from two years to life in jail, or Sharia punishments like 100 lashes of the whip or even stoning to death. If you belong to the wealthy middle classes, the likelihood of being prosecuted is extremely low. If you are born in poverty, you can expect the full force of the law.

And there's something endearingly irreconcilable between the desire for knowledge and information about the permissive society in the West among many people here, and the strict adherence to ancient religious dogmas by the same people.

The police chief is very pleased with the interview. So is his media advisor. I have been given lots of publicity material about Peshawar and the province. In the handout, there is a CD with an interview the police chief has given to the National Geographic television channel. While the cameraman is putting away the gear, Arshad and I sit down for another round of pale tea with the media advisor.

'I hear that you had an unpleasant incident on the way in,' the media advisor says.

I look at Arshad who demurely lowers his gaze. I should have known that such an incident couldn't have remained secret. By now, probably everybody at the compound knows about what happened.

'I can assure you that the perpetrator will be punished accordingly,' the advisor continues. 'The man who fired the shot is already in custody and will be interrogated.'

My mouth is dry and I ask for more tea. I know what it means to be interrogated here. If the poor chap's family doesn't have enough money to get him out, he might even be made an example of and executed. Cold shivers come down my spine.

'But I don't want to make a complaint,' I say. 'It looks like it was an accident. The man probably needs more training, if anything…'

He smiles. 'I'll let the police chief know…'

I carry the tri-pod to the van. The media advisor waves goodbye from the steps of the police headquarters and we drive away. On the way back to the hotel I am worried about another aspect of the incident. If I had been killed or injured, the BBC would want to know if I had been wearing a flak jacket. And I wasn't. Both Simpson and I thought that wearing body armour in Peshawar would be counterproductive. It would only identify us as targets and we would look very odd, indeed, walking around the city in flak jackets. So we didn't even bring ours from London.

The preparations for this trip had been fraught with difficulties. Our visas specified 'Islamabad Only' but in subsequent discussions with friends and contacts in Pakistan I was told that 'Islamabad Only' visas get you to Peshawar without a problem. I had secured a commission from the Ten O'Clock News for a piece, but didn't tell anybody about the big secret in this mission. Simpson and I were hoping to talk to the Taliban.

That's why I had suggested to Simpson that we should work with a local cameraman. First, you wouldn't have to worry about getting a visa for your cameraman. And second, it was more likely that the Taliban would agree to see you if you brought a Pakistani cameraman.

We didn't take a security advisor from London, either. We wanted to keep the mission as low profile as possible. No crew has been allowed by the BBC to 'freewheel' in Peshawar for a long time. Normally, the bosses would only approve 'facility' trips with the Pakistani army when the military takes you under its protection. You see what they want you to see.

On arrival in Islamabad on 22nd June, incidentally my birthday, a big story broke out in neighbouring Afghanistan. The commander of the US and the international force there, General Stanley McChrystal, was summoned to Washington to explain in person why he had criticised senior White House officials in a magazine interview. Simpson and I had already met McChrystal twice since he was appointed commander of ISAF (International Security Assistance Force) and commander of the US Forces in Afghanistan almost exactly a year ago. I had developed a good working relationship with his media advisor, Duncan Boothby, a former news producer for a major American television network. Only a few months ago, in January 2010, Duncan arranged an interview with McChrystal in Kabul. We didn't want a boring sit-down interview. We didn't even want to accompany him in the battlefield because we had that before. We had an unusual request and to our surprise McChrystal agreed to it. I wanted to film him in the operations room of his command centre at the ISAF headquarters in Kabul, the first time this would be done on the BBC.

He enjoyed moving around poring over a big unclassified map on a table in the middle of the room. It looked like old Soviet footage of Stalin with his generals, except that it was only Simpson to whom he revealed his bold new ideas of defeating the Taliban. I was operating the second camera, so I couldn't follow the conversation in great detail. McChrystal's mantra was that reducing Afghan civilian casualties would help win the battle for the hearts and minds of the population. He thought that the so-called 'collateral damage' during airstrikes was unacceptable. Bombing of weddings or houses full of women and children had to be avoided even though Taliban leaders were known for deliberately hiding in social gatherings. The interview, which became part of a big piece for the Ten O'Clock News, made a strong impression on editors in London. Some of them commented on the excellent 'access' we had to the top American commander in Afghanistan.

McChrystal's flirtations with the media, however, proved to be his undoing. By the early afternoon on the 22nd, news agencies around the world started quoting parts of his interview for *Rolling Stone* magazine. Yes, you heard correctly, *Rolling Stone* magazine, that propagator of 'gonzo' journalism and its most famous proponent, Hunter S. Thompson, who wrote for the magazine's political section in the 1970s. In fact, this wasn't a conventional interview. McChrystal and Boothby had allowed a freelance journalist to follow them around and record conversations. It was more of a profile peppered with details about what it's like to be the top US general in Afghanistan. Rumour had it that the journalist, Michael Hastings, apparently followed the McChrystal party not only in Afghanistan but also during drunken nights out in Paris en route to high-powered meetings, etc. The access was phenomenal. But the long article, entitled 'The Runaway General', included disparaging quotes about top US officials. Some of the remarks attributed to McChrystal and his staff mocked the Vice President, Joe Biden, the US Ambassador to Afghanistan, Karl Eikenberry, himself a former general, and the US Special Representative to Afghanistan and Pakistan, Richard Holbrooke. Incidentally, I had spotted Holbrooke at our hotel in Islamabad the other day. He was very much in the news in the 1990s when he was the mediator who brokered an agreement between the warring parties in Bosnia, the Dayton Peace Accords. Aware of his celebrity status he strutted through the hotel lobby discreetly followed by his bodyguards.

The *Rolling Stone* profile of McChrystal, which I found too long and rambling, quoted him as saying about Holbrooke: 'Oh, not another email from Holbrooke… I don't even want to open it.' Of Obama's National Security Advisor, James Jones, one of McChrystal's aides says: 'He's a clown stuck in 1985.' When asked a question about Joe Biden, McChrystal mocks: 'Who's that?' And he says he was 'betrayed' by Karl Eikenberry during a White House debate about troop requests for Afghanistan. But the most hurtful remark was reserved for President Obama. One of McChrystal's staff talks about a key meeting between the two men at the Oval Office a year ago: 'It was a 10-minute photo op… Obama didn't seem very engaged. The boss was pretty disappointed.'

What's striking about the revelations in the article is how well they fitted with the general perception of weakness and indecisiveness in the Obama administration. It highlighted the suspected divisions between the military top brass and the White House. Duncan Boothby resigned that day as a special advisor to McChrystal. The general was sacked by Obama the following day and replaced with another old acquaintance, David Petraeus, who I first met in the northern Iraqi city of Mosul in December 2003. He was then the commander of the 101st Airbourne Division stationed there.

Both Simpson and I were very fond of McChrystal. He was an intellectual soldier. But he was also known as a soldier who got things done. As head of the most secretive force in the US military history, the Joint Special Operations Command, he was credited with the capture of Saddam Hussein in December 2003, and with the killing of Abu Musab al-Zarkawi, the leader of Al-Qaida in Iraq, in June 2006. I was in charge of the BBC bureau in Baghdad at the time of Zarkawi's killing. But none of us knew about the secretive general then until he went to the house in Baquba, north-east of Baghdad, where Zarkawi was killed in a US airstrike, to identify the body personally. His unit in Iraq had the task of capturing or killing high-value targets, and his people were accused of questionable interrogation techniques and even abuse of detainees. However, he consistently delivered results. And on that hot June night in Islamabad a few days ago, Simpson and I jumped in an ordinary cab outside our hotel, breaking all the safety rules of always travelling in trusted hotel cars, and headed to the BBC office to do McChrystal's political obituary.

Simpson stuck the knife into Obama in his analysis of the McChrystal affair. He wrote: 'A stronger, more self-confident president would have given General McChrystal a public roasting, then told him in as many words to get on with the job and keep his mouth shut in the future.'

Our BBC managers in London were frantic. Those who didn't know that we were in Pakistan started asking questions about why we were there. Those who knew about it started to question the rationale of having Simpson in Islamabad and suggested we should travel to Kabul immediately to interview President Karzai. Luckily, I had a direct line to Karzai's spokesman, Wahid Omer. I rang his mobile phone and he told me that much as Karzai liked to talk to Simpson, due to the sensitivity over the sacking of McChrystal the President would not be giving any interviews for the time being. That secured our stay in Pakistan. And in the fast moving story about Washington politics, London forgot about us.

Thus on 24th June, the three of us, Simpson, cameraman Nasir and I set off on a car journey from Islamabad to Peshawar. Although our visas clearly stated 'Islamabad Only', the governor of the North-West Frontier Province was expecting us at his residence on the following day.

There were no checkpoints on the motorway. Soon after we passed Rawalpindi we crossed the mighty Indus. We were not allowed to stop on the bridge but I managed to get a glimpse of the great river. This was where Alexander the Great stopped in his quest to conquer the world and sailed down the Indus to the Arabian Sea, just east of present day Karachi.

Outside Peshawar, the motorway merged into the Peshawar Ring Road from where we took the old Grand Trunk Road, which cuts through the northern parts of the city like a knife. The G.T. Road is an ancient route across south Asia, built and rebuilt over the ages, extended at either end to stretch at present day from Chittagong in Bangladesh to Kabul in Afghanistan. The British gave it its current name when they came to India in the 17th century and it soon became the main route for trade and conquest. Kipling talked about it in his novel *Kim*: '…such a river of life as nowhere else exists in the world.'

The G.T. Road took us deeper and deeper into Peshawar. There was only one checkpoint close to the ancient Bala Hissar Fort opposite Jinnah Park but the driver said something in Urdu to the soldiers and they waved us through. The elegant red ochre fort comprising two concentric circles has dominated the city of Peshawar for centuries. Above the main entrance there is a logo: *Headquarters – Frontier Corps*. The Frontier Corps was created in 1907 at the height of the British Raj by Lord Curzon, the then viceroy of India, incorporating militias and scout units in the tribal areas along the border with Afghanistan, the most famous of which was the Khyber Rifles.

Soon after we passed the checkpoint, we saw the freshly re-built Pearl Continental Hotel to our right, nestled away from the road in the corner of Peshawar Golf Club – a sprawling golf course behind the hotel.

On the way back from the heavily fortified police headquarters I open the curtains in the van and enjoy the drive through Peshawar's streets. Deceptively soon we approach the hotel from the western end of the G.T. Road. The heat makes me tired. I have two missed calls from London on my mobile phone and I dread the conversations with my bosses. The conversation with the Foreign Editor is tortuous. He asks if we have got flak jackets. I say it borders on the insane to wear flak jackets in the city because this will draw more attention to us. And we are not planning to leave the relative safety of the city. He insists that it is mandatory to have flak jackets in Peshawar because the BBC High Risk Team has designated the city as a Category One location, which means it is considered to have the highest level of danger; in other words, it's a war zone.

Having just been in an incident I hesitate but say that this assessment is out of date. I quote what the police chief has just told me in the interview and add, 'There haven't been any incidents in Peshawar in the last six months.' However, he's adamant and we come to a compromise: he will arrange for three flak jackets to be sent by car from the BBC Islamabad Bureau; we must keep them with us at all times. But that's not the end of it. He says that no one in London knew that we were in Peshawar. Why don't we have a security advisor with us? I say that we work closely with well-connected friends, some of them former members of the Pakistani security service, the ISI, and that this way we feel better protected than having a British bodyguard with us.

'We've already seen the governor,' I say, 'and he's assured us that we are under his protection.'

I mention that I've just got an interview with the police chief. He laughs and says that this doesn't amount to much. I can see his point but go on to say that we've got an excellent fixer who gives us sensible advice. 'Also, after last year's attack on the hotel it's become the most secure place in Peshawar,' I add.

The conversation tapers and comes to a natural end. I think that I've put that problem to bed. How wrong I am. The flak jackets arrive that evening but we put them in the hotel storeroom and they stay there until the end of our assignment. Little do I know at this moment that this trip to Peshawar will become the focal point of an internal power struggle in the Newsgathering Department of BBC News. And I'll bear the brunt of it.

I am fearful of calling Simpson in the room next door. I'm not sure if he is asleep or not. So I decide to text him and give him a short summary of the conversation. He responds immediately and says that our strategy should be as follows: he'll take the blame for making us go to Peshawar without flak jackets. He'll say to the Foreign Editor that he'd arranged this trip to Peshawar with a friend of his, a former senior official at the ISI, without telling me. That's why I hadn't made plans for flak jackets. I'm sure this is done with the best possible intentions of protecting me but I don't like the sound of it. It makes me look like a hapless servant who's been taken on a trip without knowing where and to what purpose. So much for our partnership. I am prepared to take my share of responsibility.

But that's not my biggest worry at the moment. If we go back to London without a big groundbreaking story, we'll be slaughtered for wasting a portion of the licence fee and we'll be branded again as being out of control. However, if we deliver something, which will lead the news bulletins across all BBC outlets, we'll be let off the hook and the incident with the flak jackets and the 'unplanned' trip to Peshawar will be forgotten. That's why I call Arshad and ask him about how our attempts to get hold of the Taliban are progressing. His father is one of the best-connected people in this part of Pakistan. We have asked for his help to arrange an interview with the Taliban. We want the Afghan Taliban, not the Pakistani branch of it.

I'm not holding out for a direct face-to-face meeting with a Taliban representative but it's worth a try. A brief conversation with Simpson makes it clear to me that if the meeting were to happen we should do it without telling London. 'Otherwise, they will try to stop us,' he says.

The Taliban leadership often crosses the border into Pakistan. The top leader, Mullah Omar, lives in a heavily protected compound in Quetta, in Baluchistan, south-west Pakistan, I have been told by local journalists. The same people who've been to Quetta recently told me that government limousines are often seen going in and out of Mullah Omar's compound.

Legend has it that in the chaos of the civil war after the Soviet withdrawal from Afghanistan in 1989, Mullah Omar started his movement with fewer than 50 fighters, known as the Students (Taliban). Reportedly, in early 1994 Mullah Omar punished a local warlord accused of corruption and rape by hanging him from the gun of a tank. This swift justice soon gained him recognition and his movement gathered momentum. In September 1996, Kabul fell to the Taliban and in the following year the country was re-named The Islamic Emirate of Afghanistan. Mullah Omar became Afghanistan's de facto head of state. If only history could be that simple!

If you look at Pakistan from a geopolitical point of view, what would you see? It is squashed between two big unfriendly powers – its arch enemy, India, to the east, and Iran to the west. Afghanistan lies awkwardly between Iran and Pakistan. I remember talking to a friend of mine in the region back in 1995 about the unexpected advances by the then virtually unknown Taliban. 'What's happening in Afghanistan,' he said, 'is that Iran is getting a bloody nose courtesy of Pakistan.' Sunni by faith and Pashtun by ethnicity, the Taliban provided the perfect vehicle for Pakistan to counterbalance the Iranian influence in the region during the power vacuum after the Soviet withdrawal. The Persian-speaking Tajik population in the north-west of Afghanistan opposed the Taliban and formed the basis of the Northern Alliance in 2001, which fought to defeat it. Regionally, the Northern Alliance was supported by Iran, Russia and India.

In this intricate geopolitical web, Pakistan's secret service, heavily infiltrated by Islamic fundamentalists, a process that started during the rule of General Zia ul-Haq in the 1980s, became instrumental in nurturing the Taliban in the early days. In the 1990s, following the Russian withdrawal from Afghanistan, Pakistan felt abandoned by the Americans. It sent an outstanding ISI officer, known as Colonel Imam, a man with a good track record of training anti-Soviet fighters, to advise Mullah Omar and his fledgling Taliban movement. The two men knew each other. Imam, whose real name was Sultan Amir, had trained Mullah Omar in the anti-Soviet mujahideen camps on the Afghan border. In a nutshell, with the help of the ISI the Taliban swept to power in Afghanistan to provide a friendly and stable buffer zone between Pakistan and Iran.

Ironically, earlier this year Colonel Imam went to Waziristan with two other men to interview the new leader of the Pakistani Taliban, Hakimullah Mehsud. The Taliban took them hostage. One of his companions, also a former ISI officer, was executed immediately. The journalist on the team was eventually set free after his family paid a hefty ransom. Nothing was heard of Colonel Imam. A year later, in 2011, a video appeared showing Colonel Imam kneeling in front of a group of masked men. Mehsud himself says a few words and a single fighter opens fire. Imam's body slumps onto the ground, riddled with bullets. The man, known as the father of the Taliban, died of the hand of his own creation.

And he was not the only one. Hundreds of ISI officers died in attacks by the Taliban, and hundreds of ISI spies were beheaded in the tribal areas. The ISI's ambivalent attitude to terrorist groups like Lashkar-e-Taiba, responsible for the 2008 Mumbai attacks, and the Haqqani Network in Afghanistan, led to one more dramatic humiliation. It was accused of harbouring Osama bin Laden. It remains a mystery whether the ISI intentionally protected bin Laden, the most wanted man on the planet, or simply didn't look too hard for him. 'Why look for him,' remarked a former Afghan spymaster, 'if not finding him earns you billions of dollars a year, and if you did, the Americans would leave the region?'

In a country where so many mysteries have remained unsolved, from the plane crash which killed the former ruler, General Zia ul-Haq, in 1988 to the assassination of Benazir Bhutto in 2007, it's very unlikely that this one will be resolved. The fact remains that the Americans only found and killed Osama bin Laden after they stopped sharing information with the ISI.

A message comes back from Arshad's father that a face-to-face meeting with the Afghan Taliban on Pakistani territory will not be possible. I have been in direct contact with the Taliban by email in the past and know how to contact them. On a couple of occasions, Simpson interviewed on the phone, through an interpreter, a man calling himself Zabiullah Mujahed while we were in Kabul. Since 2006, the Taliban have put forward two names as their spokespeople: Qari Mohammad Yusuf and Zabiullah Mujahed. However, I have been told that other Taliban representatives use these two aliases to speak for the organisation. Arshad's father offers to put to the Taliban a few questions on Simpson's behalf. But he wants them in writing. I send him only three. Keeping it simple always works, especially when I know that the Taliban will say what they want to say, regardless of the questions. The main question is: 'Will the Taliban engage in negotiations with the Afghan government?'

But are we going to get a genuine Taliban spokesman? I trust our intermediaries with my life but the embarrassment of getting a fake Taliban spokesman will be detrimentally humiliating. We'll be the butt of all the jokes at Television Centre.

Events that eventually unfolded after our return to London revealed the vicious nature of BBC journalistic rivalries. But they did not compare with the derision heaped on MI6 for supplying a fake Taliban mullah to negotiate with President Karzai. A few months after our trip to Peshawar, in November 2010, details emerged of a secret meeting between President Karzai and a 'senior Taliban commander', organised by MI6. It turned out that the 'commander' in question was a shopkeeper from Quetta, in Pakistan. Very few people have seen the faces of senior Taliban men. They don't like their pictures taken. Anyway, the recriminations over the exposed fake mullah became vicious. The Karzai government suffering from the same embarrassment laid into MI6. It was described as pompous and very secretive. The CIA said it had nothing to do with it. MI6 got it in the neck because it tried to take the credit for arranging the 'groundbreaking' meeting before the scam was exposed. The embarrassment was exacerbated by reports that the fake mullah was paid hundreds of thousands of dollars, although British officials were quick to deny that any taxpayers' money was used to bribe the bogus negotiator.

Simpson and I are having dinner at the hotel restaurant. It's a surreal experience. We are the only guests. The restaurant is brightly lit, the napkins – brilliant white. There's no menu. The glass frontage overlooks the driveway, just where the suicide lorry struck a year ago. The back windows offer a view over the swimming pool, which reflects the night sky like a mirror. Despite the dire security situation and the lack of tourists, the pool is beautifully maintained. During the day the water is a deep emerald colour.

The buffet table looks opulent but the salads have a tangy taste and I avoid them. I also avoid the fresh vividly-coloured juices – orange, watermelon and mango. There is of course the famous lassi, made by blending yogurt with water and adding spices and salt. Normally, I would have at least one glass of delicious lassi with my meal, but this time I have to be extra careful not to succumb to a stomach bug. We haven't got much time left and I can't afford to be ill with so much work left to do. The meat dishes are delicious – I think it's the cumin, which they add to most meat dishes, that does it for me. No exercise and lots of meat, and I am beginning to put on weight. The people working at the hotel are extra pleasant. They are grateful that we are here. Our rooms are situated at the back, overlooking the swimming pool and the golf course. The very fact that I managed to get to Peshawar despite all the hurdles gives me a sense of achievement. There are very few other guests at the hotel. In better times, the PC would be buzzing with tourists. The restaurant fills up only on Friday night. It's a pleasure to watch middle-class families with very well-behaved children dressed in their best clothes enjoying a night out.

Simpson is still suffering from the stomach bug but is trying to eat as normal. His behaviour today was heroic. He managed to do a lot of work despite the illness. We went to a Madrassah, an Islamic school, where even the moderate mullah, who's advised Prince Charles on Islam, told us that he hoped the Taliban in Afghanistan would win. After that we went to interview Arshad's father, Rahimullah, at their home. Rahimullah Yusufzai is one of the most famous journalists in Pakistan. He's a respected newspaper editor and one of the few people who truly understands the Taliban. He was the first journalist to visit the Taliban in Kandahar in 1995. And apparently he was the last to interview Osama bin Laden. He looks good on camera with his white beard and is an engaging interviewee. His voice is calm and dispassionate, which makes you trust everything he says. Simpson stoically conducted the interview but I could tell he desperately needed the loo. In keeping with Islamic tradition, all female members of the family were kept out of sight but we were allowed to play with Rahimullah's one-year-old granddaughter, Arshad's baby. In the end, to the consternation of our hosts, we had to make an emergency exit. I was the only one who knew why Simpson had to go back to the hotel so urgently.

This evening in the restaurant, we are joking about today's experience. Our cameraman, Nasir, has had his dinner much earlier. He has been a revelation, very enthusiastic and competent. I like working with people like him. He considers it a privilege to work for the BBC and 'Mr Simpson'. John is very well known in Pakistan because of his reporting from Afghanistan over the last 30 years. It's so refreshing to have Nasir with us not only as a cameraman but also as a friend, advisor, translator and companion. The footage he's taken so far looks good. He's full of ideas.

Yesterday, just before sunset, Nasir and I went to take some rooftop shots of Peshawar. He was very enthusiastic about finding the right place. We climbed a tall building under construction just on the edges of the old city. There was no security, so we just went for it. The views from the top of the construction site were breathtaking. The sun turned the minarets and the flat roofs of the brick buildings into pure gold. It was exhilarating being here, enjoying the beauty of what people in London would consider a very dangerous place. Nasir had just locked the camera in one direction and had made a sign towards me with his finger on his lips to keep quiet because he was recording the call to prayer, when two burly bearded men appeared at the far end of the roof. The way they walked towards us didn't bode well. They didn't look friendly, quite the opposite – very aggressive.

Nasir kept his cool and said to me, 'When they ask, just tell them that you are from Bosnia. You are here making a film about Peshawar.'

I was impressed by his quick thinking. The cover story fitted perfectly. Nonetheless, I was a bit shaken, not so much about personal safety but about the unpleasant consequences for us in London if we got into trouble. If we were kidnapped or arrested, our detractors in London would have a field day. I could hear their nagging voices in my head: 'I told you so!'

The two men looked like local vigilantes. One of them had a handgun openly tucked into his belt. Their sunburnt faces suggested they had spent a long time out in the open. Nasir made the same sign to them to keep quiet because he was recording the call to prayer. Amazingly, they obeyed. When it stopped, he calmly started explaining to them what we were doing. I could hear the word 'Boshnia' repeated several time while he was pointing at me. I was glad I had grown a few days' stubble. We exchanged some pleasantries in English and they left us alone. When they turned back and walked away from us, I felt wobbly in the knees and had to sit down.

Watching the sun go down like a flame about to be extinguished behind the dark silhouettes of the minarets, I tried to remember the details from the Kidnap and Proof of Life form I had filled in at the BBC two years ago. What were the questions designed to establish whether I was alive if the kidnappers were unwilling to provide any other proof of my well-being? Deliberately, they were not very obvious – deeply personal and somewhat incongruous. Only the BBC, my brother and my partner knew the answers. But there on the roof in downtown Peshawar, I couldn't remember the questions. Hopefully, I would be able to answer them correctly when prompted. And hopefully, I would never find myself in such a mess. I had left instructions that no information be passed on to my mother in Bulgaria. The dementia was well entrenched and I didn't want anybody to bother her with bad news. I couldn't even remember the 'Proof of Life' codeword.

Bizarrely, the only thing I remembered was the so-called 'Duress Code', i.e. the phrase that I had to use if any public statements I had made during my captivity were made under duress or if I had been subjected to ill treatment. 'I would like to go home, I would like to go home' – the phrase had to be said twice with no interval.

'How many children do you have?' Nasir's voice jolted me out of my stupor.

'Two, a boy and a girl,' I lied.

He was satisfied with the answer.

'And does Mrs Oggy go to work?'

I didn't tell him that there was no Mrs Oggy. It was too complicated to explain. Instead, I said that Mrs Oggy was also a journalist but didn't travel like me.

He was just trying to be nice.

After the visit to the Jalozai refugee camp outside Peshawar the other day, we took the road due north to the village of Mohib Banda, on the river Kabul, the home village of the Times Square bomber, Faisal Shahzad. The day before our arrival in Pakistan, Shahzad had confessed to planting a car bomb in Times Square, on 1st May. The bomb had been ignited but failed to explode. Two New York street vendors alerted the police to smoke coming out of the vehicle. Shahzad was arrested two days later as he was trying to leave JFK on an Emirates flight to Dubai. Born into a life of privilege – his father was a senior air force officer – Shahzad, an ethnic Pashtun, was a naturalised American with two young children, both born in the United States. But he had received training in Waziristan, in the tribal belt. We wanted to talk to neighbours in the village to find out what made this 30-year-old man, who on the surface of it had achieved the American dream, perpetrate a terrorist act.

The village of Mohib Banda was an affluent place with big houses hidden behind tall mud-brick walls. The midday heat had chased every living soul, people and animals, from the unpaved streets. But the proximity of the river Kabul gave the place a lush appearance. A light breeze caressed the green leaves of the trees in the village. The precious water, which brings life into this barren land, comes from the Hindu Kush. The Kabul goes through the Afghan capital and then through the Serobi gorge flows into the city of Jalalabad before crossing into Pakistan. It runs west of Peshawar and eventually flows into the Indus.

Shahzad's house was on the main street right in the middle of the village. There was a street vendor outside the house selling fruit and sweets from a wooden cart. A few children milled around the cart. Their clean and freshly ironed shalwar kameez confirmed this was an affluent place. Unsurprisingly, there was no one in the house. Neighbours said that after Faisal's arrest last month, the family had moved out. I was expecting remorse and condemnation from the residents of Mohib Banda for what Faisal had tried to do. But there was none of that. A nicely dressed man articulated the feelings in the village. 'For as long as NATO forces remain in Afghanistan, there will be people like Faisal Shahzad to attack American and Western targets. What happens in Afghanistan has a direct effect on people's thinking here.' That level of resentment was unexpected, at least for me.

Today is our last day in Peshawar. We have battled the heat and the stomach bugs. I nearly got killed by a stray bullet outside the police headquarters. Our bosses in London have threatened to make a full investigation into how Simpson and I managed to slip through the net and arrive here, a Category One danger zone, without a BBC security advisor and no flak jackets. Our BBC colleagues at the Islamabad Bureau are resentful of the fact that we have managed to 'freewheel' in one of the most newsworthy places on their patch, something they have not been able to do.

But our 'big story' still remains elusive. And without it, punishment awaits upon our return.

We failed to get permission to travel through the Khyber Pass to the border with Afghanistan at Torkham, not even to Landi Kotal, a few miles before the border. It would've been fantastic to do a piece-to-camera at Landi Kotal, the garrison of the Khyber Rifles. Instead, today we are sending Nasir, our Pakistani cameraman, with instructions to film the road through Khyber and the mountains around it.

We want these pictures to illustrate the danger and inaccessibility of the tribal belt, which makes fighting the Taliban so difficult. We instruct him to film the Khyber Rifles Garrison at Landi Kotal.

We drive as far west as the army will permit, first along the G.T. Road past the University of Peshawar, then onto the Jamrud Road towards Kacha Gharay, a disused Afghan camp, until we reach the Peshawar Ring Road. Soon after that we are stopped at a checkpoint and not allowed any further. This is where we decide to wait for Nasir who earlier went in a separate car towards the Khyber Pass. We get out of our van to wait in the shade of the nearby trees. The atmosphere is very familiar. Lorries decorated with brightly-coloured patterns and golden festoons are being searched. There are big trucks loaded with equipment for the NATO troops in Afghanistan. But surprisingly, most of the vehicles are private cars travelling to the tribal areas.

Simpson is not feeling well. He tells me he's had another attack by the stomach bug. Arshad is with us. He gets a call from Nasir who says that he's on his way back having failed to reach Landi Kotal. The army made him turn back. He has managed to get some fantastic pictures of the Khyber Pass, though, with which we started our television film for the Ten O'Clock News two days later.

My world is falling apart. When my mobile phone rings I have no idea that this call will change everything. It's Rahimullah. It's unusual because he never rings me directly. He's had a reply from the Taliban. For security reasons we always refer to the Taliban in our conversations as Mr T, in case we are being monitored.

'Mr T has given me his answers,' Rahimullah says. 'I want to dictate them to you now.'

I motion to Simpson to get into the van. We both sit on the back seat. I indicate to him with my hand to open his notebook and then whisper just with lip movement, almost without a sound, the words: 'Taliban. Rahimullah.'

Simpson's face, which had been cringing with pain just a few seconds ago, suddenly livens up.

Rahimullah starts dictating and I repeat after him so that Simpson can write the words down in his notebook. I am so excited that I forget that the door of the van is open.

'Our consistent policy has been that we do not talk to anybody while there are occupying forces in Afghanistan. We do not want to talk to anyone – not to Karzai, not to any foreigners – until the foreign troops withdraw from Afghanistan… No talks are taking place with anyone at the moment… Why should we talk when it's not only us who believe that we're winning the war, but our enemy is also conceding that they cannot win this war… Why should we talk if we have the upper hand and the foreign forces are considering withdrawal, and there are differences in the ranks of our enemies?'

As we expected, the Taliban response is in the form of a statement and not direct answers to our questions. The nature of this interview by proxy means that we cannot challenge their assertions but it's good enough in the circumstances. Mr T has saved our bacon in the last hours before our departure. We are due to leave Peshawar for Dubai early the next morning.

The statement is from our old friend Zabiullah Mujahed. I have never met him but I have a faint idea about what he looks like – a slight man with a youthful face and a wispy beard, white turban, intense sorrowful eyes full of angst. This is how an Afghan friend of mine, who's met Zabiullah, has described him. The strongly-worded statement will certainly make the top of the news bulletins. It will touch a raw nerve with politicians on both sides of the Atlantic, and with commanders on the ground trying to degrade Taliban military capability. No one is talking about defeating Mr T any more. Rahimullah said in his interview with Simpson the other day that after the NATO withdrawal, the Taliban will be strong enough to seize parts of Afghanistan, not all of it but a significant part, and with it the prospect of a partitioned Afghanistan becomes very real.

I am already planning in my head how to sell the story to London. With the McChrystal resignation, the debate about troop withdrawal and the uncertainty about the Afghan army's ability to control the country, this response from the Taliban is the missing piece of the jigsaw. And we can definitely advertise it as a response to Simpson's direct questions, which is undoubtedly true. I think we've managed to get off the hook by a whisker.

Nasir is tired from his journey up the Khyber but he has to do a piece-to-camera at the checkpoint. Simpson holds a piece of paper with Mr T's statement in his hand and the viewer can see traffic to and from the Khyber Pass behind him.

But that's not the end of our work here. I have plans for a bigger, half-hour documentary for BBC World News, the BBC's international channel. It's so rare that any BBC crew spends a week in Peshawar that it will be a shame if we don't use all our material, interviews, street shots, rooftop shots and vox pops – short interviews with unnamed ordinary people which the Americans call 'man-on-the-street'. Our total material so far exceeds the limit of the usual three-minute piece for the Ten O'Clock News. And I've got the title for the documentary in my head already: *Pakistan and the Great Game*.

Next stop is the old city of Peshawar where I suggest we do a different piece-to-camera for the documentary. However, not everyone is friendly. Some people don't like the camera. Simpson stands out with his white hair and Western looks. Arshad's presence is reassuring. His long black beard and intelligent face command respect among ordinary people in the street. Nonetheless, we decide to spend only 20 minutes in the hustle and bustle of the old city. Car engine noise and the hooting of motorcycles weaving through the traffic blend with the loud voices of street vendors and ordinary conversations in a wonderful cacophony of sounds. I want to immerse myself in this busy life and sample it properly. But it's not safe, Arshad tells us. The danger of kidnapping is very real. We must rush and record our material before news of our presence gets out to the Taliban and the Al-Qaida types or just to ordinary criminals. The latter could easily estimate the potential re-sell value of a BBC television crew to Al-Qaida or Taliban buyers.

I look up and savour the sight of the old merchant houses, once opulently decorated but now falling into disrepair. These precious twenty minutes in downtown Peshawar during the 'golden hour', every photographer's dream, when the dying sunlight gently kisses the unbaked brick walls of the old houses, their beautifully carved doors and wooden latticed balconies, will remain the enduring memory of this trip.

I am waiting in the office of the BBC's Head of Newsgathering on the fifth floor of the old Television Centre in White City. The grilling hasn't started yet. It's quite clever of them to delay the inquisition until the memory of our big success has faded.

Our Taliban story from Peshawar led the news on all BBC outlets from the minute our plane touched down in London. Simpson was still recovering from the stomach bug but admirably coped with the demand for interviews and pieces for radio and television. We were on a high. No one mentioned flak jackets, security concerns and BBC safety rules. Some sniggered and said they could have got a statement from the Taliban from the safety of their desks in London. Some at the World Service dug out a report from the Taliban website, the Voice of Jihad, which said that the Taliban 'had not made these remarks to the BBC directly or indirectly'. This was duly passed on to me for comment. Instead of shooting from the hip, I held back and contacted Rahimullah. A week or so after our report, I received the following email directly from Zabiullah Mujahed:

> *Subject: Salam*
> *Dear oggy boytchev Hop u will be ok.*
> *1st of all I want 2 tell u that my English isn't good. I'm sorry 4 this.*
> *Mr. there was some confusion regarding the recent bbc interview with me. I want 2 clarify that we did receive the questions from Mr john simpson of bbc through Mr rahemullah usufzae and our shoura give the answers in accordance with the Taliban policy and this has been the declared policy of the Islamic emirate of Afghanistan.*
> *Zabuillahmujahed. Taliban spokesman*

I must admit I was shocked to receive this email not only because it was sent to my BBC email address but also because Zabiullah bothered to answer at all. I deliberately sat on it for 24 hours enjoying the fact that the Taliban had been drawn into an internal BBC rivalry. When I finally forwarded it to several of the top brass, including the head of the World Service, there was no response. The matter was swept under the carpet.

Rahimullah told me that the Taliban were conducting their own investigation into the affair and that the confusion was probably due to the fact that sometimes more than one person operates as Zabiullah Mujahed.

But this is not why I am in the office of my top boss at the BBC. I have been summoned to give an account of how and why we turned up in Peshawar. Simpson has refused to attend. Reluctantly, I have come alone with maps and hard copies of email exchanges. The BBC did approve our trip to Islamabad. We did inform them from Islamabad that there was an opportunity to travel to Peshawar, which we had arranged through trusted friends. The confusion lies in the fact that by the time the BBC machine came round to making a decision, we had already arrived in Peshawar. Once there, even the BBC bosses thought it was unnecessary to pull us out. Indecision paid off. We got a big story.

In my safety briefing, I open a map of the North-West Frontier Province and explain that the Pakistani army has recently captured the strategic point of Ferozkhel in Orakzai tribal area, south-west of Peshawar. Controlling Ferozkhel means that the army controls access to Peshawar from the tribal belt. The recent offensive in Bajaur to the north-west of Peshawar has had the same effect. There are also more checkpoints controlling the entry into the city itself. The Head of the High Risk Team, a former military man, listens with great interest and looks at the map very carefully. The others yawn with boredom. Then I'm told by the Foreign Editor, a little hyperactive bald-headed man, that whatever we do in the future, any Simpson trip, will have to be subjected to the same scrutiny as everybody else.

'There's a feeling that Simpson and you are out of control, that there's one rule for you and another one for everybody else,' he says, a clear reference to complaints from the Islamabad Bureau.

Then his deputy, a horsey woman irritated by our relative autonomy, wades in. 'We've always told our resident correspondent in Islamabad that Peshawar is out of bounds. How come that you felt it was safe for you? We just want to know for future reference.'

'We trusted our hosts implicitly and we kept a low profile. In this way, you can go anywhere in Pakistan, if you want to,' I reply.

The Head of Newsgathering wants to know why we didn't take flak jackets. I say that in my judgement it's more likely that you'll contract some exotic disease or die in a car crash than get shot in Peshawar.

She looks at me as if I'm telling her a joke.

'The highest risk for foreign crews in Peshawar is kidnapping,' I continue, 'and flak jackets will not help you with that.'

'How about car bombs or suicide bombers?' she insists.

I say that we had assessed the latest reports carefully before we set off. There hadn't been any explosion in Peshawar in the last six months for the reasons that I had already outlined, and that if we had walked the streets of Peshawar in body armour, we would've looked like Martians.

The Foreign Editor still bangs on about how there can't be one rule for Simpson and another one for everybody else. 'He has to be treated like any other correspondent.'

At that point I ignore all sensible career advice, which instinctively tells me not to argue with my direct boss and say, 'Well, if Simpson had listened to instructions from the BBC he would never have got on Ayatollah Khomeini's plane from Paris to Tehran in 1979 because everybody thought the aircraft would be shot down. He ignored direct instructions from the Head of BBC News and stayed on in Baghdad during the first Gulf War in 1991 when everybody else was pulled out. If he had obeyed BBC instructions, he would never have stayed on in Belgrade during the NATO bombing in 1999. He's made a career out of ignoring BBC rules.'

The Head of the High Risk Team, who's new to the BBC, looks visibly impressed. The Foreign Editor shakes his head. The boss of Newsgathering smiles and changes the subject. 'So how are you, anyway?'

'Well, I'm not very well, really,' I say. 'My GP thinks I have contracted leishmaniasis, a flesh-eating disease caused by a parasite transmitted by the sand fly. But I'm not sure. We are doing tests at the moment.'

Everybody squirms. That precipitates an early end of the meeting. We stand up and I detect that all of them have suddenly moved away from me to avoid contagion. No one shakes my hand. The Head of the High Risk Team then steps forward, gets closer to me, grabs me by the hand and says, 'I'm not afraid to shake your hand. Take care, mate.'

I am relieved that I don't have to have a social conversation with any of them after the meeting. The fear of contagion makes them disappear swiftly.

Leishmaniasis was eventually ruled out by the tests.

CAIRO, EGYPT, FEBRUARY 2011

Simpson and I walk through the deserted arrivals hall of Cairo airport. It's eerily quiet. The only other passengers on the British Airways flight from London are several camera crews, some of them American. The Arab Spring is in full swing. At the moment, all the anger is focused on Mubarak and his family. The demonstrators demand his resignation. The army, which controls every aspect of Egyptian society, is about to make the ultimate sacrifice: ditch the leader who is one of them, and whose main purpose during his reign has been to preserve the army's dominant position inherited from the founder of modern Egypt, Gamal Abdel Nasser. The first reaction from the army high command was to order police to shoot at demonstrators. It didn't work, so they withdrew the police from the streets to demonstrate to the population that only IT can control law and order. In the ensuing power vacuum looting and vigilante gangs sprung up in equal measure. It killed Egypt's tourist industry. But we are now getting reports that the US, the single largest contributor to Egypt's military budget, has issued an ultimatum: get rid of Mubarak or we'll withdraw military aid. The US gives Egypt's military on average about two billion dollars a year; it's the second largest recipient of US military aid after Israel. When money talks, things tend to happen. Hence, we are back in Cairo.

We were here only a few days ago but had left because, like many other journalists, we thought that Mubarak would sit this crisis out. On our last day here three nights previously, we nearly got lynched by a vigilante mob in the countryside around Saqqara, an archaeological site about twenty miles south-west of Cairo. We were expecting to find supporters of the Muslim Brotherhood in what looked like a religiously conservative village but were shocked to discover how deep the infiltration of the state security apparatus was even in rural parts of the country. As we drove deeper into the countryside, the atmosphere became more and more hostile. Government propaganda on television and in the newspapers told Egyptians that foreign news crews were Israeli agents and were here not to report the news but to spy for Israel. We interviewed people, young and old, outside a local shop and they all told us that the Tahrir Square demonstrators were townsfolk who didn't care about the countryside. The country people wanted things to get back to 'normal'. Mubarak had been doing a good job defending the country from foreign enemies.

I first noticed that something was not quite right when young teenagers and even children started to take pictures of us with their mobile phones. This wasn't an act of 'we like you, let's take a picture of you'. It was more like 'we want to photograph the faces of foreign spies'. Then just before we tried to cross a little bridge, a big lorry blocked our way. When I turned back, there was another one blocking us from behind. We were trapped. Unfortunately, our translator wasn't a local man. He was a British Palestinian, who had moved his young family to Cairo. His accent aroused even more suspicion.

Our first vehicle, in which we had a security adviser, had gone over the bridge and had the chance to escape but chose to stop and wait for us thus making it possible for the crowd to seize it, too.

I turned to Simpson: 'The crowd is turning ugly.'

Our in-joke didn't produce any smiles this time. People of all ages surrounded the car and began to rock it. They wanted to overturn it with us inside. It was an unpleasant experience. The driver, a local Egyptian guy who I hired from outside the Marriott Hotel in Zamalek, unlocked the doors and got out. That took the crowd by surprise. It stopped rocking the vehicle and turned its attention to the camera, trying to seize it from the cameraman's hands through the open window. The cheerleader, a small dark-skinned man with a short army haircut, demanded our tapes. It was obvious that he wasn't just an ordinary vigilante but some type of police informant.

I said to the cameraman, 'Just open the camera and give him the empty tape.'

We had already switched the tapes and I had hidden our footage in some old rags under the front passenger seat. The tape was out of the camera but the little over-zealous man wasn't satisfied and began rummaging through the glove compartment.

While he was doing that I leant over to Simpson next to me in the back seat and whispered in his ear, 'You've got to divert their attention somehow. I've got 20 thousand dollars of BBC money in my bag. I don't want to have to explain to people in London that it had been stolen by an angry mob in Egypt.'

The reason I had the money with me was that the hotel was unsafe. There were rumours that in the general breakdown of law and order, some hotel staff had begun to take liberties with guests' property. There was no safety box in my room. I dreaded the thought of being robbed in such a silly way so I carried the money with me.

Simpson got out of the car. Once again, like many times before, his big frame and white hair made the crowd step back. People subconsciously responded to authority. He casually took his iPhone out of his pocket and started filming over the heads of the surrounding mob. No one stopped him. Something in the mood of the crowd had changed. I thought that this might be due to Simpson's presence but from my vantage point in the back seat of our four-by-four Mitsubishi I saw the crowd parting to clear the way for an army jeep. The jeep's driver revved the engine nudging his way slowly through the thick crowd. People rushed to both sides in front of the machine in a panic. I never thought that I would be so happy to be taken into the custody of the Egyptian army.

An army captain got into the passenger seat of our vehicle and said in reasonable English that we shouldn't worry. He would get us out. The mob reluctantly withdrew from around our vehicle and we drove over the bridge, following the army jeep. And just when I thought that it was all over, I saw that we were being followed by a motorcade of pick-up trucks loaded with angry men. The vigilantes had not gone away.

We were taken to an abandoned police station. Two soldiers ushered us into a large single-storey building. No one kept the crowd away. A rag tag mob filled the courtyard. People pressed their faces to the windows of our room banging on the panes with their fists. The army did nothing to stop that. The captain was very relaxed, from which I inferred that he was deliberately tolerating this harassment to make us feel insecure.

A lengthy identification process started. We had to give our press cards to a thin man in civilian clothes who copied our names on a piece of paper. He took his time. It was exasperating to watch every letter of our names copied in rickety Latin script followed by the phonetic equivalent in Arabic. Their interest visibly increased when our translator produced an Egyptian ID card. A long interrogation process ensued. Eventually, the man walked out with the piece of paper in his hand. More people started to file into the room. Initially, I thought that they were just ordinary men from the crowd who wanted to take a good look at us. But among them I spotted the small dark man with the short army haircut who was the vigilante cheerleader by the bridge. It suddenly all made sense. The people by the door who looked like ordinary members of the crowd were in fact plainclothes policemen, the eyes and ears of the regime.

They were angry because their little world of relative security had been shattered by the demonstrations in Tahrir Square. They had incited the crowd to shake us up a bit. I was glad that the army was now in control. Reassuringly, there were two armed soldiers at the door preventing the angry crowd from entering the room. And I was glad that we were due to fly home the following day.

Today is 10th February. We are in the baggage hall of Cairo airport, which we only left a few days ago. By the end of the day President Mubarak had made a defiant speech on national television in which he vowed to stay in power until elections in September. Although he promised to transfer some powers to his newly appointed vice president, Omar Suleiman, his former security chief, the nature of the speech called into question our decision to come back.

The streets are empty like I've never seen them before. The usual Cairo gridlock has disappeared. The taxi takes the airport road and in no time we are on the lush island of Gezira on the Nile. We are booked like the rest of the media pack at the Marriott Hotel, situated in the well-to-do area of Zamalek. The hotel was built on the site of a former palace dating back to the opening of the Suez Canal in 1869. Many of the dignitaries who came to the opening celebrations stayed at the Gezira Palace, as it was known at the time. The views from the main terrace over the Nile are unparalleled. I first stayed here during the bizarre two-stage funeral of Yasser Arafat in November 2004. Cairo was the venue of a military funeral on 11th November, attended by many heads of state and government, while he was actually buried in Ramallah later on the same day.

The first thing to do after our arrival at the Marriott is to meet our new driver and fixer, Hamza, an architecture graduate, who I had approached on the phone before leaving London. We had accidentally met on our previous trip to Cairo. He struck me as a highly intelligent young man who spoke excellent English. His family had good connections with the Muslim Brotherhood. I'm still in email contact with him. Our British-Palestinian fixer who we hired in Tahrir Square during the demonstrations the previous week had been poached by another part of the BBC.

Hamza is very keen to work because he's been unemployed since his graduation two years ago. He's already waiting for us at the hotel lobby. He is tall with a fair complexion and a longish, almost biblical, black beard.

This is a difficult assignment for us. We are in the shadow of the BBC's Middle East Editor, Jeremy Bowen, who is doing all the main pieces. Simpson's been allocated the castrated role of either doing follow-up pieces or live injects, summarising the main topics of the day and providing interpretation of the day's events. I have noticed before that when rapid change engulfs a country or a whole region, audiences in the UK and worldwide like to hear an opinion. Not many BBC correspondents are prepared to volunteer an opinion. Simpson always does. That's why his appearances on television are so memorable.

The BBC has an enormous team on the ground this time and the main news bulletins are co-presented from here by George Alagiah. It's not ideal for us to be on the sidelines but both Simpson and I are happy to be here witnessing history in the making. On one occasion we make a wrong call and choose to stay in Tahrir Square. The Ten O'Clock News refuses to take Simpson live from there and instead go for Bowen from our main live position on the Corniche. This creates a combustible atmosphere in our partnership. I implicitly blame myself for the wrong call. Although he doesn't say it, Simpson does, too. Nonetheless, I am happy to be here where my new life started 25 years ago.

Simpson and I don't like mixing with other journalists on our foreign trips. I detest the fake camaraderie. We are both fiercely competitive and dislike the sharing of ideas with other people. Also, wars and revolutions tend to attract the same people and after a while I find their stories rather boring.

For most of the British public Simpson is a national treasure – a towering personality with international fame. For some of our colleagues at the BBC, often driven by envy, he is a ruthless operator who frequently puts himself at the centre of the story. I like that. My job has been to navigate the choppy waters of office politics and get the most out of him as a box-office asset. I like to mix with irreverent, slightly edgy, alternative types with strong views, and there aren't many of those at the BBC. It tends to employ the acquiescent, compliant types, who sometimes hide their true selves behind a wall of aggressive behaviour. After many years at the corporation, I have hardly made any lasting friends here – except Simpson. All my other friends work elsewhere.

At least the Gezira Palace is big enough for us to choose a quiet place away from the oversized BBC team and have a solitary dinner. I mention to Simpson that it is 25 years since I first came here and instead of returning to communist Bulgaria I bought a ticket on Egypt Air to Heathrow and asked for political asylum. During the years we've worked together, I have briefly spoken about my defection but he's never been very inquisitive, perhaps not to sound too intrusive. And I, on the other hand, haven't been forthcoming with details about how exactly it happened, always brushing aside his questions with a joke, 'You will read it all in my book, eventually.'

Tonight he is in a mood to find out more. And I would like to tell him more because I know we only have a couple of months left as a team.

'How did you manage to get on a plane without a British visa? You wouldn't be able to pull that one off now,' he says.

'I simply asked the shipping agent to buy a one-way ticket for me. I gave him cash. He assumed that I'd be joining another Bulgarian ship in Britain. I might've mentioned casually the Port of Tilbury.'

'But how did you actually get on the plane without a visa?'

'Well, I was just lucky that on that day there was a national police strike here. All over Egypt, the army had taken over from the police, including the immigration service at Cairo airport. My passport was inspected by a young army conscript who spoke no English. I was lucky. It could've turned out totally different and I could've ended up in an Egyptian jail or deported back to Bulgaria. Not sure which one would've been worse.'

Simpson smiles. He doesn't ask about why I left Bulgaria. He's been to the old Soviet bloc often enough to know the answer.

'Did you tell your parents before you left Bulgaria that you wouldn't be coming back?'

'No, I didn't. I didn't want to worry them. I had secretly transferred my savings into my mother's account. I had obtained an international driving licence and took my hard currency with me, all 200 US dollars of it. This was a lot of money for me at the time.'

'So, why did you choose London?'

'Well, flying from Cairo to London was the most inconspicuous route. Anywhere else, like Frankfurt, or Amsterdam, or Zurich would've aroused suspicion with the shipping agent. He was Egyptian but after all he was an agent of a Bulgarian shipping company. Moreover, I had studied English at school and was a great Anglophile. I still am.'

'Was it hard leaving your parents, knowing that you might never see them again? At that time, although Gorbachev had just come to power, no one believed that communism would collapse so spectacularly and so soon.'

'It was very similar to what's happening now!' I say. 'Only a few months ago no one would've predicted that Mubarak would be rattled by some student demonstrations. Because I do think he'll go sooner or later. We've talked about the mechanics of revolutions. They are fascinating. What did Lenin say: "Give me just one generation of youth and I'll transform the world" or "When the ruling classes find it impossible to maintain their domination…"'

'Come on, Oggy, you are such an incorrigible Marxist. You can take the boy out of communism but you can't take communism out of the boy…'

'It is true, though. Look at the enormous security apparatus here. It finds it impossible to deal with a few thousand students. Something intangible has changed, at this particular moment the ruling elite doesn't want to shoot young enlightened people and – bingo, we have a revolutionary situation.'

Simpson looks at me pensively as if his mind is somewhere else.

'But, as we both know,' I continue, 'revolutions are never won by the people who ignite the first spark. You witnessed how it started in Iran in 1978, and where it ended.'

'But you have such a Marxist approach to history,' Simpson says. 'Let's go back to your story. Were you scared when you boarded the plane for London?'

'Of course I was. I couldn't sleep the night before the flight. I couldn't eat. All I managed was a bowl of soup and a bit of bread. As I was lying in bed at the Novotel at Cairo airport, I was expecting the proverbial knock on the door. With hindsight, I understand that I had overestimated the long arm of the communist security service. But nonetheless, I thought they could burst into my room in the middle of the night and ask: "What are you doing here? Where do you think you're going?"'

I may be imagining it, but I think I spot a little tear in the corner of one of Simpson's eyes. We are now alone in the restaurant. Everybody else has gone.

'So you arrived at Heathrow. How did the Brits let you in? What did you tell them?' Simpson persists.

'Well, I told them that my father was interned for 18 years. He was forced to do hard manual labour. He kept his head down, married a girl from a poor family and by 1965 was considered a reformed character. A brief amnesty allowed him to return to the capital. He still couldn't get a proper job and had to work on construction sites until he was well into his seventies. That had scarred me for life and I couldn't wait for an opportunity to escape. They questioned me at Heathrow for five days and let me in.'

A moment of silence…

'But why was he interned? What did he do?'

'He was accused of being a British spy.'

Another moment of silence…

'And was he?' Simpson fixes his gaze on me. This is very unusual because during all the years we've worked together he's very rarely looked directly into my eyes. 'I mean, was he a spy?' he continues.

'I don't really know because he never told us explicitly, perhaps to protect us. He was a very reticent character. He never talked about himself but as a child I had teased out of him some gems. For example, I knew that as a young man during the war he moved in pro-American Jewish circles. He let slip once that in the winter of 1941 he helped someone jump over the wall of the British embassy in Sofia to pass on information to the Allies that Bulgaria was about to join the Axis. He told me that when he was questioned by the secret police in 1948, he was shown photographs of him meeting the British military attaché in a Sofia café. But I don't think they had any hard evidence. Evidence was never something the commies worried about when they wanted to eliminate someone. But there were other entangled and contradictory elements in his life story. He was born in northern Greece and his family there fought on the side of the communist resistance against the Nazis. One of his brothers was publicly executed as a resistance fighter. Perhaps, that's why his life was spared.'

Simpson is engrossed in the story, which I've never shared with him before.

'When I was 14,' I continue, 'I found some letters in an old suitcase in the attic. Typed on fine paper, they were part of a business correspondence in English between my father and two trading companies, one in London and the other one in Manchester. When I asked him, he said that between 1945 and 1948 he had a trading firm specialising in imports of English fabric. He said that the suitcase had been in safe keeping with one of my uncles during his internment. I never heard him mention that again and the letters mysteriously disappeared.'

'Did you try to find out more later, after the fall of communism?'

'Of course. When the new government opened the archives he saw his file compiled by the communist secret service but there was nothing substantial in it. He thought that most of the file had been destroyed. He was shocked, though, to find out that he'd been on the watch list as late as the early 1980s. There were reports from secret agents tailing him to and from work on various construction sites, and watching our family, too. But there was nothing about the period 1945-1948. There were no photographs of him and foreign diplomats.'

'So, to come back to our previous conversation, did the Brits ask you about why you wanted to escape from Bulgaria? After all, you had a good education, a good job, the commies even allowed you to travel abroad.' Simpson is playing devil's advocate.

'Yes, they did. And I told them a joke, a very popular joke in Bulgaria at the time. It goes like this: "Two dogs meet in no-man's-land on the Bulgarian-Turkish border having crawled under the electric fences. This was the border between NATO and the Warsaw Pact. The Bulgarian dog is well fed, with a nice shiny coat. The Turkish dog is emaciated and scraggy.

"I want to escape to Turkey," says the Bulgarian dog.

"But why? You've got enough to eat, and your master keeps you clean. Why do you want to do that?"

"Because I want to be allowed to bark from time to time," the Bulgarian dog replies."'

Simpson laughs uneasily. There's a bit of sadness in his laughter. Oh, how well he knows what's it like be allowed to bark!

'So, they questioned you for five days and let you in... Did you at any point have any doubts about coming to Britain?'

'In the first days after my arrival, I succumbed to a severe bout of flu. My immune system must have been shattered by the nervous strain of the defection. I had a fever for many days, lying in a shared dingy room in a hostel in Victoria. I had no money for food, no friends and my optimism was evaporating rapidly. But I came through to the other side and never looked back.'

'Did you tell you parents about your doubts?'

'Of course not! It would've been unfair, having excluded them from the decision about my defection. I called them from a public telephone box at Victoria a few days after my arrival in London. They said they had already been interrogated by the police. My father was very aggressive when he spoke to me, which normally masks deep distress. I guess he was distraught because he thought he would never see me again. He was 73 at the time. My mum, 20 years younger, was surprisingly upbeat. Five years later they came to see me in London. No one could've predicted that the world would change so dramatically so quickly. And here we go again, more dramatic changes on the way…'

'It's not the same,' Simpson says. 'What happened in 1989 was momentous. This is just a blip.'

11th February. We're off to Tahrir Square again. The BBC has rented a flat in one of the buildings on the south-western side overlooking the square. It's difficult to estimate how many people are in the square but there must be thousands of them, angered by Mubarak's defiant speech last night in which he vowed to stay on until the next presidential election in September.

Just after 6 pm local time my mobile phone rings. Simpson and I are walking between two locations – the Tahrir Square live position and the rooftop broadcasting operation in the Corniche from where the main bulletins are being presented. It's George Alagiah. He asks to speak to Simpson without telling me what it's about. Simpson takes my phone and listens for a few seconds then covers it with his other hand and says quietly: 'He's resigned. It's just been announced on television.'

I know it's all over. Not for Egypt but for us. We'll be here for another two days max and then back to London. It is, however, a momentous event. The most powerful leader in the Middle East has been brought down by popular demonstrations. Gaddafi in Libya and Assad in Syria will be quaking in their boots tonight.

While Simpson is doing endless two-ways, fireworks are going off in Tahrir Square in the distance and soldiers are being carried on the shoulders of jubilant demonstrators. I feel deflated. Revolutions are not meant to end like this. The military top brass has sacrificed Mubarak in an effort to keep the status quo. I can't help but remember a quote from a book I had read surreptitiously in Bulgaria, *The Leopard*, by the Italian writer, Giuseppe di Lampedusa, made immortal in a 1960s Visconti film: 'If we want things to stay the same, things will have to change.' The old Duke was talking about the need for the aristocracy to change if it wanted to avoid a republic. The same thing was often said when communism was collapsing in Eastern Europe in 1989. During the first public demonstrations, the communist leadership, the military and the secret police just wanted to introduce some peripheral reforms so that they could stay in power. But when that failed, they joined the revolution to preserve their economic power and privileges. The economic system changed, the faces at the top were replaced but economic and political power stayed essentially with the same groups. No mass bloodshed, no witch-hunt, no radical rearrangement of the social strata like in the Russian Revolution of 1917, or more recently, the Iranian Revolution of 1979.

It's symptomatic that Mubarak's resignation has been announced by the vice-president, Omar Suleiman, a former intelligence chief, and not by Mubarak himself. There is no doubt in my mind that Mubarak has been removed because of pressure from the White House, who threatened to withdraw its military aid unless he went. He has been sacrificed in order to preserve the regime. But history is unforgiving. Egypt now faces two stark choices: fake democracy with undiminished power of the military, or free elections, which will bring the Muslim Brotherhood to power.

In the following hours, we try to interview a leading member of the Brotherhood but he refuses to be filmed on camera. We do the interview over the telephone, which isn't very exciting. The organisation still doesn't know how things will develop and is keeping a low profile. It's biding its time in order to step in untainted by recent violence. However, we have noticed more and more Brotherhood supporters, women with hijabs and men in conservative Islamic clothes and beards joining the demonstrations as private citizens. In the current climate of anger against a corrupt government and greedy ruling family, the Brotherhood's original message 'Islam is the solution', the establishment of an Islamic state governed by Sharia, has become very appealing.

The movement was founded in 1928 by a schoolteacher, Hassan al-Banna, to promote Islamic morals and charity work among the poor, but quickly became involved in politics. The Muslim Brotherhood, or al-Ikhwan al-Muslimun, set up branches throughout Egypt, each running a mosque, a school and a sporting club. It was modelled on a political party and its membership grew rapidly, especially among the young and those who sought to end British colonial influence. By the 1940s the organisation was thought to have had two million followers and its ideas began to spread across the Arab world. But al-Banna had a greater vision for his organisation. He created a paramilitary wing, the so-called 'Special Apparatus', clearly copying the Russian revolutionary structures, which joined the campaign against British interests with bombings and assassinations. Although Egypt had gained nominal independence in 1922, Britain had continued to play a dominant role in the country's political life and its relations with the rest of the world, retaining control of the Suez Canal. In 1948 the pro-British government of Egypt dissolved the Brotherhood and in the following year al-Banna was assassinated by unknown gunmen. Four years later, in 1952, the Brotherhood supported a *coup d'état* by young men calling themselves the Free Officers led by the charismatic Gamal Abdel Nasser. Another future president of Egypt, Anwar Sadat, was the liaison officer between Nasser's Free Officers and the Brotherhood. The coup resulted in the abolition of the monarchy and the establishment of the modern day republic of Egypt. A failed assassination attempt against Nasser in 1954 was blamed on the Brotherhood and the organisation was banned and thousands of members were sent to prison and tortured. The Brotherhood started to operate underground. That prompted a change in its strategy and ideology. An Egyptian poet, Sayyid Qutb, became the voice of the new radical Brotherhood. He advocated Jihad against what he called 'ignorant' societies obsessed with 'materialism, violence and sexual pleasures'. His writings, especially his work *Milestones* which was published in 1964, inspired future radical Islamist groups, including Islamic Jihad and Al-Qaida. Qutb was put on trial for sedition and executed in 1966, thus making him a martyr for many in the Islamic world.

I look across Cairo's evening skyline unable to foresee the turbulence that will beset Egypt in the next few years. The Facebook and Twitter generation will feel cheated but won't give up. I listen to Simpson's last two-way for the day, in which he says that after today's events President Assad of Syria should be very worried, indeed. The contagion of revolution seems unstoppable tonight. Only five years ago Simpson and I were sitting in one of Assad's palaces in Damascus waiting to interview him. He suddenly walked in. Tall, lanky, with curious agile eyes, he seemed almost shy. He didn't look like a vicious dictator whose hands were dripping with blood. We shook hands. He looked straight into my eyes and said, 'So you are the producer. What does a producer do?' His voice was mild and muffled.

'Oh, I make sure that everything works,' I said.

'Well, you research the country and its political scene, and brief Simpson about the questions. No?'

'That too,' I said, 'but there are much more mundane tasks like organising visas, flights, cars and drivers, camera crews and making sure we have a roof over our heads when we travel.' I tried to downplay my role.

No other world leader we'd interviewed had expressed such interest in what I did. After the interview, he agreed to all my requests for filming a walkabout with Simpson in the palace gardens and without any fuss allowed himself to be directed during second and third takes of the shots.

After an exhausting evening, our driver takes the Nile Corniche towards the '15th of May' bridge – the quickest route to the Marriott in Zamalek. It's after midnight but the streets are still buzzing with people. Cars and pick-up trucks carrying youths with green bandanas waving the national flag criss-cross the city. Simpson and I sit in the back of the four-by-four congratulating ourselves on witnessing a historic moment. Suddenly, the vehicle grinds to a halt at a makeshift checkpoint. A young man with a fierce face and a handgun in his belt demands that the car be searched. Simpson protests. The people around the vehicle get angry. They are holding sticks and metal pipes in their hands and the atmosphere is very menacing. One of them explains in reasonable English that because of the breakdown of law and order there's been widespread looting. They want to see if there are any looted goods in the back of our car. We find this logic preposterous and try to argue with them but soon realise that this is only designed to intimidate us.

Who are these people? Obviously, they don't share the popular exultation. Our driver says that the best thing to do is to let them search the car. We are at their mercy. We could be beaten to death, robbed or injured and there's nothing anyone can do to prevent it. There's no one to call. We just hope that all goes well. Our captors are enjoying their newly found power. They search the back of the car and ask questions about the purpose of various bits of equipment. Then they demand to search our bags. This is when Simpson gets very angry but the driver and the cameraman try to calm him down. He reluctantly lets the vigilantes peer into his leather rucksack. Unexpectedly, they show some respect and don't rummage through it. The mood has changed. They have asserted their authority and have lost interest in us. There are other vehicles with passengers to be intimidated in the queue behind us. I wonder how quickly the army will be able to bring these vigilante activities under control.

We take the approach to the bridge, named after the start of the Arab-Israeli War in 1948. The car drives into the relative safety of Zamalek. When we walk through the hotel lobby, I notice that the large portrait of Mubarak still hangs above the reception desk.

We stay one more day in Cairo. It's amazing how quickly interest in the story wanes. The media interest now shifts towards Libya. We tour Tahrir Square and its surroundings unhindered. In the courtyard of a government building next to the square we see a number of burnt-out police vehicles. Demonstrators and volunteers are sweeping the debris in the streets in a noble attempt to clean up their city. We see the signs of the break-in into the Museum of Egyptian Antiquities, or the Egyptian Museum as it's commonly known. The red ochre neoclassical building was one of the most protected sites in Cairo and yet during the unrest a gang managed to steal valuable objects. The army is now guarding it, and has been hailed again as the great saviour of the nation.

The British Airways flight from Cairo is in the afternoon. Simpson, our translator Hamza and I decide to use the morning for a bit of sightseeing. Hamza recommends that we go to Al Azhar Mosque, one of the most significant mosques in the Islamic world. Situated a short drive north-east of Tahrir Square, in the middle of old Cairo, it is the heart of one of the most prestigious Islamic universities, the Al Azhar University – the main centre for Arabic literature and Islamic learning in the world. Downtown Cairo is deserted. People are reluctant to leave their homes. They are apprehensive about the uncertain future. We are the only visitors in the mosque. The four minarets piercing the blue sky were built at different times and represent different architectural styles over the last thousand years. The marble-paved courtyard glistens in the sun and the surrounding arches look as light as an embroidery. Someone volunteers to take us around and we immerse ourselves in the calm of this wonderful spiritual building.

No foreign trip is complete without buying souvenirs, regardless of the historic events that we have witnessed. In a shop nearby, Hamza helps me haggle with the shopkeeper. I eventually buy a set of six alabaster jars at a fraction of the asking price. With an hour to spare before we head for the airport, we sit down in a street café for a glass of fresh mint tea.

Incongruously, I say to Simpson, 'Do you know what? Cairo this morning reminds me of Olivia Manning's description of the city in *The Levant Trilogy*.'

He doesn't say anything, waiting for me to continue.

'I am impressed by the tranquility of this city at the moment despite the turbulent historic events. The reason I mention Olivia Manning is that she describes how normal life for British Council workers was in Cairo while some of the fiercest battles of the Second World War were taking place in the desert just a short distance away from here. The characters in her book collected their salaries, conducted their love affairs, had their professional jealousies…'

'How do you know Olivia Manning?' Simpson interrupts me.

'Not from the television series. I was introduced to her work by a second-hand book dealer in Hampstead. There is a small bookshop in Flask Walk, crammed to the ceiling with all sorts of books. It is chaotic, but the man knows exactly where everything is. You just have to ask. He likes talking. We talk about Bulgakov, Gore Vidal, Vera Brittain, and Anthony Burgess. I bought a nice early edition of *Earthly Powers* there. He recommended *The Levant Trilogy*. Then I read *The Balkan Trilogy*.'

Hamza feels excluded and Simpson changes the subject. 'Moments like these are what make our job so rewarding,' and he sips from his glass, looking at the empty street. It's pleasant and quiet, and no one would've guessed that only yesterday the city was in the grips of revolutionary upheaval. 'I wouldn't change my job for all the gold in the world…'

Hamza asks whether the job could be sometimes dangerous.

'Yeah, it can be.' Simpson sighs and recounts in great detail the 'friendly fire' incident in April 2003 when he was bombed by an American plane while travelling with a convoy of Kurdish special forces advancing on Saddam Hussein's army. We had managed to get into the self-governing territory of northern Iraq through neighbouring Turkey. Being stuck there for more than a month with very little to report, we, like many other journalists, felt frustrated and tried to break into Iraq proper. That convoy was such an opportunity. The intention was to get closer to Saddam's army positions. Simpson cheerfully recalls how he heard a whistling sound before the anti-tank missile struck the convoy. He was injured by shrapnel and had a perforated eardrum. Our translator, Kamran, was killed.

'Oggy came to pick us up with an ambulance,' he adds.

This is how the story has been re-told now. He didn't say that we had had a heated argument the previous day. I refused to join the Kurdish convoy and stayed behind with the BBC satellite dish and the engineers operating it. During our exchange on the phone, which was witnessed by some of our colleagues, he told me that he never wanted to work with me again. In the evening before the incident, Simpson did call me and apologised for the things he had said in the heat of the moment. I only murmured that we had all got very tired and frustrated. The argument was never mentioned between the two of us again.

In the fresh February morning in downtown Cairo, I didn't tell Hamza that Kamran, who was gravely injured when shrapnel from the explosion cut off his leg, died in my arms while I was transferring him from the back of a Kurdish truck to an American ambulance. I didn't tell Hamza that despite that argument with Simpson we worked together again only a few days later. Our whole team, including the satellite dish, moved gradually from the Kurdish-controlled zone to the cities of Kirkuk, Mosul and Tikrit, as the regime disintegrated. We were able to send our films and do live broadcasts with our satellite equipment.

I didn't tell Hamza that the 'friendly fire' incident was not the only one in which BBC colleagues died during the fateful assignment in northern Iraq. Three days earlier, an Iranian cameraman working as part of our team died in a landmine explosion near the city of Suleymania, close to the Iranian border. The team of three had parked their vehicle in a meadow with unmarked landmines, legacy of the Iran-Iraq war. A close colleague of mine, Stuart, lost his leg in the same incident.

Instead, I tell Hamza a funny story about how in Kirkuk I had left Simpson in a hotel room to file a report on a satellite telephone to London. When a few minutes later I passed by the door, which was left ajar, I saw Simpson lying unconscious on the floor. He had collapsed from exhaustion and acute pain due to a perforated eardrum from the explosion. I still remember the intensity of the hot wave that hit my brain when I saw him on the floor. I thought that he had died. I tell Hamza that I ordered two of our Kurdish armed escorts to go and fetch a doctor in the middle of the night. By the time the doctor arrived, Simpson had regained consciousness. The poor doctor had been dragged out of bed and thought that he would be executed by the Kurds for working in a hospital for Saddam's senior officials. He was ashen faced. I tried to assure him that no harm would come to him. He gave Simpson an injection of painkillers and we all continued with our work.

Hamza is looking at us with eyes wide open. We have another glass of mint tea and then set off for the airport. By the time we reach the airport road, traffic has picked up again, and despite the revolution we are back to Cairo's normal gridlock.

EPILOGUE

LONDON, AUGUST 2013

Since my last assignment for the BBC two years ago, it has been strange to watch the foreign news on television instead of being out there, witnessing it first-hand. This summer, the 89-year-old Mugabe won another term in office, having outmanoeuvred his opponents once again. There were cries of foul play and vote rigging, but the African nations supported his victory while there was only token condemnation from the West.

Back in 2008 after our first trip to Zimbabwe, Simpson and I went back twice for two rounds of elections. We were in the thick of it, working undercover. We changed locations every few days to avoid arrest. In a daredevil act reminiscent of a Boy's Own adventure, we secretly interviewed the opposition leader, Morgan Tsvangerai, while everybody was attending Mugabe's inauguration ceremony. We became part of the story, which many at the BBC didn't like. This summer's coverage of the Zimbabwean elections was solid, professional and competent but unexciting. No analysis, no punch, no drive. At least, this is what I thought.

I watched with trepidation every news report on the presidential elections in Iran. There was no BBC presence there and I must admit to a bit of schadenfreude on my part. I wanted to believe that my contacts in Iran could have secured visas for Simpson and myself to be in Tehran for the event. A few months later, on a different occasion, I tried again but my confidence was punctured when I failed to get the visas despite the initial euphoria when our applications were accepted. That was my last attempt to get back into Iran with Simpson. The Green Revolution of four years ago had been suppressed with an iron fist. A new president, Hassan Rouhani, known as the 'diplomatic sheikh' was inaugurated. Glasgow educated – his thesis was on Sharia – and a former nuclear negotiator, he's employed conciliatory rhetoric since he came to office. But rhetoric is all he's got since there's no real power vested in the office of the President. According to the constitution he holds the second highest position in the power structure, but in reality he comes third. It is the unelected Supreme Leader at the top who controls the armed forces and makes all decisions on security, defence and foreign policy. Next comes the Guardian Council, which vets all presidential candidates, while the president is the face Iran presents to the outside world.

This summer, we learned that the Americans were to start peace negotiations with the Taliban in Doha, in the Gulf state of Qatar. After 12 years of fighting and with the loss of more than 2,000 American and 400 British soldiers, the Americans were forced to the negotiating table with the Taliban. People may legitimately wonder what the whole business of invading Afghanistan was all about.

The sectarian violence in Iraq has reached heights that have not been seen since the dark days of 2006-2007 when a thousand people died each month in Baghdad alone. Car bombs are targeted at shopping areas, a move designed to inflict the maximum number of casualties. Coverage on the main BBC bulletins has been reduced to one-liners.

A long-awaited report by the WHO on congenital deformities and cancers in Iraq as covered by our story from Fallujah was due to be published in November 2012. Inexplicably, it still hasn't been released prompting speculations of interference and efforts to suppress it.

Al-Qaida is still alive and kicking despite the killing of Osama bin Laden two and a half years ago. US intelligence claims to have intercepted messages between top commanders and prevented major attacks in Yemen. This seems to vindicate those who advocate spending money on intelligence and counter-terrorism rather than on war.

Hopes for a stable democratic Libya post-Gaddafi have not materialised. Britain's close links with Gaddafi have also come under the spotlight since I left Tripoli. A long-time Gaddafi opponent, Abdel Hakim Belhaj, leader of the Libyan Islamic Fighting Group (LIFG), who was instrumental in overthrowing the regime, is suing a former British spy, Sir Mark Allen, and the British government. He is claiming unlawful 'extraordinary rendition' (transferring people from one jurisdiction to another) and torture. The case dates back to 2004 when preparations were made for the historic rapprochement between Gaddafi and Tony Blair. MI6 and the CIA delivered Belhaj to Gaddafi as a gift-wrapped present just in time before the meeting. A letter by Sir Mark Allen to Gaddafi's feared head of intelligence, Musa Kusa, was found in the rubble of the Libyan Intelligence Agency destroyed by NATO bombs in Tripoli. It congratulated Musa Kusa for the 'safe arrival of the air cargo'.

A decade ago MI5 believed that Belhaj's group, LIFG, was involved in recruiting young British Muslims to fight jihad in Iraq. In the new Libya that Britain helped create, Belhaj is a senior commander. He has indicated that he'll accept an apology, admission of liability and a token payment of one pound each from Sir Mark Allen and the former foreign secretary, Jack Straw. The UK has already agreed to pay over two million pounds to another Libyan dissident from the Gaddafi years, Sami al Saadi, for his unlawful extraordinary rendition.

A year after the fall of Tripoli, the American ambassador to Libya died in an attack by an angry mob on the US consulate in Benghazi. The death of Chris Stevens, a highly regarded American diplomat, sent shock waves through the American administration. The new Libya hasn't turn out the way it was meant to be.

It's been a disappointing summer for the Facebook and Twitter generation in the Middle East as the Arab Spring went into a tailspin. Two years ago enthusiastic Arab youths went out in numbers to protest against corrupt and autocratic governments. They thought they could change the way they live – they asked for democratic elections and a role in shaping the future of their countries. Instead, the ballot box delivered power into the hands of Islamist parties who see politics as a direct extension of religion.

In Egypt, free elections brought the Muslim Brotherhood to power. But fear that the country would turn into an Islamic republic, a Sunni version of Iran, made the military establishment panic. President Morsi was overthrown just over a year after taking the reigns of government.

Tunisia, where the Spring began, has been rocked by uncertainty and two high-profile political assassinations. The moderate Islamist Ennahda party, originally inspired by the Muslim Brotherhood, governs in coalition with two non-religious parties. The murder of the secular opposition leader Chokri Belaid and the left-wing politician Mohamed Brahmi shook the urban liberal sections of Tunisian society. Although the Ennahda party has promised not to ban alcohol or impose the veil, there is palpable pressure from ultra-conservative Muslims known as Salafis for the introduction of Sharia.

A vicious civil war has gripped Syria and destabilised the region. Supported by Russia and Iran (and Iran's proxy, Hezbollah, in Lebanon), President Assad, who many in the West had written off when the rebellion started two and a half years ago, is making gains against a fractured opposition. The curious case of a jihadist fighter cutting the chest of an opponent and biting into his heart, all captured on video, was given as an example of the kind of people who might rule Syria one day if President Assad were to be removed. A glum-looking President Putin made this point at the G8 summit in Belfast this summer. Both Russia and China are determined not to allow a repeat of how the Libyan conflict was handled. They still have the bitter aftertaste of being hoodwinked by the West into voting at the UN for intervention to protect civilians, which then not so subtly morphed into a mission of regime change. Russia even brokered a deal allowing the West to destroy Syria's chemical weapons – a masterstroke, which extended Assad's political life.

In Turkey, often cited as a model of how it is possible to reconcile democracy and economic growth with Islamic sensibilities, an environmental protest earlier this summer turned into widespread student demonstrations against what they see as an encroachment of Islam on their liberties pursued by an increasingly authoritarian prime minister.

Saif al Islam, Gaddafi's son, has been put on trial in the city of Zintan, in western Libya. The new government has resisted requests by the International Criminal Court for extradition to The Hague where he's wanted on charges of war crimes. A trial in Libya could result in the death penalty. Gone are his Western looks – a thick black beard and a tribal robe with a desert scarf across the face completes his image transformation.

Simpson went to Zintan without me in May this year to report on Saif's appearance in court. He then all but disappeared from the Ten O'Clock News. There is a new programme on BBC1 – *The Editors* – which he presents. It's scheduled once a month. Sadly, it's shown on the last Monday of every month at the graveyard time of 11.30 pm. I only watched it a few times on the BBC iPlayer. I stopped because it made me anxious – I still miss working with him.

I haven't seen him for at least a year, although we keep in touch by email and SMS. It's a pity when you think how intense our relationship was. Sometimes my emails remain unanswered for weeks, sometimes – ignored. At other times, he writes the sweetest, friendliest messages. I did not invite him to my civil partnership event last year because I was never open with him about my private life. Although I've been with my partner for over 20 years, I couldn't find the right moment to tell him. Unsure about his reaction, I didn't dare to upset our successful business partnership. Perhaps I didn't tell him for the same reason I didn't tell my father – I was desperate for his approval.

By accident, I found out from his monthly column in the British Airways in-flight magazine that he had sold his flat in Paris. It was a lovely stylish little place in the 7th Arrondissement, not far from the Eiffel Tower. He told me he had bought it when, in his words, 'one of my books did rather well'. Inexplicably, I felt sadness at the news. Not only did I feel privileged to have been invited to the flat, but it was at the centre of one of our most memorable jokes. We were in Mexico City a few years ago editing a piece for the Ten O'Clock News on the government's war against the drug cartels. In a hotel room, we were watching some exciting footage on a laptop of an assault by the army against a drug gang featuring very real and very loud gunfire when Simpson's phone rang. He answered and his face immediately changed, initially with mild annoyance, followed by visible anger. 'It's the concierge of our flat in Paris,' he whispered, covering the phone with his palm. 'They're going to bust our front door and seize the furniture because we're late with our council tax.' Then in a moment of epiphany he gestured to our cameraman to resume the gunfire footage on the laptop and moved his phone close to it so that the concierge could hear. 'Oh mon dieu, Monsieur Simpson, où êtes-vous?' came a worried voice from the other end of the line. 'Je dirai au conseil que vous êtes dans une guerre, c'est pourquoi vous êtes en retard avec le paiement…' All three of us were red in the face trying to hold back our laughter. 'I can't hear you…' Simpson shouted and put his phone closer to the speakers. The gunfire continued. 'I'll call you when I'm out of here.' He severed the line to Paris. The hotel room was still echoing with the sound of machine guns. I rolled with laughter on the floor, our cameraman's face looked as if it was going to explode and Simpson roared with tears of joy in his eyes. Bizarrely, of all the experiences of danger, anger, fear and resentment I had at various times while working with him, this remains for me the most memorable moment of our time together.

My mother doesn't call me any more. She is now in a nursing home in Sofia. I try to visit every six months. Her metallic voice has lost its strength. She holds my hand and looks at me with vacant eyes. She talks about my dad as if he's still alive. And most of her memories are from happy days in her childhood town of Red Riverbank. She is as content as she has been throughout her uneventful life. She's always placed limits on her ambitions and this has provided for a steady and secure life.

It was my father who unfurled the possibilities of limitless ambition in front of me in the dark days of conformity in communist Bulgaria. 'Taking risks is what makes life worth living,' he'd say. 'You always have to aim higher than anybody else expects of you.'

I wonder if he wanted to achieve through me what he had failed to accomplish in his own life. A blessing or a curse, the constant discontentment with the status quo, which I inherited from him, has defined me.

He died halfway through my career at the BBC. For many years the memory of his death has haunted me. It was a warm October afternoon in Sofia. The blue sky of an Indian summer sparkled through the open hospital window. He had had a stroke and was lying paralysed in bed. The room was big. I caught the whiff of death in the pungent smell of disinfectant. A white screen had been placed ominously around one of the beds in the corner. My father didn't want me to see him like this – powerless and frail – and tried to cut the visit short. I had come from London to see him but had to go back the following morning for an urgent job. His mouth was curved in a grotesque involuntary semi-smile as though the stroke had captured his sardonic character. He said he was sorry I had to fly from London to see him like this. I didn't know what to reply. During the few seconds of silence that followed he closed his eyes as if to shut the world out.

'Are you planning to get married soon?' he said without opening his eyes. It felt as if his corpse had spoken.

'All in due course,' I said.

His eyes opened. 'It's a pity I'm not going to live to see your bride,' he said, trying to put the stress on 'bride' but his paralyzed mouth only muffled the word. 'Is she going to be blonde or dark?' he added, fixing his agile eyes on mine.

'I don't know,' I said and moved my gaze to the open window. This is not the right moment, I thought. Sadness and discontent overwhelmed me. I wished him well and prepared to leave. At the door, I looked back across the room. His eyes had followed me. And for the first time I felt that there was no mockery in them. They were soft and gentle. He knew that he would never see me again. It was a relief that I didn't have to go through the motions of a final farewell. I only said: 'See you soon.'

In hindsight, I wish I had said: 'I love you, Dad.' But more than anything, I wish he'd said: 'I love you, son.' He only shut his eyes and turned his head away.